OTHER BOOKS I

MW00876492

Available on Amazon

Claim These Free Resources that Will Help You Unleash the Power of Your Words and Speak with Confidence. Visit www.speakforsuccesshub.com/toolkit for Access.

18 Free PDF Resources

30 Free Video Lessons

2 Free Workbooks

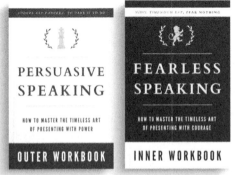

Claim These Free Resources that Will Help You Unleash the Power of Your Words and Speak with Confidence. Visit www.speakforsuccesshub.com/toolkit for Access.

18 Free PDF Resources

12 Iron Rules for Captivating Story, 21 Speeches that Changed the World, 341-Point Influence Checklist, 143 Persuasive Cognitive Biases, 17 Ways to Think On Your Feet, 18 Lies About Speaking Well, 137 Deadly Logical Fallacies, 12 Iron Rules For Captivating Slides, 371 Words that Persuade, 63 Truths of Speaking Well, 27 Laws of Empathy, 21 Secrets of Legendary Speeches, 19 Scripts that Persuade, 12 Iron Rules For Captivating Speech, 33 Laws of Charisma, 11 Influence Formulas, 219-Point Speech-Writing Checklist, 21 Eloquence Formulas

30 Free Video Lessons

We'll send you one free video lesson every day for 30 days, written and recorded by Peter D. Andrei. Days 1-10 cover authenticity, the prerequisite to confidence and persuasive power. Days 11-20 cover building self-belief and defeating communication anxiety. Days 21-30 cover how to speak with impact and influence, ensuring your words change minds instead of falling flat. Authenticity, self-belief, and impact – this course helps you master three components of confidence, turning even the most high-stakes presentations from obstacles into opportunities.

2 Free Workbooks

We'll send you two free workbooks, including long-lost excerpts by Dale Carnegie, the mega-bestselling author of *How to Win Friends and Influence People* (5,000,000 copies sold). *Fearless Speaking* guides you in the proven principles of mastering your inner game as a speaker. *Persuasive Speaking* guides you in the time-tested tactics of mastering your outer game by maximizing the power of your words. All of these resources complement the Speak for Success collection.

THE

PSYCHOLOGY

OF

PERSUASION

HOW TO USE PROVEN SPEAKING PATTERNS
TO MAKE YOUR IDEAS IRRESISTIBLE

Peter Andrei

THE

PSYCHOLOGY

OF

PERSUASION

SPEAK FOR SUCCESS COLLECTION BOOK

SPEAK
TRUTH
WELL
PRESS

A SUBSIDIARY OF SPEAK TRUTH WELL LLC
800 Boylston Street
Boston, MA 02199

SPEAK
TRUTH
WELL LLC

SPEAK FOR SUCCESS COLLECTION

Printed in the United States of America
40 39 38 37 36 35 34 33 32 31

While the author has made every effort to provide accurate internet addresses at the time of publication, neither the publisher nor the author assumes any responsibility for errors, or for changes that occur after publication. Further, the publisher does not have any control over and does not assume any responsibility for author or third-party websites or their content.

www.speakforsuccesshub.com/toolkit

FREE RESOURCES FOR OUR READERS

We believe in using the power of the internet to go above and beyond for our readers. That's why we created the free communication toolkit: 18 free PDF resources, 30 free video lessons, and even 2 free workbooks, including long-lost excerpts by Dale Carnegie, the mega-bestselling author of *How to Win Friends and Influence People*. (The workbooks help you put the most powerful strategies into action).

We know you're busy. That's why we designed these resources to be accessible, easy, and quick. Each PDF resource takes just 5 minutes to read or use. Each video lesson is only 5 minutes long. And in the workbooks, we bolded the key ideas throughout, so skimming them takes only 10 minutes each.

Why give so much away? For three reasons: we're grateful for you, it's useful content, and we want to go above and beyond. Questions? Feel free to email Peter directly at pandreibusiness@gmail.com.

www.speakforsuccesshub.com/toolkit

WHY DOES THIS HELP YOU?

I

The PDF resources cover topics like storytelling, logic, cognitive biases, empathy, charisma, and more. You can dig deeper into the specific topics that interest you most.

II

Many of the PDF resources are checklists, scripts, example-compilations, and formula-books. With these practical, step-by-step tools, you can quickly create messages that work.

III

With these free resources, you can supplement your reading of this book. You can find more specific guidance on the areas of communication you need to improve the most.

IV

The two workbooks offer practical and actionable guidance for speaking with complete confidence (*Fearless Speaking*) and irresistible persuasive power (*Persuasive Speaking*).

V

You can even learn from your phone with the free PDFs and the free video lessons, to develop your skills faster. The 30-lesson course reveals the secrets of building confidence.

VI

You are reading this because you want to improve your communication. These resources take you to the next level, helping you learn how to speak with power, impact, and confidence. We hope these resources make a difference. They are available here:

www.speakforsuccesshub.com/toolkit

From the desk of Peter Andrei
Speak Truth Well LLC
800 Boylston Street
Boston, MA 02199
pandreibusiness@gmail.com

May 15, 2021

What is Our Mission?

To whom it may concern:

The Wall Street Journal reports that public speaking is the world's biggest fear – bigger than being hit by a car. According to Columbia University, this pervasive, powerful, common phobia can reduce someone's salary by 10% or more. It can reduce someone's chances of graduating college by 10% and cut their chances of attaining a managerial or leadership position at work by 15%.

If weak presentation kills your good ideas, it kills your career. If weak communication turns every negotiation, meeting, pitch, speech, presentation, discussion, and interview into an obstacle (instead of an opportunity), it slows your progress. And if weak communication slows your progress, it tears a gaping hole in your confidence – which halts your progress.

Words can change the world. They can improve your station in life, lifting you forward and upward to higher and higher successes. But they have to be strong words spoken well: rarities in a world where most people fail to connect, engage, and persuade; fail to answer the question "why should we care about this?"; fail to impact, inspire, and influence; and, in doing so, fail to be all they could be.

Now zoom out. Multiply this dynamic by one thousand; one million; one billion. The individual struggle morphs into a problem for our communities, our countries, our world. Imagine the many millions of paradigm-shattering, life-changing, life-saving ideas that never saw the light of day. Imagine how many brilliant convictions were sunk in the shipyard. Imagine all that could have been that failed to be.

Speak Truth Well LLC solves this problem by teaching ambitious professionals how to turn communication from an obstacle into an engine: a tool for converting "what could be" into "what is." There is no upper limit: inexperienced speakers can become self-assured and impactful; veteran speakers can master the skill by learning advanced strategies; masters can learn how to outperform their former selves.

We achieve our mission by producing the best publications, articles, books, video courses, and coaching programs available on public speaking and communication, and at non-prohibitive prices. This combination of quality and accessibility has allowed Speak Truth Well to serve over 70,000 customers in its year of launch alone (2021). Grateful as we are, we hope to one day serve millions.

Dedicated to your success,

Peter Andrei

Peter Andrei
President of Speak Truth Well LLC
pandreibusiness@gmail.com

PROLOGUE:

This three-part prologue reveals my story, my work, and the practical and ethical principles of communication. It is not a mere introduction. It will help you get more out of the book. It is a preface to the entire 15-book Speak for Success collection. It will show you how to use the information with ease, confidence, and fluency, and how to get better results faster. If you would like to skip this, flip to page 50, or read only the parts of interest.

I

page XIII

MY STORY AND THE STORY OF THIS COLLECTION

how I discovered the hidden key to successful communication, public speaking, influence, and persuasion

II

page XXIV

THE 15-BOOK SPEAK FOR SUCCESS COLLECTION

confidence, leadership, charisma, influence, public speaking, eloquence, human nature, credibility – it's all here

III

page XXIX

THE PRACTICAL TACTICS AND ETHICAL PRINCIPLES

how to easily put complex strategies into action and how to use the power of words to improve the world

MY STORY AND THE STORY OF THIS COLLECTION

how I discovered the hidden key to successful communication, public speaking, influence, and persuasion (by reflecting on a painful failure)

HOW TO GAIN AN UNFAIR ADVANTAGE IN YOUR CAREER, BUSINESS, AND LIFE BY MASTERING THE POWER OF YOUR WORDS

I WAS SITTING IN MY OFFICE, TAPPING A PEN against my small wooden desk. My breaths were jagged, shallow, and rapid. My hands were shaking. I glanced at the clock: 11:31 PM. "I'm not ready." Have you ever had that thought?

I had to speak in front of 200 people the next morning. I had to convince them to put faith in my idea. But I was terrified, attacked by nameless, unreasoning, and unjustified terror which killed my ability to think straight, believe in myself, and get the job done.

Do you know the feeling?

After a sleepless night, the day came. I rose, wobbling on my tired legs. My head felt like it was filled with cotton candy. I couldn't direct my train of thoughts. A rushing waterfall of unhinged, self-destructive, and meaningless musings filled my head with an uncompromising cacophony of anxious, ricocheting nonsense.

"Call in sick."

"You're going to embarrass yourself."

"You're not ready."

I put on my favorite blue suit – my "lucky suit" – and my oversized blue-gold wristwatch; my "lucky" wristwatch.

"You're definitely not ready."

"That tie is ugly."

"You can't do this."

The rest went how you would expect. I drank coffee. Got in my car. Drove. Arrived. Waited. Waited. Waited. Spoke. Did poorly. Rushed back to my seat. Waited. Waited. Waited. Got in my car. Drove. Arrived home. Sat back in my wooden seat where I accurately predicted "I'm not ready" the night before.

Relieved it was over but disappointed with my performance, I placed a sheet of paper on the desk. I wrote "MY PROBLEMS" at the top, and under that, my prompt for the evening: "What did I do so badly? Why did everything feel so off? Why did the speech fail?"

"You stood in front of 200 people and looked at... a piece of paper, not unlike this one. What the hell were you thinking? You're not fooling anyone by reading a sentence and then looking up at them as you say it out loud. They know you're reading a manuscript, and they know what that means. You are unsure of yourself. You are unsure of your message. You are unprepared. Next: Why did you speak in that odd, low, monotone voice? That sounded like nails on a chalkboard. And it was inauthentic. Next: Why did you open by talking about yourself? Also, you're not particularly funny. No more jokes. And what was the structure of the speech? It had no structure. That, I feel, is probably a pretty big problem."

I believed in my idea, and I wanted to get it across. Of course, I wanted the tangible markers of a successful speech. I wanted action. I wanted the speech to change something in the real world. But my motivations were deeper than that. I wanted to see people "click" and come on board my way of thinking. I wanted to captivate the audience. I wanted to speak with an engaging, impactful voice, drawing the audience in, not repelling them. I wanted them to remember my message and to remember me. I wanted to feel, for just a moment, the thrill of power. But not the petty, forceful power of tyrants and dictators; the justified power – the earned power – of having a good idea and conveying it well; the power of Martin Luther King and John F. Kennedy; a power harnessed in service of a valuable idea, not the personal privilege of the speaker. And I wanted confidence: the quiet strength that comes from knowing your words don't stand in your way, but propel you and the ideas you care about to glorious new mountaintops.

Instead, I stood before the audience, essentially powerless. I spoke for 20 painful minutes – painful for them and for me – and then sat down. I barely made a dent in anyone's consciousness. I generated no excitement. Self-doubt draped its cold embrace over me. Anxiety built a wall between "what I am" and "what I could be."

I had tried so many different solutions. I read countless books on effective communication, asked countless effective communicators for their advice, and consumed countless courses on powerful public speaking. Nothing worked. All the "solutions" that didn't really solve my problem had one thing in common: they treated communication as an abstract art form. They were filled with vague, abstract pieces of advice like "think positive thoughts" and "be yourself." They confused me more than anything else. Instead of illuminating the secrets I had been looking for, they shrouded the elusive but indispensable skill of powerful speaking in uncertainty.

I knew I had to master communication. I knew that the world's most successful people are all great communicators. I knew that effective communication is the bridge between "what I have" and "what I want," or at least an essential part of that bridge. I knew that without effective communication – without the ability to influence, inspire, captivate, and move – I would be all but powerless.

I knew that the person who can speak up but doesn't is no better off than the person who can't speak at all. I heard a wise man say "If you can think and speak and write, you are absolutely deadly. Nothing can get in your way." I heard another wise man say "Speech is power: speech is to persuade, to convert, to compel. It is to bring another out of his bad sense into your good sense." I heard a renowned psychologist say "If you look at people who are remarkably successful across life, there's various reasons. But one of them is that they're unbelievably good at articulating what they're aiming at and strategizing and negotiating and enticing people with a vision forward. Get your words together... that makes you unstoppable. If you are an effective writer and speaker and communicator, you have all the authority and competence that there is."

When I worked in the Massachusetts State House for the Department of Public Safety and Homeland Security, I had the opportunity to speak with countless senators, state representatives, CEOs, and other successful people. In our conversations, however brief, I always asked the same question: "What are the ingredients of your success? What got you where you are?" 100% of them said effective communication. There was not one who said anything else. No matter their field – whether they were entrepreneurs, FBI agents, political leaders, business leaders, or multimillionaire donors – they all pointed to one skill: the ability to convey powerful words in powerful ways. Zero exceptions.

Can you believe it? It still astonishes me.

My problem, and I bet this may be your obstacle as well, was that most of the advice I consumed on this critical skill barely scratched the surface. Sure, it didn't make matters worse, and it certainly offered some improvement, but only in inches when I needed progress in miles. If I stuck with the mainstream public speaking advice, I knew I wouldn't unleash the power of my words. And if I didn't do that, I knew I would always accomplish much less than I could. I knew I would suffocate my own potential. I knew I would feel a rush of crippling anxiety every time I was asked to give a presentation. I knew I would live a life of less fulfillment, less success, less achievement, more frustration, more difficulty, and more anxiety. I knew my words would never become all they could be, which means that I would never become all I could be.

To make matters worse, the mainstream advice – which is not wrong, but simply not deep enough – is everywhere. Almost every article, book, or course published on this subject falls into the mainstream category. And to make matters worse, it's almost impossible to know that until you've spent your hard-earned money and scarce time with the resource. And even then, you might just shrug, and assume that shallow, abstract advice is all there is to the "art" of public speaking. As far as I'm concerned, this is a travesty.

I kept writing. "It felt like there was no real motive; no real impulse to action. Why did they need to act? You didn't tell them. What would happen if they didn't? You didn't tell them that either. Also, you tried too hard to put on a formal façade; you spoke in strange, twisted ways. It didn't sound sophisticated. And your mental game was totally off. You let your mind fill with destructive, doubtful, self-defeating thoughts. And your preparation was totally backward. It did more to set bad habits in stone than it did to set you up for success. And you tried to build suspense at one point but revealed the final point way too early, ruining the effect."

I went on and on until I had a stack of papers filled with problems. "That's no good," I thought. I needed solutions. Everything else I tried failed. But I had one more idea: "I remember reading a great speech. What was it? Oh yeah, that's right: JFK's inaugural address. Let me go pull it up and see why it was so powerful." And that's when everything changed.

I grabbed another sheet of paper. I opened JFK's inaugural address on my laptop. I started reading. Observing. Analyzing.

Reverse-engineering. I started writing down what I saw. Why did it work? Why was it powerful? I was like an archaeologist, digging through his speech for the secrets of powerful communication. I got more and more excited as I kept going. It was late at night, but the shocking and invaluable discoveries I was making gave me a burst of energy. It felt like JFK – one of the most powerful and effective speakers of all time – was coaching me in his rhetorical secrets, showing me how to influence an audience, draw them into my narrative, and find words that get results.

"Oh, so that's how you grab attention."

"Aha! So, if I tell them this, they will see why it matters."

"Fascinating – I can apply this same structure to my speech."

Around 3:00 in the morning, an epiphany hit me like a ton of bricks. That night, a new paradigm was born. A new opportunity emerged for all those who want to unleash the unstoppable power of their words. This new opportunity changed everything for me and eventually, tens of thousands of others. It is now my mission to bring it to millions, so that good people know what they need to know to use their words to achieve their dreams and improve the world.

Want to hear the epiphany?

The mainstream approach: Communication is an art form. It is unlike those dry, boring, "academic" subjects. There are no formulas. There are no patterns. It's all about thinking positive thoughts, faking confidence, and making eye contact. Some people are naturally gifted speakers. For others, the highest skill level they can attain is "not horrible."

The consequences of the mainstream approach: Advice that barely scratches the surface of the power of words. Advice that touches only the tip of the tip of the iceberg. A limited body of knowledge that blinds itself to thousands of hidden, little-known communication strategies that carry immense power; that blinds itself to 95% of what great communication really is. Self-limiting dogmas about who can do what, and how great communicators become great. Half the progress in twice the time, and everything that entails: missed opportunities, unnecessary and preventable frustration and anxiety, and confusion about what to say and how to say it. How do I know? Because I've been there. It's not pretty.

My epiphany, the new Speak for Success paradigm: Communication is as much a science as it is an art. You can study words that changed the world, uncover the hidden secrets of their power, and apply these proven principles to your own message. You can discover precisely what made great communicators great and adopt the same strategies. You can do this without being untrue to yourself or flatly imitating others. In fact, you can do this while being truer to yourself and more original than you ever have been before. Communication is not unpredictable, wishy-washy, or abstract. You can apply predictable processes and principles to reach your goals and get results. You can pick and choose from thousands of little-known speaking strategies, combining your favorite to create a unique communication approach that suits you perfectly. You can effortlessly use the same tactics of the world's most transformational leaders and speakers, and do so automatically, by default, without even thinking about it, as a matter of effortless habit. That's power.

The benefits of the Speak for Success paradigm: Less confusion. More confidence. Less frustration. More clarity. Less anxiety. More courage. You understand the whole iceberg of effective communication. As a result, your words captivate others. You draw them into a persuasive narrative, effortlessly linking your desires and their motives. You know exactly what to say. You know exactly how to say it. You know exactly how to keep your head clear; you are a master of the mental game. Your words can move mountains. Your words are the most powerful tools in your arsenal, and you use them to seize opportunities, move your mission forward, and make the world a better place. Simply put, you speak for success.

Fast forward a few years.

I was sitting in my office at my small wooden desk. My breaths were deep, slow, and steady. My entire being – mind, body, soul – was poised and focused. I set my speech manuscript to the side. I glanced at the clock: 12:01 AM. "Let's go. I'm ready."

I had to speak in front of 200 people the next morning. I had to convince them to put faith in my idea. And I was thrilled, filled with genuine gratitude at the opportunity to do what I love: get up in front of a crowd, think clearly, speak well, and get the job done.

I slept deeply. I dreamt vividly. I saw myself giving the speech. I saw myself victorious, in every sense of the word. I heard applause. I saw their facial expressions. I rose. My head was clear. My mental game was pristine. My mind was an ally, not an obstacle.

"This is going to be fun."

"I'll do my best, and whatever happens, happens."

"I'm so lucky that I get to do this again."

I put on my lucky outfit: the blue suit and the blue-gold watch.

"Remember the principles. They work."

"You developed a great plan last night. It's a winner."

"I can't wait."

The rest went how you would expect. I ate breakfast. Got in my car. Drove. Arrived. Waited. Waited. Waited. Spoke. Succeeded. Walked back to my seat. Waited. Waited. Waited. Got in my car. Drove. Arrived home. Sat back in my wooden seat where I accurately predicted "I'm ready" the night before.

I got my idea across perfectly. My message succeeded: it motivated action and created real-world change. I saw people "click" when I hit the rhetorical peak of my speech. I saw them leaning forward, totally hushed, completely absorbed. I applied the proven principles of engaging and impactful vocal modulation. I knew they would remember me and my message; I engineered my words to be memorable. I felt the thrilling power of giving a great speech. I felt the quiet confidence of knowing that my words carried weight; that they could win hearts, change minds, and help me reach the heights of my potential. I tore off the cold embrace of self-doubt. I defeated communication anxiety and broke down the wall between "what I am" and "what I could be."

Disappointed it was over but pleased with my performance, I placed a sheet of paper on the desk. I wrote "Speak Truth Well" and started planning what would become my business.

To date, we have helped tens of thousands of people gain an unfair advantage in their career, business, and life by unleashing the power of their words. And they experienced the exact same transformation I experienced when they applied the system.

If you tried to master communication before but haven't gotten the results you wanted, it's because of the mainstream approach; an approach that tells you "smiling at the audience" and "making eye contact" is all you need to know to speak well. That's not exactly a malicious lie – they don't know any better – but it is completely incorrect and severely harmful.

If you've been concerned that you won't be able to become a vastly more effective and confident communicator, I want to put those fears to rest. I felt the same way. The people I work with felt the same way. We just needed the right system. One public speaking book written by the director of a popular public speaking forum – I won't name names – wants you to believe that there are "nine public speaking secrets of the world's top minds." Wrong: There are many more than nine. If you feel that anyone who would boil down communication to just nine secrets is either missing something or holding it back, you're right. And the alternative is a much more comprehensive and powerful system. It's a system that gave me and everyone I worked with the transformation we were looking for.

Want to Talk? Email Me:

PANDREIBUSINESS@GMAIL.COM

This is My Personal Email.
I Read Every Message and
Respond in Under 12 Hours.

Visit Our Digital Headquarters:

WWW.SPEAKFORSUCCESSHUB.COM

See All Our Free Resources,
Books, Courses, and Services.

THE 15-BOOK SPEAK FOR SUCCESS COLLECTION

confidence, leadership, charisma, influence, public speaking, eloquence, human nature, credibility – it's all here, in a unified collection

MASTER EVERY ASPECT OF COMMUNICATION

T HE BESTSELLING SPEAK FOR SUCCESS COLLECTION covers every aspect of communication. Each book in the collection includes diagrams that visualize the essential principles, chapter summaries that remind you of the main ideas, and checklists of the action items in each section, all designed to help you consult the set as a reference.

This series is a cohesive, comprehensive set. After writing the first book, I realized how much information I couldn't fit into it. I wrote the second. After writing the second, the same thing happened. I wrote the third. The pattern continued. As of this writing, there are fifteen books in the collection. After writing each book, I felt called to write another. It is the ultimate communication encyclopedia.

Aside from a small amount of necessary overlap on the basics, each book is a distinct unit that focuses on an entirely new set of principles, strategies, and communication secrets. For example, *Eloquence* reveals the secrets of language that sounds good; *Trust is Power* reveals the secrets of speaking with credibility; *Public Speaking Mastery* reveals a blueprint for delivering speeches.

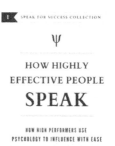

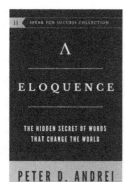
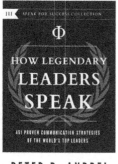
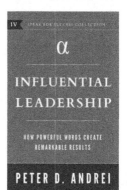
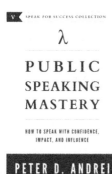
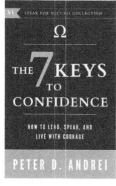

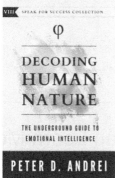
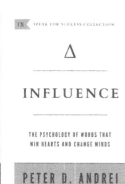

"*The most complete and comprehensive collection of communication wisdom ever compiled.*" – *Amazon Customer*

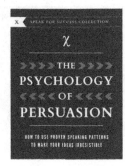
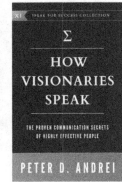
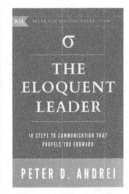

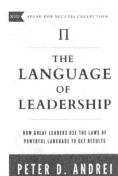
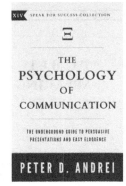

"I love the diagrams and summary checklists. I have all 15 on my shelf, and regularly refer back to them." – Amazon Customer

You Can Learn More Here:
www.speakforsuccesshub.com/series

........................A Brief Overview................................

- I wrote *How Highly Effective People Speak* to reveal the hidden patterns in the words of the world's most successful and powerful communicators, so that you can adopt the same tactics and speak with the same impact and influence.

- I wrote *Eloquence* to uncover the formulas of beautiful, moving, captivating, and powerful words, so that you can use these exact same step-by-step structures to quickly make your language electrifying, charismatic, and eloquent.

- I wrote *How Legendary Leaders Speak* to illuminate the little-known five-step communication process the top leaders of the past 500 years all used to spread their message, so that you can use it to empower your ideas and get results.

- I wrote *Influential Leadership* to expose the differences between force and power and to show how great leaders use the secrets of irresistible influence to develop gentle power, so that you can move forward and lead with ease.

- I wrote *Public Speaking Mastery* to shatter the myths and expose the harmful advice about public speaking, and to offer a proven, step-by-step framework for speaking well, so that you can always speak with certainty and confidence.

- I wrote *The 7 Keys to Confidence* to bring to light the ancient 4,000-year-old secrets I used to master the mental game and speak in front of hundreds without a second of self-doubt or anxiety, so that you can feel the same freedom.

- I wrote *Trust is Power* to divulge how popular leaders and career communicators earn our trust, speak with credibility, and use this to rise to new heights of power, so that you can do the same thing to advance your purpose and mission.

- I wrote *Decoding Human Nature* to answer the critical question "what do people want?" and reveal how to use this knowledge to develop unparalleled influence, so that people adopt your idea, agree with your position, and support you.

- I wrote *Influence* to unearth another little-known five-step process for winning hearts and changing minds, so that you can know with certainty that your message will persuade people, draw support, and motivate enthusiastic action.

- I wrote *The Psychology of Persuasion* to completely and fully unveil everything about the psychology behind "Yes, I love it! What's the next step?" so that you can use easy step-by-step speaking formulas that get people to say exactly that.

- I wrote *How Visionaries Speak* to debunk common lies about effective communication that hold you back and weaken your words, so that you can boldly share your ideas without accidentally sabotaging your own message.

- I wrote *The Eloquent Leader* to disclose the ten steps to communicating with power and persuasion, so that you don't miss any of the steps and fail to connect, captivate, influence, and inspire in a crucial high-stakes moment.

- I wrote *The Language of Leadership* to unpack the unique, hidden-in-plain-sight secrets of how presidents and world-leaders build movements with the laws of powerful language, so that you use them to propel yourself forward.

- I wrote *The Psychology of Communication* to break the news that most presentations succeed or fail in the first thirty seconds and to reveal proven, step-by-step formulas that grab, hold, and direct attention, so that yours succeeds.

- I wrote *The Charisma Code* to shatter the myths and lies about charisma and reveal its nature as a concrete skill you can master with proven strategies, so that people remember you, your message, and how you electrified the room.

- **Learn more: www.speakforsuccesshub.com/series**

III

PRACTICAL TACTICS AND ETHICAL PRINCIPLES

how to easily put complex strategies into action and how to use the power of words to improve the world in an ethical and effective way

MOST COMMUNICATION BOOKS

HAVE YOU READ ANOTHER BOOK ON COMMUNICATION? If you have, let me remind you what you probably learned. And if you haven't, let me briefly spoil 95% of them. "Prepare. Smile. Dress to impress. Keep it simple. Overcome your fears. Speak from the heart. Be authentic. Show them why you care. Speak in terms of their interests. To defeat anxiety, know your stuff. Emotion persuades, not logic. Speak with confidence. Truth sells. And respect is returned."

There you have it. That is most of what you learn in most communication books. None of it is wrong. None of it is misleading. Those ideas are true and valuable. But they are not enough. They are only the absolute basics. And my job is to offer you much more.

Einstein said that "if you can't explain it in a sentence, you don't know it well enough." He also told us to "make it as simple as possible, but no simpler." You, as a communicator, must satisfy both of these maxims, one warning against the dangers of excess complexity, and one warning against the dangers of excess simplicity.

And I, as someone who communicates about communication in my books, courses, and coaching, must do the same.

THE SPEAK FOR SUCCESS SYSTEM

The Speak for Success system makes communication as simple as possible. Other communication paradigms make it even simpler. Naturally, this means our system is more complex. This is an unavoidable consequence of treating communication as a deep and concrete science instead of a shallow and abstract art. If you don't dive into learning communication at all, you miss out. I'm sure you agree with that. But if you don't dive *deep*, you still miss out.

THE FOUR QUADRANTS OF COMMUNICATION

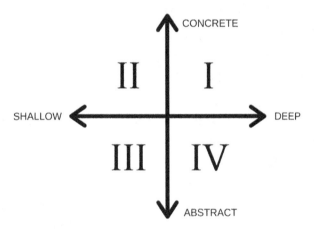

FIGURE VIII: There are four predominant views of communication (whether it takes the form of public speaking, negotiation, writing, or debating is irrelevant). The first view is that communication is concrete and deep. The second view is that communication is concrete and shallow. The third view is that communication is shallow and abstract. The fourth view is that communication is deep and abstract.

WHAT IS COMMUNICATION?

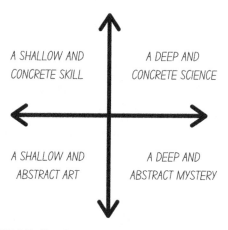

FIGURE VII: The first view treats communication as a science: "There are concrete formulas, rules, principles, and strategies, and they go very deep." The second view treats it as a skill: "Yes, there are concrete formulas, rules, and strategies, but they don't go very deep." The third view treats it as an art: "Rules? Formulas? It's not that complicated. Just smile and think positive thoughts." The fourth view treats it as a mystery: "How are some people such effective communicators? I will never know…"

WHERE WE STAND ON THE QUESTION

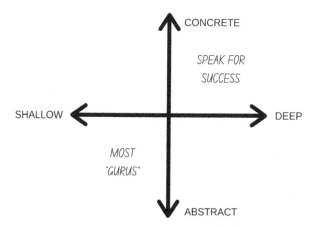

FIGURE VI: Speak for Success takes the view that communication is a deep and concrete science. (And by "takes the view," I mean "has discovered.") Most other communication writers, thought-leaders, public speaking coaches, and individuals and organizations in this niche treat communication as a shallow and abstract art.

This doesn't mean the Speak for Success system neglects the basics. It only means it goes far beyond the basics, and that it doesn't turn simple ideas into 200 pages of filler. It also doesn't mean that the Speak for Success system is unnecessarily complex. It is as simple as it can possibly be.

In this book, and in the other books of the Speak for Success collection, you'll find simple pieces of advice, easy formulas, and straightforward rules. You'll find theories, strategies, tactics, mental models, and principles. None of this should pose a challenge. But you'll also find advanced and complicated strategies. These might.

What is the purpose of the guide on the top of the next page? To reveal the methods that make advanced strategies easy. When you use the tactics revealed in this guide, the difficulty of using the advanced strategies drops dramatically. They empower you to use complicated and unfamiliar persuasive strategies with ease. If the 15-book Speak for Success collection is a complete encyclopedia of communication, to be used like a handbook, then this guide is a handbook for the handbook.

A SAMPLING OF EASY AND HARD STRATEGIES

Easy and Simple	Hard and Complicated
Use Four-Corner Eye Contact	The Fluency-Magnitude Matrix
Appeal to Their Values	The VPB Triad
Describe the Problem You Solve	The Illusory Truth Effect
Use Open Body Language	Percussive Rhythm
Tell a Quick Story	Alliterative Flow
Appeal to Emotion	Stacking and Layering Structures
Project Your Voice	The Declaratory Cascade
Keep it as Simple as Possible	Alternating Semantic Sentiments

THE PRACTICAL TACTICS

$$\blacktriangleright\!\!\!-\!\!\!\Diamond\!\!-\!\!\!\blacktriangleleft$$

ECOGNIZE THAT, WITH PRACTICE, YOU can use any strategy extemporaneously. Some people can instantly use even the most complex strategies in the Speak for Success collection after reading them just once. They are usually experienced communicators, often with competitive experience. This is not an expectation, but a possibility, and with practice, a probability.

CREATE A COMMUNICATION PLAN. Professional communication often follows a strategic plan. Put these techniques into your plan. Following an effective plan is not harder than following an ineffective one. Marshall your arguments. Marshall your rhetoric. Stack the deck. Know what you know, and how to say it.

DESIGN AN MVP. If you are speaking on short notice, you can create a "minimum viable plan." This can be a few sentences on a notecard jotted down five minutes before speaking. The same principle of formal communication plans applies: While advanced strategies may overburden you if you attempt them in an impromptu setting, putting them into a plan makes them easy.

MASTER YOUR RHETORICAL STACK. Master one difficult strategy. Master another one. Combine them. Master a third. Build out a "rhetorical stack" of ten strategies you can use fluently, in impromptu or extemporaneous communication. Pick strategies that come fluently to you and that complement each other.

PRACTICE THEM TO FLUENCY. I coach a client who approached me and said he wants to master every strategy I ever compiled. That's a lot. As of this writing, we're 90 one-hour sessions in. To warm up for one of our sessions, I gave him a challenge: "Give an impromptu speech on the state of the American economy, and after you stumble, hesitate, or falter four times, I'll cut you off. The challenge is to see how long you can go." He spoke for 20 minutes without a single mistake. After 20 minutes, he brought the impromptu speech to a perfect, persuasive, forceful, and eloquent conclusion. And he naturally and fluently used advanced strategies throughout his impromptu speech. After he closed the speech (which he did because he wanted to get on with the session), I asked him if he thought deeply about the strategies he used. He said no. He used them thoughtlessly. Why? Because he practiced them. You can too. You can practice them on your own. You don't need an audience. You don't need a coach. You don't even need to speak. Practice in your head. Practice ones that resonate with you. Practice with topics you care about.

KNOW TEN TIMES MORE THAN YOU INTEND TO SAY. And know what you do intend to say about ten times more fluently than you need to. This gives your mind room to relax, and frees up cognitive bandwidth to devote to strategy and rhetoric in real-time. Need to speak for five minutes? Be able to speak for 50. Need to read it three times to be able to deliver it smoothly? Read it 30 times.

INCORPORATE THEM IN SLIDES. You can use your slides or visual aids to help you ace complicated strategies. If you can't remember the five steps of a strategy, your slides can still follow them. Good slides aren't harder to use than bad slides.

USE THEM IN WRITTEN COMMUNICATION. You can read your speech. In some situations, this is more appropriate than impromptu or extemporaneous speaking. And if a strategy is difficult to remember in impromptu speaking, you can write it into your speech. And let's not forget about websites, emails, letters, etc.

PICK AND CHOOSE EASY ONES. Use strategies that come naturally and don't overload your mind. Those that do are counterproductive in fast-paced situations.

TAKE SMALL STEPS TO MASTERY. Practice one strategy. Practice it again. Keep going until you master it. Little by little, add to your base of strategies. But never take steps that overwhelm you. Pick a tactic. Practice it. Master it. Repeat.

MEMORIZE AN ENTIRE MESSAGE. Sometimes this is the right move. Is it a high-stakes message? Do you have the time? Do you have the energy? Given the situation, would a memorized delivery beat an impromptu, in-the-moment, spontaneous delivery? If you opt for memorizing, using advanced strategies is easy.

USE ONE AT A TIME. Pick an advanced strategy. Deliver it. Now what? Pick another advanced strategy. Deliver it. Now another. Have you been speaking for a while? Want to bring it to a close? Pick a closing strategy. For some people, using advanced strategies extemporaneously is easy, but only if they focus on one at a time.

MEMORIZE A KEY PHRASE. Deliver your impromptu message as planned, but add a few short, memorized key phrases throughout that include advanced strategies.

CREATE TALKING POINTS. Speak from a list of pre-written bullet-points; big-picture ideas you seek to convey. This is halfway between fully impromptu speaking and using a script. It's not harder to speak from a strategic and persuasively-advanced list of talking points than it is to speak from a persuasively weak list. You can either memorize your talking points, or have them in front of you as a guide.

TREAT IT LIKE A SCIENCE. At some point, you struggled with a skill that you now perform effortlessly. You mastered it. It's a habit. You do it easily, fluently, and thoughtlessly. You can do it while you daydream. Communication is the same. These tactics, methods, and strategies are not supposed to be stuck in the back of your mind as you speak. They are supposed to be ingrained in your habits.

RELY ON FLOW. In fast-paced and high-stakes situations, you usually don't plan every word, sentence, and idea consciously and deliberately. Rather, you let your subconscious mind take over. You speak from a flow state. In flow, you may flawlessly execute strategies that would have overwhelmed your conscious mind.

LISTEN TO THE PROMPTS. You read a strategy and found it difficult to use extemporaneously. But as you speak, your subconscious mind gives you a prompt:

"this strategy would work great here." Your subconscious mind saw the opportunity and surfaced the prompt. You execute it, and you do so fluently and effortlessly.

FOLLOW THE FIVE-STEP CYCLE. First, find truth. Research. Prepare. Learn. Second, define your message. Figure out what you believe about what you learned. Third, polish your message with rhetorical strategies, without distorting the precision with which it conveys the truth. Fourth, practice the polished ideas. Fifth, deliver them. The endeavor of finding truth comes before the rhetorical endeavor. First, find the right message. Then, find the best way to convey it.

CREATE YOUR OWN STRATEGY. As you learn new theories, mental models, and principles of psychology and communication, you may think of a new strategy built around the theories, models, and principles. Practice it, test it, and codify it.

STACK GOOD HABITS. An effective communicator is the product of his habits. If you want to be an effective communicator, stack good communication habits (and break bad ones). This is a gradual process. It doesn't happen overnight.

DON'T TRY TO USE THEM. Don't force it. If a strategy seems too difficult, don't try to use it. You might find yourself using it anyway when the time is right.

KNOW ONLY ONE. If you master one compelling communication strategy, like one of the many powerful three-part structures that map out a persuasive speech, that can often be enough to drastically and dramatically improve your impact.

REMEMBER THE SHORTCOMING OF MODELS. All models are wrong, but some are useful. Many of these complex strategies and theories are models. They represent reality, but they are not reality. They help you navigate the territory, but they are not the territory. They are a map, to be used if it helps you navigate, and to be discarded the moment it prevents you from navigating.

DON'T LET THEM INHIBIT YOU. Language flows from thought. You've got to have something to say. And *then* you make it as compelling as possible. And *then* you shape it into something poised and precise; persuasive and powerful; compelling and convincing. Meaning and message come first. Rhetoric comes second. Don't take all this discussion of "advanced communication strategies," "complex communication tactics," and "the deep and concrete science of communication" to suggest that the basics don't matter. They do. Tell the truth as precisely and boldly as you can. Know your subject-matter like the back of your hand. Clear your mind and focus on precisely articulating exactly what you believe to be true. Be authentic. The advanced strategies are not supposed to stand between you and your audience. They are not supposed to stand between you and your authentic and spontaneous self – they are supposed to be integrated with it. They are not an end in themselves, but a means to the end of persuading the maximum number of people to adopt truth. Trust your instinct. Trust your intuition. It won't fail you.

MASTERING ONE COMMUNICATION SKILL

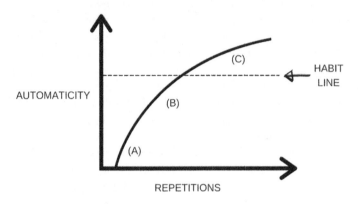

FIGURE V: Automaticity is the extent to which you do something automatically, without thinking about it. At the start of building a communication habit, it has low automaticity. You need to think about it consciously (A). After more repetitions, it gets easier and more automatic (B). Eventually, the behavior becomes more automatic than deliberate. At this point, it becomes a habit (C).

MASTERING COMMUNICATION

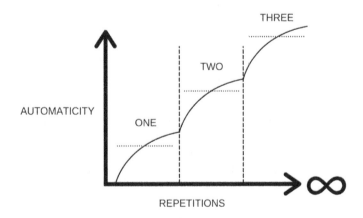

FIGURE IV: Layer good communication habits on top of each other. Go through the learning curve over and over again. When you master the first good habit, jump to the second. This pattern will take you to mastery.

THE FOUR LEVELS OF KNOWING

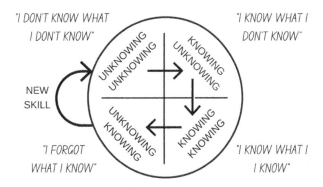

FIGURE III: First, you don't know you don't know it. Then, you discover it and know you don't know it. Then, you practice it and know you know it. Then, it becomes a habit. You forget you know it. It's ingrained in your habits.

REVISITING THE LEARNING CURVE

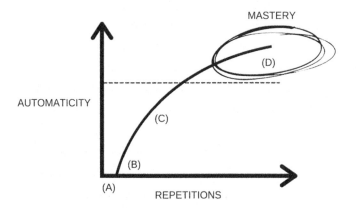

FIGURE II: Note the stages of knowing on the learning curve: unknowing unknowing (A), knowing unknowing (B), knowing knowing (C), unknowing knowing (D).

WHAT'S REALLY HAPPENING?

Have you ever thought deeply about what happens when you communicate? Let's run through the mile-high view.

At some point in your life, you bumped into an experience. You observed. You learned. The experience changed you. Your neural networks connected in new ways. New rivers of neurons began to flow through them.

The experience etched a pattern into your neurobiology representing information about the moral landscape of the universe; a map of *where we are, where we should go, and how we should make the journey.* This is meaning. This is your message.

Now, you take the floor before a crowd. Whether you realize it or not, you want to copy the neural pattern from your mind to their minds. You want to show them where we are, where we should go, and how we should make the journey.

So, you speak. You gesture. You intone. Your words convey meaning. Your body language conveys meaning. Your voice conveys meaning. You flood them with a thousand different inputs, some as subtle as the contraction of a single facial muscle, some as obvious as your opening line. Your character, your intentions, and your goals seep into your speech. Everyone can see them. Everyone can see you.

Let's step into the mind of one of your audience members. Based on all of this, based on a thousand different inputs, based on complex interactions between their conscious and nonconscious minds, the ghost in the machine steps in, and by a dint of free will, acts as the final arbiter and makes a choice. A mind is changed. You changed it. And changing it changed you. You became more confident, more articulate, and deeper; more capable, more impactful, and stronger.

Communication is connection. One mind, with a consciousness at its base, seeks to use ink or pixels or airwaves to connect to another. Through this connection, it seeks to copy neural patterns about the present, the future, and the moral landscape. Whatever your message is, the underlying connection is identical. How could it not be?

IS IT ETHICAL?

By "it," I mean deliberately using language to get someone to do or think something. Let's call this rhetoric. We could just as well call it persuasion, influence, communication, or even leadership itself.

The answer is yes. The answer is no. Rhetoric is a helping hand. It is an iron fist. It is Martin Luther King's dream. It is Stalin's nightmare. It is the "shining city on the hill." It is the iron curtain. It is "the pursuit of happiness." It is the trail of tears. It is "liberty, equality, and brotherhood." It is the reign of terror. Rhetoric is a tool. It is neither good nor evil. It is a reflection of our nature.

Rhetoric can motivate love, peace, charity, strength, patience, progress, prosperity, common sense, common purpose, courage, hope, generosity, and unity. It can also sow the seeds of division, fan the flames of tribalism, and beat back the better angels of our nature.

Rhetoric is the best of us and the worst of us. It is as good as you are. It is as evil as you are. It is as peace-loving as you are. It is as hate-mongering as you are. And I know what you are. I know my readers are generous, hardworking people who want to build a better future for themselves, for their families, and for all humankind. I know that if you have these tools in your hands, you will use them to achieve a moral mission. That's why putting them in your hands is my mission.

Joseph Chatfield said "[rhetoric] is the power to talk people out of their sober and natural opinions." I agree. But it is also the power to talk people out of their wrong and harmful opinions. And if you're using rhetoric to talk people out of their sober opinions, the problem isn't rhetoric, it's you.

In the *Institutes of Rhetoric*, Roman rhetorician Quintilian wrote the following: "The orator then, whom I am concerned to form, shall be the orator as defined by Marcus Cato, a good man, skilled in speaking. But above all he must possess the quality which Cato places first and which is in the very nature of things the greatest and most important, that is, he must be a good man. This is essential not merely on account of the fact that, if the powers of eloquence serve only to lend arms to crime, there can be nothing more pernicious than eloquence to public and private welfare alike, while I myself, who have labored to the best of my ability to contribute something of the value to oratory, shall have rendered the worst of services to mankind, if I forge these weapons not for a soldier, but for a robber."

Saint Augustine, who was trained in the classical schools of rhetoric in the 3rd century, summed it up well: "Rhetoric, after all, being the art of persuading people to accept something, whether it is true or false, would anyone dare to maintain that truth should stand there without any weapons in the hands of its defenders against falsehood; that those speakers, that is to say, who are trying to convince their hearers of what is untrue, should know how to get them on their side, to gain their attention and have them eating out of their hands by their opening remarks, while these who are defending the truth should not? That those should utter their lies briefly, clearly, plausibly, and these should state their truths in a manner too boring to listen to, too obscure to understand, and finally too repellent to believe? That those should attack the truth with specious arguments, and assert falsehoods, while these should be incapable of either defending the truth or refuting falsehood? That those, to move and force the minds of their hearers into error, should be able by their style to terrify them, move them to tears, make them laugh, give them rousing encouragement, while these on behalf of truth stumble along slow, cold and half asleep?"

THE ETHICS OF PERSUASION

REFER BACK TO THIS ETHICAL GUIDE as needed. I created this in a spirit of humility, for my benefit as much as for the benefit of my readers. And you don't have to choose between efficacy and ethics. When I followed these principles, my words became more ethical *and* more powerful.

FOLLOW THESE TWELVE RULES. Do not use false, fabricated, misrepresented, distorted, or irrelevant evidence to support claims. Do not intentionally use specious, unsupported, or illogical reasoning. Do not represent yourself as informed or as an "expert" on a subject when you are not. Do not use irrelevant appeals to divert attention from the issue at hand. Do not cause intense but unreflective emotional reactions. Do not link your idea to emotion-laden values, motives, or goals to which it is not related. Do not hide your real purpose or self-interest, the group you represent, or your position as an advocate of a viewpoint. Do not distort, hide, or misrepresent the number, scope, or intensity of bad effects. Do not use emotional appeals that lack a basis of evidence or reasoning or that would fail if the audience examined the subject themselves. Do not oversimplify complex, gradation-laden situations into simplistic two-valued, either/or, polar views or choices. Do not pretend certainty where tentativeness and degrees of probability would be more accurate. Do not advocate something you do not believe (Johannesen et al., 2021).

APPLY THIS GOLDEN HEURISTIC. In a 500,000-word book, you might be able to tell your audience everything you know about a subject. In a five-minute persuasive speech, you can only select a small sampling of your knowledge. Would learning your entire body of knowledge result in a significantly different reaction than hearing the small sampling you selected? If the answer is yes, that's a problem.

SWING WITH THE GOOD EDGE. Rhetoric is a double-edged sword. It can express good ideas well. It can also express bad ideas well. Rhetoric makes ideas attractive; tempting; credible; persuasive. Don't use it to turn weakly-worded lies into well-worded lies. Use it to turn weakly-worded truths into well-worded truths.

TREAT TRUTH AS THE HIGHEST GOOD. Use any persuasive strategy, unless using it in your circumstances would distort the truth. The strategies should not come between you and truth, or compromise your honesty and authenticity.

AVOID THE SPIRIT OF DECEIT. Wrong statements are incorrect statements you genuinely believe. Lies are statements you know are wrong but convey anyway. Deceitful statements are not literally wrong, but you convey them with the intent to mislead, obscure, hide, or manipulate. Hiding relevant information is not literally lying (saying you conveyed all the information would be). Cherry-picking facts is not literally lying (saying there are no other facts would be). Using clever innuendo to twist reality without making any concrete claims is not literally lying (knowingly making a false accusation would be). And yet, these are all examples of deceit.

ONLY USE STRATEGIES IF THEY ARE ACCURATE. Motivate unified thinking. Inspire loving thinking. These strategies sound good. Use the victim-perpetrator-benevolence structure. Paint a common enemy. Appeal to tribal psychology. These strategies sound bad. But when reality lines up with the strategies that sound bad, they become good. They are only bad when they are inaccurate or move people down a bad path. *But the same is true for the ones that sound good.* Should Winston Churchill have motivated unified thinking? Not toward his enemy. Should he have avoided appealing to tribal psychology to strengthen the Allied war effort? Should he have avoided painting a common enemy? Should he have avoided portraying the victimization of true victims and the perpetration of a true perpetrator? Should he have avoided calling people to act as the benevolent force for good, protecting the victim and beating back the perpetrator? Don't use the victim-perpetrator-benevolence structure if there aren't clear victims and perpetrators. This is demagoguery. Painting false victims disempowers them. But if there are true victims and perpetrators, stand up for the victims and stand against the perpetrators, calling others to join you as a benevolent force for justice. Don't motivate unified thinking when standing against evil. Don't hold back from portraying a common enemy when there is one. Some strategies might sound morally suspect. Some might sound inherently good. But it depends on the situation. Every time I say "do X to achieve Y," remember the condition: "if it is accurate and moves people up a good path."

APPLY THE TARES TEST: truthfulness of message, authenticity of persuader, respect for audience, equity of persuasive appeal, and social impact (TARES).

REMEMBER THE THREE-PART VENN DIAGRAM: words that are authentic, effective, and true. Donald Miller once said "I'm the kind of person who wants to present my most honest, authentic self to the world, so I hide backstage and rehearse honest and authentic lines until the curtain opens." There's nothing dishonest or inauthentic about choosing your words carefully and making them more effective, as long as they remain just as true. Rhetoric takes a messy marble brick of truth and sculpts it into a poised, precise, and perfect statue. It takes weak truths and makes them strong. Unfortunately, it can do the same for weak lies. But preparing, strategizing, and sculpting is not inauthentic. Unskillfulness is no more authentic than skillfulness. Unpreparedness is no more authentic than preparedness.

APPLY FITZPATRICK AND GAUTHIER'S THREE-QUESTION ANALYSIS. For what purpose is persuasion being employed? Toward what choices and with what consequences for individual lives is it being used? Does the persuasion contribute to or interfere with the audience's decision-making process (Lumen, 2016)?

STRENGTHEN THE TRUTH. Rhetoric makes words strong. Use it to turn truths strong, not falsities strong. There are four categories of language: weak and wrong, strong and wrong, weak and true, strong and true. Turn weak and true language into strong and true language. Don't turn weak and wrong language into strong and wrong language, weak and true language into strong and wrong language, or strong and true language into weak and true language. Research. Question your assumptions. Strive for truth. Ensure your logic is impeccable. Defuse your biases.

START WITH FINDING TRUTH. The rhetorical endeavor starts with becoming as knowledgeable on your subject as possible and developing an impeccable logical argument. The more research you do, the more rhetoric you earn the right to use.

PUT TRUTH BEFORE STYLE. Rhetorical skill does not make you correct. Truth doesn't care about your rhetoric. If your rhetoric is brilliant, but you realize your arguments are simplistic, flawed, or biased, change course. Let logic lead style. Don't sacrifice logic to style. Don't express bad ideas well. Distinguish effective speaking from effective rational argument. Achieve both, but put reason and logic first.

AVOID THE POPULARITY VORTEX. As Plato suggested, avoid "giving the citizens what they want [in speech] with no thought to whether they will be better or worse as a result of what you are saying." Ignore the temptation to gain positive reinforcement and instant gratification from the audience with no merit to your message. Rhetoric is unethical if used solely to appeal rather than to help the world.

CONSIDER THE CONSEQUENCES. If you succeed to persuade people, will the world become better or worse? Will your audience benefit? Will you benefit? Moreover, is it the best action they could take? Or would an alternative help more? Is it an objectively worthwhile investment? Is it the best solution? Are you giving them all the facts they need to determine this on their own?

CONSIDER SECOND- AND THIRD-ORDER IMPACTS. Consider not only immediate consequences, but consequences across time. Consider the impact of the action you seek to persuade, as well as the tools you use to persuade it. Maybe the action is objectively positive, but in motivating the action, you resorted to instilling beliefs that will cause damage over time. Consider their long-term impact as well.

KNOW THAT BAD ACTORS ARE PLAYING THE SAME GAME. Bad actors already know how to be persuasive and how to spread their lies. They already know the tools. And many lies are more tempting than truth and easier to believe by their very nature. Truth waits for us to find it at the bottom of a muddy well. Truth is complicated, and complexity is harder to convey with impact. Use these tools to give truth a fighting chance in an arena where bad actors have a natural advantage. Use your knowledge to counter and defuse these tools when people misuse them.

APPLY THE FIVE ETHICAL APPROACHES: seek the greatest good for the greatest number (utilitarian); protect the rights of those affected and treat people not as means but as ends (rights); treat equals equally and nonequals fairly (justice); set the good of humanity as the basis of your moral reasoning (common good); act consistently with the ideals that lead to your self-actualization and the highest potential of your character (virtue). Say and do what is right, not what is expedient, and be willing to suffer the consequences of doing so. Don't place self-gratification, acquisitiveness, social status, and power over the common good of all humanity.

APPLY THE FOUR ETHICAL DECISION-MAKING CRITERIA: respect for individual rights to make choices, hold views, and act based on personal beliefs and values (autonomy); the maximization of benefits and the minimization of harms, acting for the benefit of others, helping others further their legitimate interests; taking action to prevent or remove possible harms (beneficence); acting in ways that cause no harm, avoid the risk of harm, and assuring benefits outweigh costs (non-maleficence); treating others according to a defensible standard (justice).

USE ILLOGICAL PROCESSES TO GET ETHICAL RESULTS. Using flawed thinking processes to get good outcomes is not unethical. Someone who disagrees should stop speaking with conviction, clarity, authority, and effective paralanguage. All are irrelevant to the truth of their words, but impact the final judgment of the audience. You must use logic and evidence to figure out the truth. But this doesn't mean logic and evidence will persuade others. Humans have two broad categories of cognitive functions: system one is intuitive, emotional, fast, heuristic-driven, and generally illogical; system two is rational, deliberate, evidence-driven, and generally logical. The best-case scenario is to get people to believe right things for right reasons (through system two). The next best case is to get people to believe right things for wrong reasons (through system one). Both are far better than letting people believe wrong things for wrong reasons. If you don't use those processes, they still function, but lead people astray. You can reverse-engineer them. If you know the truth, have an abundance of reasons to be confident you know the truth, and can predict the disasters that will occur if people don't believe the truth, don't you have a responsibility to be as effective as possible in bringing people to the truth? Logic and evidence are essential, of course. They will persuade many. They should have persuaded you. But people can't always follow a long chain of reasoning or a complicated argument. Persuade by eloquence what you learned by reason.

HELP YOUR SELF-INTEREST. (But not at the expense of your audience or without their knowledge). Ethics calls for improving the world, and you are a part of the world – the one you control most. Improving yourself is a service to others.

APPLY THE WINDOWPANE STANDARD. In Aristotle's view, rhetoric reveals how to persuade and how to defeat manipulative persuaders. Thus, top students of rhetoric would be master speakers, trained to anticipate and disarm the rhetorical tactics of their adversaries. According to this tradition, language is only useful to the extent that it does not distort reality, and good writing functions as a "windowpane," helping people peer through the wall of ignorance and view reality. You might think this precludes persuasion. You might think this calls for dry academic language. But what good is a windowpane if nobody cares to look through it? What good is a windowpane to reality if, on the other wall, a stained-glass window distorts reality but draws people to it? The best windowpane reveals as much of reality as possible while drawing as many people to it as possible.

RUN THROUGH THESE INTROSPECTIVE QUESTIONS. Are the means truly unethical or merely distasteful, unpopular, or unwise? Is the end truly good, or does it simply appear good because we desire it? Is it probable that bad means will achieve the good end? Is the same good achievable using more ethical means if we are creative, patient, and skillful? Is the good end clearly and overwhelmingly better than any bad effects of the means used to attain it? Will the use of unethical means to achieve a good end withstand public scrutiny? Could the use of unethical means be justified to those most affected and those most impartial? Can I specify my ethical criteria or standards? What is the grounding of the ethical judgment? Can I justify the reasonableness and relevancy of these standards for this case? Why are these the best criteria? Why do they take priority? How does the communication succeed or fail by these standards? What judgment is justified in this case about the degree of ethicality? Is it a narrowly focused one rather than a broad and generalized one? To whom is ethical responsibility owed – to which individuals, groups, organizations, or professions? In what ways and to what extent? Which take precedence? What is my responsibility to myself and society? How do I feel about myself after this choice? Can I continue to "live with myself?" Would I want my family to know of this choice? Does the choice reflect my ethical character? To what degree is it "out of character?" If called upon in public to justify the ethics of my communication, how adequately could I do so? What generally accepted reasons could I offer? Are there precedents which can guide me? Are there aspects of this case that set it apart from others? How thoroughly have alternatives been explored before settling on this choice? Is it less ethical than some of the workable alternatives? If the goal requires unethical communication, can I abandon the goal (Johannesen et al., 2007)?

VIEW YOURSELF AS A GUIDE. Stories have a hero, a villain who stands in his way, and a guide who helps the hero fulfill his mission. If you speak ineffectively, you are a nonfactor. If you speak deceitfully, you become the villain. But if you convey truth effectively, you become the guide in your audience's story, who leads them, teaches them, inspires them, and helps them overcome adversity and win. Use your words to put people on the best possible path. And if you hide an ugly truth, ask yourself this: "If I found out that *my* guide omitted this, how would I react?"

APPLY THE PUZZLE ANALOGY. Think of rhetoric as a piece in the puzzle of reality. Only use a rhetorical approach if it fits with the most logical, rational, and evidence-based view of reality. If it doesn't, it's the wrong puzzle piece. Try another.

KNOW THAT THE TRUTH WILL OUT. The truth can either come out in your words, or you can deceive people. You can convince them to live in a fantasy. And that might work. Until. Until truth breaks down the door and storms the building. Until the facade comes crashing down and chaos makes its entry. Slay the dragon in its lair before it comes to your village. Invite truth in through the front door before truth burns the building down. Truth wins in the end, either because a good person spreads, defends, and fights for it, or because untruth reveals itself as such by its consequences, and does so in brutal and painful fashion, hurting innocents and perpetrators alike. Trust and reputation take years to create and seconds to destroy.

MAXIMIZE THE TWO HIERARCHIES OF SUCCESS: honesty *and* effectiveness. You could say "Um, well, uh, I think that um, what we should... should uh... do, is that, well... let me think... er, I think if we are more, you know... fluid, we'll be better at... producing, I mean, progressing, and producing, and just more generally, you know, getting better results, but... I guess my point is, like, that, that if we are more fluid and do things more better, we will get better results than with a bureaucracy and, you know how it is, a silo-based structure, right? I mean... you know what I mean." Or, you could say "Bravery beats bureaucracy, courage beats the status quo, and innovation beats stagnation." Is one of those statements truer? No. Is one of them more effective? Is one of them more likely to get positive action that instantiates the truth into the world? Yes. Language is not reality. It provides signposts to reality. Two different signposts can point at the same truth – they can be equally and maximally true – and yet one can be much more effective. One gets people to follow the road. One doesn't. Maximize honesty. Then, insofar as it doesn't sacrifice honesty, maximize effectiveness. Speak truth. And speak it well.

KNOW THAT DECEPTION SINKS THE SHIP. Deception prevents perception. If someone deceives everyone onboard a ship, blinding them in a sense, they may get away with self-serving behavior. But eventually, they get hurt by the fate they designed. The ship sinks. How could it not? The waters are hazardous. If the crew is operating with distorted perceptions, they fail to see the impending dangers in the deep. So it is with teams, organizations, and entire societies.

APPLY THE WISDOM OF THIS QUOTE. Mary Beard, an American historian, author, and activist, captured the essence of ethical rhetoric well: "What politicians do is they never get the rhetoric wrong, and the price they pay is they don't speak the truth as they see it. Now, I will speak truth as I see it, and sometimes I don't get the rhetoric right. I think that's a fair trade-off." It's more than fair. It's necessary.

REMEMBER YOUR RESPONSIBILITY TO SOCIETY. Be a guardian of the truth. Speak out against wrongdoing, and do it well. The solution to evil speech is not less speech, but more (good) speech. Create order with your words, not chaos. Our civilization depends on it. Match the truth, honesty, and vulnerable transparency of your words against the irreducible complexity of the universe. And in this complex universe, remember the omnipresence of nuance, and the dangers of simplistic ideologies. (Inconveniently, simplistic ideologies are persuasive, while nuanced truths are difficult to convey. This is why good people need to be verbally skilled; to pull the extra weight of conveying a realistic worldview). Don't commit your whole mind to an isolated fragment of truth, lacking context, lacking nuance. Be precise in your speech, to ensure you are saying what you mean to say. Memorize the logical fallacies, the cognitive biases, and the rules of logic and correct thinking. (Conveniently, many rhetorical devices are also reasoning devices that focus your inquiry and help you explicate truth). But don't demonize those with good intentions and bad ideas. If they are forthcoming and honest, they are not your enemy. Rather, the two of you are on a shared mission to find the truth, partaking in a shared commitment to reason and dialogue. The malevolent enemy doesn't care about the truth. And in this complex world, remember Voltaire's warning to "cherish those who seek the truth but beware of those who find it," and Aristotle's startling observation that "the least deviation from truth [at the start] is multiplied a thousandfold." Be cautious in determining what to say with conviction. Good speaking is not a substitute for good thinking. The danger zone is being confidently incorrect. What hurts us most is what we know that just isn't so. Remember these tenets and your responsibility, and rhetoric becomes the irreplaceable aid of the good person doing good things in difficult times; the sword of the warrior of the light.

KNOW THAT DECEPTION IS ITS OWN PUNISHMENT. Knowingly uttering a falsehood is a spoken lie of commission. Having something to say but not saying it is a spoken lie of omission. Knowingly behaving inauthentically is an acted-out lie of commission. Knowingly omitting authentic behavior is an acted-out lie of omission. All these deceptions weaken your being. All these deceptions corrupt your own mind, turning your greatest asset into an ever-present companion you can no longer trust. Your conscience operates somewhat autonomously, and it will call you out (unless your repeated neglect desensitizes it). You have a conscious conscience which speaks clearly, and an unconscious conscience, which communicates more subtly. A friend of mine asked: "Why do we feel relieved when we speak truth? Why are we drawn toward it, even if it is not pleasant? Do our brains have something that makes this happen?" Yes, they do: our consciences, our inner lights, our inner north stars. And we feel relieved because living with the knowledge of our own deceit is often an unbearable burden. You live your life before an audience of one: yourself. You cannot escape the observation of your own awareness; you can't hide from yourself. Everywhere you go, there you are. Everything you do, there you are. Some of the greatest heights of wellbeing come from performing well in this one-man theater, and signaling virtue to yourself; being someone you are proud to be (and grateful to observe). Every time you lie, you tell your subconscious mind that your character is too weak to contend with the truth. And this shapes your character accordingly. It becomes true. And then what? Lying carries its own punishment, even if the only person who catches the liar is the liar himself.

BE A MONSTER (THEN LEARN TO CONTROL IT). There is nothing moral about weakness and harmlessness. The world is difficult. There are threats to confront, oppressors to resist, and tyrants to rebuff. (Peterson, 2018). There are psychopaths, sociopaths, and Machiavellian actors with no love for the common good. There is genuine malevolence. If you are incapable of being an effective deceiver, then you are incapable of being an effective advocate for truth: it is the same weapon, pointed in different directions. If you cannot use it in both directions, can you use it at all? Become a monster, become dangerous, and become capable of convincing people to believe in a lie... and then use this ability to convince them to believe in the truth. The capacity for harm is also the capacity for harming harmful entities; that is to say, defending innocent ones. If you can't hurt anyone, you can't help anyone when they need someone to stand up for them. Words are truly weapons, and the most powerful weapons in the world at that. The ability to use them, for good *or* for bad, is the prerequisite to using them for good. There is an archetype in our cultural narratives: the well-intentioned but harmless protagonist who gets roundly defeated by the villain, until he develops his monstrous edge and integrates it, at which point he becomes the triumphant hero. Along similar lines, I watched a film about an existential threat to humanity, in which the protagonist sought to convey the threat to a skeptical public, but failed miserably because he lacked the rhetorical skill to do so. The result? The world ended. Everyone died. The protagonist was of no use to anyone. And this almost became a true story. A historical study showed that in the Cuban Missile Crisis, the arguments that won out in the United States mastermind group were not the best, but those argued with the most conviction. Those with the best arguments lacked the skill to match. The world (could have) ended. The moral? Speak truth... well.

MASTERING COMMUNICATION, ONE SKILL AT A TIME

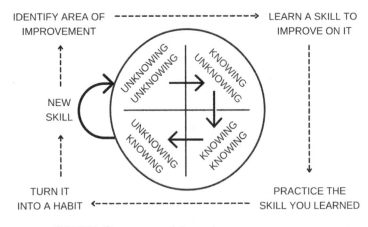

FIGURE I: The proven path to mastery.

psychology

....

noun

> the scientific study of the human mind and its
> functions, especially those affecting behavior in a
> given context

persuasion

....

noun

> the action or fact of persuading someone or of being
> persuaded to do or believe something; to move by
> argument, entreaty, or expostulation to a belief,
> position, or course of action

CONTENTS

HOW TO PERSUADE: 171

HOW TO INFORM: 225

HOW TO INSPIRE: 267

BEFORE YOU GO...

Rhetoric, Motivated by Love, Guided by Reason, and Aimed at Truth, Is a Powerful Force for the Greatest Good.

POLITICAL DISCLAIMER

Throughout this book, and throughout all my books, I draw examples of communication strategies from the political world. I quote from the speeches of many of America's great leaders, like JFK and MLK, as well as from more recent political figures of both major parties. Political communication is ideal for illustrating the concepts revealed in the books. It is the best source of examples of words that work that I have ever found. I don't use anything out of the political mainstream. And it is by extensively studying the inaugural addresses of United States Presidents and the great speeches of history that I have discovered many of the speaking strategies I share with you.

My using the words of any particular figure to illustrate a principle of communication is not necessarily an endorsement of the figure or their message. Separate the speaker from the strategy. After all, the strategy is the only reason the speaker made an appearance in the book at all. Would you rather have a weak example of a strategy you want to learn from a speaker you love, or a perfect example of the strategy from a speaker you detest?

For a time, I didn't think a disclaimer like this was necessary. I thought people would do this on their own. I thought that if people read an example of a strategy drawn from the words of a political figure they disagreed with, they would appreciate the value of the example as an instructive tool and set aside their negative feelings about the speaker. "Yes, I don't agree with this speaker or the message, but I can clearly see the strategy in this example and I now have a better understanding of how it works and how to execute it." Indeed, I suspect 95% of my readers do just that. You probably will, too. But if you are part of the 5% who aren't up for it, don't say I didn't warn you, and please don't leave a negative review because you think I endorse this person or that person. I don't, as this is strictly a book about communication.

THE

PSYCHOLOGY

OF

PERSUASION

HOW TO USE PROVEN SPEAKING PATTERNS
TO MAKE YOUR IDEAS IRRESISTIBLE

SPEAK FOR SUCCESS COLLECTION BOOK

THE PSYCHOLOGY OF PERSUASION CHAPTER

I

INSTANT INFLUENCE:

The Little-Known Secret of Words that Work

THE STRANGEST SECRET – FOREWORD

L ET ME TELL YOU THE STRANGEST STORY AND the strangest secret. I have a vivid memory of this moment burned into my head. My mind always wanders back to it. It's the moment everything changed. I'll tell you exactly what happened. Then I'll tell you exactly why this changes everything about persuasive presentation, compelling communication, and powerful public speaking.

I was a college student when it happened. Much of my life since has been spent developing the single critical insight that slapped me in the face one fateful day.

Let's begin.

I was watching reruns of Bill Clinton's debate against Bush. Why? Because I'm odd like that. I'm fascinated by public speaking and communication; so fascinated that I ended up winning 32 awards as a competitive public speaker, coaching hundreds of mentees, and winning national speech competitions.

And in this particular moment I was feeling a little nostalgic for my competitive debating days. So, that's why I was watching Clinton's most compelling debate moment while I should have been in Microeconomics class. I analyzed every single word, intonation, and gesture. Every single muscle shift in his facial expression meant something specific and, to me, something he strategically selected for a particular impact.

I'll admit something shameful. I was cocky. I was arrogant. I thought I knew everything there was to know about public speaking.

I thought every technique Clinton used was something I had already discovered, I had already used as a competitive public speaker, and I had already written about in my first book, originally printed under the title *How to Master Public Speaking.*

And I had good reason to think so. Need I reiterate my public speaking accomplishments? I won't, I'll spare you; just know I'd be happy to list them out again. The point is this: I was arrogant and felt like I knew everything there was to know about public speaking.

Inclusive pronouns like "we," which put him and his audience on a team, fighting for the same cause together? Check. Knew about them. Used them. Wrote about them.

Portraying both empathy and authority, the qualities of a true leader? Check. Knew about them. Used them. Wrote about them.

Narrow-eyed eye contact with the head tilted slightly up to create captivating intensity, and outward gestures to draw the audience in? Check. Knew about them. Used them. Wrote about them.

So far, this was all old news. But as I watched Clinton speak, I realized an incredible secret. Something so big, so obvious, and so powerful, but at the same time so subtle, secret, and hidden, that my brain couldn't completely process it. I re-winded the video. One more time. A third time. A fourth.

Trust me on this: I don't like not knowing things. And in this moment, I realized that there was something so incredible that I hadn't known all this time (talk about getting knocked down a few pegs). It's okay: I needed it (and probably still do). Pride cometh before destruction, and a haughty spirit before a fall.

Just one problem. Bill Clinton was a single data point. A very interesting data point, but a lonely one. I needed to know if I had stumbled upon the motherload or not. I needed to know if this was just a passing accident or a deliberate, intentional, and accessible example of a secret that would revolutionize communication theory.

Turns out it wasn't just a passing trend.

Video after video.

Transcript after transcript.

Speaker after speaker.

From Martin Luther King, to Bernie Sanders, to JFK, to Barack Obama, to Ronald Reagan, to Mahatma Ghandi, to Hillary Clinton, to Donald Trump, and hundreds of other legendary speakers, I saw what I saw in Bill Clinton repeated again and again.

But more significantly, I analyzed example after example of failed speeches; speeches that fell flat; speeches that didn't motivate; speeches that lacked power; speeches that were, in a word, "meh." And not only did successful speeches consistently use this secret: The unsuccessful ones consistently did not.

EVERYTHING WAS POINTING TO ONE UNKNOWN

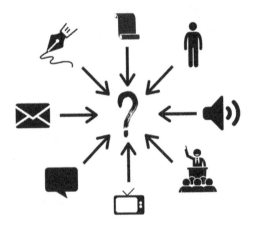

FIGURE 1: Years of studying communication contributed to the realization that there was one fundamental secret of effective persuasion that I had missed.

Like I said, I don't like not knowing things. And for someone who has had as much experience as I have on the subject of public speaking, and who has written a book on the subject, it was sobering. I realized, in a swift moment, that I didn't know 80% of public speaking like I thought, but only 20%. And the worst part? That 20% wasn't even the most important stuff.

But as dismayed as I was, I was also excited; thrilled, even. Why? Because I found something new. I went online and searched diligently to see if anyone else discovered what I discovered that fateful day. And to be truthful, some other people have stumbled upon it, but they only recognize the tip of the iceberg. And if you stick around, I'm going to give you the whole damn iceberg, from top to bottom. Let me tell you this: It's a massive iceberg.

THIS BOOK TAKES A UNIQUE DIVE INTO THE SECRET

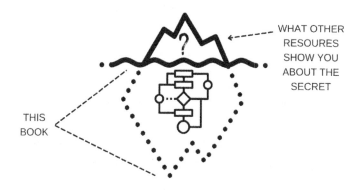

FIGURE 2: To the best of my knowledge, no other resource reveals the information this book reveals.

Why should you care? Because this secret will take the anxiety out of public speaking. This secret will make persuasion easy. This secret will make presentations 50% done for you before you even start. This secret can be used in presentations, public speeches, meetings, conversations, writing; you name it. If it's communication, this secret will revolutionize everything you thought you knew about it, and maximize your impact and influence.

I bet you want to know the secret. Are you still reading this right now? If so, it's because this introduction itself was an example of the secret in action.

Now, let me tell you the big secret. In a word, just a single word, which means the difference between failed and successful communication, and in a gross oversimplification of what I've discovered, here's the powerful, hidden, little-known secret: structure.

In this book, you will learn everything I've discovered about this secret. I hold nothing back. You will be able to take advantage of the secret in an extremely specific way, tailored exactly to your life and your communication needs.

THIS IS THE BEST PART

Don't let me fool you. Throughout this book, and in basically anything I ever wrote or recorded on the subjects of communication, persuasion, influence, and leadership (which are all really one subject), I present information through the lens of public speaking. Why? Because that's my background. That's how I got my start. My journey as a competitive public speaker is what led me on this journey; the journey of compiling the frameworks and strategies leaders need to communicate with influence. This background informs all my work and colors all my writing. But remember this: Whenever I describe a strategy through the lens of giving a public speech or presentation, it applies to virtually all professional communication.

KEY INSIGHT:

The Medium Is Not the Message, and the Message Is Not the Medium. The Medium Is a Piece of the Message.

OUT OF MANY, ONE

FIGURE 3: Most of these principles work for virtually all forms of communication (occasionally requiring just a modicum of adaptation).

Proposals. Emails. Pitches. Interviews. Meetings. Informal (but high-stakes) conversations. Whatever form of communication you can think of, it's all really one and the same when you strip away the superficial differences. It's all transmitting an idea from your mind into another mind (or millions of other minds). So, if I say "the problem-solution structure is a simple and compelling framework you can use to create a fast and psychologically irresistible persuasive punch in your speech," know that what I'm really saying is this: "The problem-solution structure is a simple and compelling framework you can use to create a fast and psychologically irresistible persuasive punch in all communication, no matter its superficial form."

..............................Chapter Summary..................................

- There is one little-known secret undergirding the legendary messages delivered by legendary speakers.

- This secret applies to all communication: emails, pitches, conversations, debates, speeches, presentations, etc.
- The hidden secret is structure: the idea that effective communication breaks down into step-by-step processes.
- If you understand this secret, you will be vastly more influential, persuasive, and impactful in your speech.
- If you understand this secret, you will know exactly what to say in every communication situation.
- If you understand this secret, communication will be "done for you," simply requiring that you fill in the structure steps.

KEY INSIGHT:

Structures Help You Argue on Behalf of Truth with Precision, Poise, and Elegance.

The Medium Behind All Mediums Is Human Connection. Part of the Purpose of a Rhetorical Structure Is Shaping and Deepening that Connection.

Claim These Free Resources that Will Help You Unleash the Power of Your Words and Speak with Confidence. Visit www.speakforsuccesshub.com/toolkit for Access.

18 Free PDF Resources

12 Iron Rules for Captivating Story, 21 Speeches that Changed the World, 341-Point Influence Checklist, 143 Persuasive Cognitive Biases, 17 Ways to Think On Your Feet, 18 Lies About Speaking Well, 137 Deadly Logical Fallacies, 12 Iron Rules For Captivating Slides, 371 Words that Persuade, 63 Truths of Speaking Well, 27 Laws of Empathy, 21 Secrets of Legendary Speeches, 19 Scripts that Persuade, 12 Iron Rules For Captivating Speech, 33 Laws of Charisma, 11 Influence Formulas, 219-Point Speech-Writing Checklist, 21 Eloquence Formulas

Claim These Free Resources that Will Help You Unleash the Power of Your Words and Speak with Confidence. Visit www.speakforsuccesshub.com/toolkit for Access.

30 Free Video Lessons

We'll send you one free video lesson every day for 30 days, written and recorded by Peter D. Andrei. Days 1-10 cover authenticity, the prerequisite to confidence and persuasive power. Days 11-20 cover building self-belief and defeating communication anxiety. Days 21-30 cover how to speak with impact and influence, ensuring your words change minds instead of falling flat. Authenticity, self-belief, and impact – this course helps you master three components of confidence, turning even the most high-stakes presentations from obstacles into opportunities.

Claim These Free Resources that Will Help You Unleash the Power of Your Words and Speak with Confidence. Visit www.speakforsuccesshub.com/toolkit for Access.

2 Free Workbooks

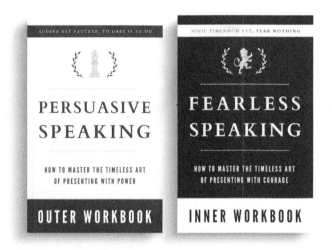

We'll send you two free workbooks, including long-lost excerpts by Dale Carnegie, the mega-bestselling author of *How to Win Friends and Influence People* (5,000,000 copies sold). *Fearless Speaking* guides you in the proven principles of mastering your inner game as a speaker. *Persuasive Speaking* guides you in the time-tested tactics of mastering your outer game by maximizing the power of your words. All of these resources complement the Speak for Success collection.

SPEAK FOR SUCCESS COLLECTION BOOK

THE PSYCHOLOGY OF PERSUASION CHAPTER

II

THE FOUNDATION:

Revealing the Basics Truths of
Effective Communication

MODELS OF COMMUNICATION

M OST PEOPLE DON'T KNOW THE BASIC THEORIES of effective communication. This is deeply unfortunate. The one covered in this book, "structure-theory," is just one of many. And it will make more sense to you and be more useful if we support it with the context of some other theories.

Just remember two things. First, there are many more communication models than these. We are just going through the most relevant ones. Second, we are going wide, covering a lot of theories, but not necessarily expounding too deeply on any one theory. I suspect that by the time you learn the 29 theories, you will be a drastically better communicator, you will avoid common communication mistakes, and you will be able to persuade with ease and confidence.

1.1: THE PUBLIC SPEAKING TRIAD

I coined this as the public speaking triad. But, in truth, it should be called the communication triad. The theory goes like this: For all communication to succeed, the communicator must connect to the receivers of the communication and to his or her message, the receivers must connect to the communicator and to his or her message, and the message must connect to the communicator and to the receivers. Everything else about communication comes down to the foundation of this single concept.

Let me put it more simply: For successful communication to occur, the communicator(s), the receiver(s), and the message(s) must all connect. Each one of those three must be connected to the other two. If any one of the connections breaks, the entire piece of communication fails and falls apart.

THE ESSENCE OF COMPELLING COMMUNICATION

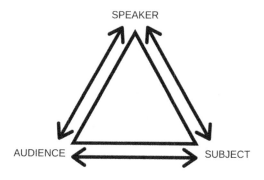

FIGURE 4: Successful communication connects speaker with subject, audience with subject, and speaker with audience, in no particular order.

In the context of public speaking, for a persuasive speech, the speaker must connect to the message to draw upon a reserve of emotional energy when communicating, and the speaker must connect to the audience to understand their preexisting beliefs, pain-points, and mental states. The audience must connect to the speaker so that the speaker can meet the audience's trust threshold, and the audience must connect to the idea by seeing it as relevant to their lives; as a solution to a problem they have. And finally, the idea must connect to the speaker, because the speaker must have some compelling stake in the idea, and thorough knowledge of it (plus the ability to convey this knowledge), while it must connect to the audience because, if it is not relevant to them, they won't care.

One last key: The connections usually grow together, and usually fall together. If you improve one of the connections, the others tend to follow suit immediately. I call this the "rising tide" effect.

1.2: THE COMMUNICATION TOOLBOX AND THREE-LAYER COMMUNICATION

How do you build the public speaking triad? Think about it: You know exactly what you need to accomplish for your communication to succeed. So, how do you do it?

It depends on the medium. In writing, you have only words, which means you can fully apply structure theory since it deals with only words. But when speaking, you have words, body language, and your voice. You aren't communicating with one language, but three. You have the language of your words (English, for example), the language of your body, and the language of your voice. Right now, I am communicating with you just with my "word language." If I were speaking to you in a lecture hall, or a seminar, or a training, I would be using three languages: words, body, and voice.

EVERYONE SPEAKS THREE LANGUAGES

FIGURE 5: Your "public speaking toolbox" or "communication toolbox" consists of the three components of your communication: your words, body language, and vocal tonalities. Nearly every piece of communication advice relates to improving one of these three tools.

So, to summarize, the public speaking triad is the three-way connection between speaker, audience, and message, and you build it with your words, body language, and vocal tonalities.

HOW YOU GUARANTEE COMPELLING COMMUNICATION

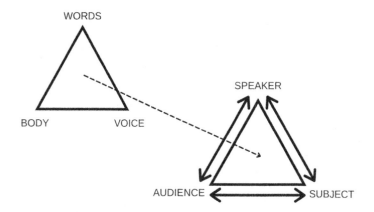

FIGURE 6: You form the three connections in the public speaking triad by using your three languages. You interconnect the speaker, audience, and subject by using your words, body language, and voice. As we will shortly see, this is not yet the complete picture.

The vast majority of communication advice deals with this theory alone. Any tip or piece of advice you receive has to do with empowering your words, body language, and voice in some way.

Think about this book, which teaches you exactly how to organize your words for maximum impact based on the psychology of communication we are discussing now. Which part of the public speaking toolbox does it deal with? Which of your languages does it empower? Your words.

For your word language, use "secrecy" phrases. Use words like "secret, hidden, little-known, never-before-seen, classified, unknown, forbidden, underground." These secrecy phrases build mystery and intrigue, and play into natural, innate human curiosity. "Security" phrases are powerful too: "proven, guaranteed, time-tested, scientific," are four examples. There are so many different categories of words that impact your audience in different ways. These are just two of them. See how these types of words strengthen the speaker to audience and idea to audience connections?

For your body language, use open body language. What's open body language? Simply put, open body language is when you open your torso, face your audience, and keep your hands out in open sight. This open body language is a symbol buried deep into our subconscious psychologies by evolution, and it communicates that "this person can be trusted." See how this improves the speaker to audience connection?

For your vocal language, use breaking-rapport tonality. This is when the pitch (and if you want, pace and volume) of your voice go down at the end of your statements. These make you seem confident in yourself and your ideas. They also signal and create a sense of "conclusion." The sharper the breaking-rapport, the more conclusive and believable a statement sounds. See how this improves the speaker to audience connection?

There are thousands of techniques that fall under each of the strategies. They are rooted firmly in human psychology. Why does technique X produce effect Y in humans? Because our psychologies have evolved to interpret the signal X to mean Y. And overriding human psychology is not something people can easily do, even to themselves, which is why these strategies are so powerful.

You will learn plenty of these strategies in this book; strategies falling under the "word language" bucket. You will learn a few thousand in my other books, which fall under each of the three buckets.

1.3: ACTIVATION, CONTROL, ALIGNMENT

You are aware, at this point, that you have three languages when you are speaking, and that you use them to create a three-way connection between three elements: the speaker, the audience, and the idea. By my estimation, you are already ahead of 90% of people at this point.

Let me throw you another trifecta: your three languages must all be activated, in your deliberate control, and in alignment with one another. If these three conditions are not met, your communication will not be effective. It won't accomplish its purpose. But what do activation, control, and alignment mean? Let's dive into this theory.

Activation: Your three languages must all be activated. You must be using them. If you are speaking, your word language is activated. However, if your vocal language is fully monotonous and you don't move your body at all, your other two languages are not activated.

Control: Your three languages must all be in your deliberate control. You must be able to say to yourself while you're communicating that, "If I do X with [insert language], effect Y will happen to my audience." You must be confident in this, and you must also be able to actually execute X, whatever technique it might stand for.

Alignment: Once you activate your three languages and once you bring them under your deliberate control, you must bring them all in alignment. The three ways human beings convey meaning must be conveying the same meaning.

KEY INSIGHT:

Make Your Languages of Body & Voice Echo the Message of Your Words.

HOW TO PROPERLY USE YOUR THREE LANGUAGES

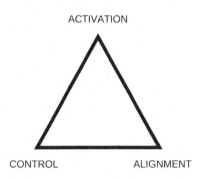

FIGURE 7: To properly apply your three languages, you must activate them, control them, and align them. You must be using them, directing them, and conveying the same message with each of them.

Think about it: If a speaker is speaking confident words with a confident voice but is portraying total insecurity with their body language, are they communicating effectively? Nope. Not a chance. Why not? Because their three languages are not in alignment.

Imagine another scenario: A speaker is speaking engaging words with engaging body language, but a monotone vocal tonality. What happens? If you have ever listened to this type of communication, you already know. The audience tunes out.

Misalignment ruins the speaker to audience connection. Why? Because the audience doesn't necessarily trust words alone. People can easily manipulate their words. As a result, the audience looks to two other languages which are not easily manipulated: the voice and body languages. If these two align, the trust threshold is passed (for most people, under most circumstances). If not? The connection is instantly harmed.

BRINGING IT ALL TOGETHER

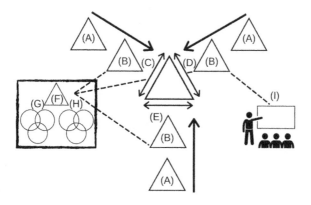

FIGURE 8: Even this complex diagram leaves out a great deal of nuance. But it brings together some of the previous theories. You must activate, control, and align (A) your words, voice, and body language (B) to connect the speaker and the audience (C), the speaker and the subject (D), and the audience and the subject (E). With your words (B), you must appeal to ethos, pathos, and logos (F) while using the new, simple, relevant triad (G) to achieve saliency, intensity, and stability (H). You can also conceive of presentation slides or other visual material (I) as another "language," which makes four.

1.4: TRIAD INGREDIENTS

Each of the connections in the triad is strengthened by a set of characteristics.

Speaker to audience: The speaker can help the audience, the speaker can provide a solution to the audience's problem, the speaker understands the audience.

Speaker to idea: The speaker thoroughly understands the idea, the speaker has an incentive to spread the idea, the speaker believes in the idea.

Audience to speaker: The audience trusts, knows, and likes the speaker, the audience sees the speaker as an authority figure, and the audience feels that the speaker has empathy for them and understands their pain.

Audience to idea: The audience believes the idea has value to them, the audience finds the idea to be a solution to a problem, and the audience trusts the idea.

Idea to speaker: The idea has impacted the speaker's life in a significant way (or the speaker has impacted the idea's life in a significant way, as an expert does for the ideas in his field).

Idea to audience: The idea is relevant to the audience's life (or the audience is relevant to the idea's life, as is the case for an idea that the audience must help spread).

KEY INSIGHT:

"There Are Three Things to Aim at In Public Speaking: First, to Get Into Your Subject, Then to Get Your Subject Into Yourself, And Lastly, to Get Your Subject Into the Heart of Your Audience." – Alexander Gregg

---

THE COMMON ASPECTS OF THE TRIAD

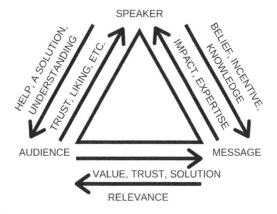

FIGURE 9: While every public speaking triad is unique depending on the characteristics of its parts, almost all demand some key elements to form the connections.

1.5: PURPOSEFUL COMMUNICATION

If you understand and use purposeful communication in your writing and speaking, communication will instantly become something you enjoy. Purposeful communication is, in its simplest form, just a mental model of how to view communication. All these theories are.

All communication (at least, all communication worth engaging in) must have a purpose. Communication is effective if it fulfills that purpose. Communication is ineffective if it does not fulfill that purpose. There is a "starting state," which describes the world before your communication. There is a "finishing state," which describes the world after your communication if its purpose has been fulfilled. In truly purposeful communication, every single word, sentence, paragraph, structural component, pause, vocal intonation, gesture – every single use of your three languages – must be specifically, strategically, and deliberately designed to move in a straight line from the starting state to the finishing state.

And don't take "straight line" to necessarily suggest a forceful, direct approach lacking all measures of subtlety or nuance. Why? Because, sometimes, and probably most of the time, the straightest line (that is, the most effective path), from starting state to ending state, is one that contains subtlety and nuance.

THE MEANING OF PURPOSEFUL COMMUNICATION

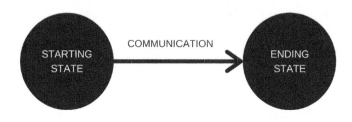

FIGURE 10: Purposeful communication is geared toward moving the world from what it is to what you want it to be.

Does the foundation of this theory make sense to you? Every action you take when you're communicating, as this theory dictates, must be designed to move the world closer to your desired outcome.

When I edit speeches or persuasive writing, I run through this following process for cleaning, simplifying, and empowering language. This process is informed by the theory of purposeful communication. First, take a sentence you're editing, or the first one in the speech. Identify the one purpose of that sentence clearly (in a sentence, perhaps) as it relates to your one overarching purpose. Go through each word, phrase, and unit of meaning, and decide if it helps toward that purpose, or detracts away from that purpose. If it does help, does it help enough to justify keeping it when keeping it dilutes the power of the other stuff that potentially helps more, or if it takes the place of another unit of meaning that would help more? Remove detractors, keep helpers. Repeat for next sentence. Repeat multiple times if you'd like, slowly chiseling to perfection. Apply this strategy at different levels of meaning. Apply it to words, pieces of sentences, sentences, sequences of sentences, paragraphs, ideas, etc.

HOW TO ITERATE YOUR COMMUNICATION TO PERFECTION

FIGURE 11: This simple, easy, fast, and elegant process allows you to iterate your communication to perfection, vastly improving your influence in the process.

Of course, there is a "step zero" to this process, which is to identify a worthwhile purpose in the first place.

In *The Way of the Wolf,* Jordan Belfort describes a similar theory of persuasive communication in this way: "On the straight line, directly on it, every single word, every single statement, sentence, everything is fulfilling the open to close purpose. No free words, no time for stupid statements, no time to go off to Pluto and talk about the price of tea in China. Being in-control, specifically directly on the line, is directed, powerful; your words have meaning, and the meaning is to create massive certainty in the audience's minds. Every word has a purpose."

If your communication doesn't have a purpose, then don't communicate. It's that simple. But if it does have a purpose, you better make sure every single use of your three languages moves you toward fulfilling that purpose.

1.6: THREE-PART MODEL

All communication has three parts: a beginning, a middle, and an end. Shocking, right?

Technically, everything has a beginning, an end, and a time in between the beginning and the end that we label as the middle.

But you must remember that each of the three parts has its own distinct goals. This is the basis of structure theory. Let's break down an example of this into a hierarchy of structures.

Level one structure. Beginning – get attention in a way that is relevant to the content of the speech, middle – close the gap between starting state and finishing state, and end – ensure that the audience follows through on creating the finishing state.

Level two structure. Beginning: APP – establish empathy, authority, and create curiosity, middle: DDD trifecta – create a strong desire in your audience to perform your suggested action, ending: SBA – end on a note most likely to create high audience follow-through.

Level three structure. APP: agree – create empathy, promise – portray authority, preview – create curiosity and a mental "open-loop," DDD trifecta: desire – make your audience want a certain thing, dissonance – show your audience how they are missing what they desire and create cognitive discomfort, decision – suggest the necessary decision that will realize the desire and end the dissonance, SBA: summarize – re-cement the factual information in your audience's minds to create logical certainty, benefits – repeat the tantalizing benefits to set you up for the next step, action – describe to your audience the action you want them to take.

REVEALING THE LEVELS OF STRUCTURE

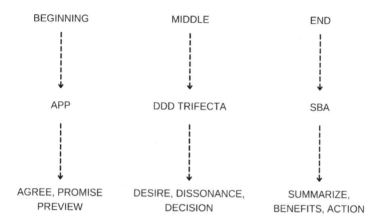

FIGURE 12: At the beginning, use the APP: agree, promise, and preview. At the middle, use the DDD trifecta: instigate desire, create dissonance, and inspire a decision. At the end, use the SBA trifecta: summarize, promise benefits, and present a next action. This is an example of a structure breaking down into sub-structures.

See how we filled in the "beginning, middle, and end" with those formulas? See how those formulas broke down into sub-structures, with distinct steps that fulfill secondary purposes? See how the secondary purposes ultimately come together to fulfill the primary purpose?

After you learn these formulas, instead of seeing persuasive communication as a confusing soup of random statements, you'll see it as an organized, orderly set of structures that clearly move the world from its starting state to your chosen finishing state.

1.7: CONE OF ATTENTION

Every single audience has a set of subjects that, if you communicate about these subjects, results in them narrowing their attention to only focus on you. This is "top of cone" communication, near the vertex of the cone, where its volume is smaller; where it is narrower. If you speak about these "top of cone" subjects, your audience will narrowly focus on you. Think about it: A cone is narrower at the top. It includes fewer things, and if you're lucky, the cone of attention will be so narrow it only includes you and your message. Of course, it has nothing to do with luck, and everything to do with deliberately choosing the correct inputs.

On the flip side, every single audience has a set of subjects that, if you speak about them, will completely dilute their attention away from you. These are "bottom of cone," where its volume is larger; where it includes more things – distractions – and not only you.

Here's where it gets tricky: There is no universal cone.

Here's where it gets simpler: There is a sort of universal vertex.

Imagine a bunch of different cones overlapping only at the top, flaring out in different directions but meeting in a shared vertex.

You are probably wishing there was some sort of universal cone; that there was some sort of universal key unlocking every single person equally, and grabbing everyone's attention to the same degree. The core psychological human desires are that key. If you speak about the core human desires, you will almost always be "top of cone," and your audience – and almost any audience – will give you their narrow attention. If you speak without invoking the core human desires, that's a problem. You'll be "bottom of cone," and you won't earn undivided attention.

That said, every single audience has a different cone. In other words, they want different external things, but they want those different external things (the body of the cone) because they satisfy the same core desires (the overlapping vertex of the cone). A financier on Wallstreet wants to hit the next hot stock to satisfy the same desires as a fisherman in East Asia seeking a full net of fish. Sure, these are drastically different means, but to the same primordial psychological ends.

HOW TO ENSURE PEOPLE PAY ATTENTION

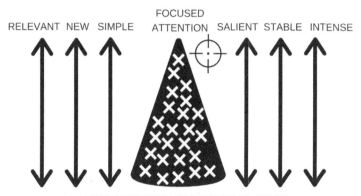

FIGURE 13: At the top of the cone, you bring your audience to a state of focused attention, including only one item: you. As the cone broadens toward the bottom, it includes more items: you, their car repairs, their weekend plans, the price of tea in China, etc. Aim to bring your audience to the top of the cone by applying the new, relevant, simple triad and achieving saliency, intensity, and stability. These qualities generally bring you "top of cone."

Let me put it this way: Many of us want the same things, but we go about achieving those things in different ways. There are means (what we want to achieve) and ends (why we want to achieve those things). While the means differ wildly, the ends are often very similar. They are a set of core human desires and needs.

Why am I telling you this? Because of the cone of audience attention, of course. If you know your audience's means and ends, invoke them both. You'll be right there near the vertex of the cone. If you don't know the means, then identify the ends and invoke those. That will get you very close, and because most of these core desires are widely shared, they are the unifying point for diverse cones of attention; they are where different cones of attention, flaring out in different directions and belonging to wildly different people, meet.

How do you identify the core desires at play? Use the "many-fold-why."

A financier wants to hit the next hot stock. Why? To make money. Why do they want more money? To afford nicer things, and to feel financial security. Here, we branch.

The "nicer-things" branch: Why do they want to afford nicer things? To have a more attractive outward appearance. Why do they want that? For social status and prestige. You have isolated two core motivating desires of that financier.

The "financial security" branch: Why do they want financial security? To be safe no matter what happens. Why do they want that? To be free to do whatever they want, and free from fear. You have isolated two more.

Now we know the exact motivating factors that will make an audience of financiers (and probably fishermen too) listen in. We have the exact, core, psychological human desires that will immediately take you to the "top of cone," where effective communication happens because you met its prerequisite: attaining attention.

Remember this: Social status, prestige, freedom to act, and freedom from fear are all key motivating desires that describe why the fisherman wants a full net. What is inherently valuable about a bunch of flopping fish trapped in a rope net in the middle of the ocean? Nothing. It is only valuable because it fulfills the deeper desires of the fisherman. Want to know why someone does something? Look at the impacts of their action. You will find that the wide and infinite array of diverse human action often boils down to satisfying the same core desires, which is where disparate and diverse cones of attention belonging to disparate and diverse people unite.

UNDERSTANDING THE TWO TYPES OF AUDIENCES

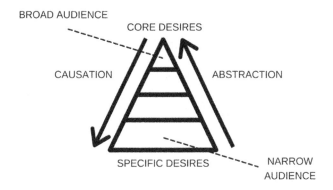

FIGURE 14: A broad audience with no clear-cut defining characteristics share their core desires, while a narrow audience with clear-cut commonalities (like sharing a profession) are much more likely to share specific desires.

THE PYRAMID OF DESIRE AND THE PYRAMID OF SCOPE

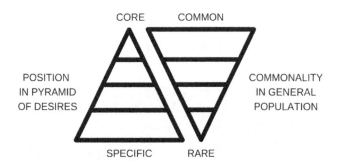

FIGURE 15: The core desires are more common, and any particular specific desire is less common. The closer you

are to core desires – the higher the level of abstraction at
which you define a desire – the more common it is.

You bought (or borrowed or stole) this book because you want to
be more influential. What could give you more influence in
communication than what I just told you?

1.8: THE RIGHT THINGS THE RIGHT WAY

Your words are important, but so is how you look and sound saying
them. We talked about your three languages. This theory is an
extension of that theory.

Everyone can say the right things. Only a person who is
confident and authentic can say the right things in the right ways.

There are those who manipulate themselves and inauthentically
say the right things in the right ways, and they are those who can't say
the right things or say them in the right ways no matter what. Don't
be either of those people.

Your words impact your audience consciously and
subconsciously. They inherently pass the traffic stop of the conscious,
logical, analytical mind on their way to the subconscious mind. At
this traffic stop, their influence dulls, and they often arrive at the
subconscious mind a quivering shadow of what they once were, if
they weren't rejected and sent away altogether. Structure theory and
certain uses of language bypass this intrinsic limitation.

THE TWO LEVELS OF EFFECTIVE COMMUNICATION

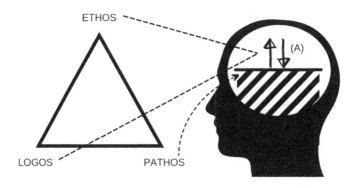

FIGURE 16: Influence occurs on both a conscious and subconscious (also called unconscious or non-conscious) level. The repetitive thoughts of the conscious mind influence the subconscious mind, while the state of the subconscious mind influences the conscious mind, often "tossing up" thoughts to the conscious mind. Some are great, some are distracting, some are nonsensical. Certain strategies are particularly suited for hitting at one of the two minds in particular: ethos and logos hit the conscious mind, while pathos tends to exert more influence over the subconscious mind. Use both.

Your body language and vocal tonalities skip that traffic stop. They are a one-way street with no speed limit taking you directly to your audience's subconscious minds. And which mind has more power over someone? The subconscious one, which researchers estimate makes up between 70% and 94% of our cognition.

Can you imagine someone thinking "I disagree with this idea because [insert reasoned, conscious objection]?" Of course you can. It happens all the time. This is the conscious filter reacting to words.

Can you imagine someone consciously thinking "This speaker is engaged, authentic, and wearing a big smile; he is loud, confident, and self-assured; he is maintaining eye-contact, using vocal emphasis appropriately, and gesturing with intent. As a result, I think his point is compelling?" Or on the flip side, can you imagine someone consciously thinking "This speaker is engaged, authentic, and wearing a big smile; he is loud, confident, and self-assured; he is presenting eye-contact, using vocal emphasis appropriately, and gesturing with intent. I am going to ignore this when judging his point?" I can hardly imagine either of them occurring in the real world, because these characteristics of the speaker – unlike most (but not all) of the speaker's words – pass the conscious filter. They are largely perceived subconsciously, and thus their impact is largely subconscious as well. The advantage of this is that these inputs pass the skepticism of the conscious filter.

1.9: SELF-INTEREST AND "WIIFM?"

If you want to communicate with persuasion and influence, appeal to people's self-interest and answer the question "what's in it for me?" or "WIIFM?"

THE ONLY WAY TO MOTIVATE ENTHUSIASTIC ACTION

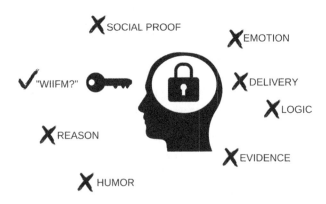

FIGURE 17: In many cases, the only effective persuasive gateway is appealing to the "WIIFM" question. In these

> cases, everything else (reason, humor, evidence, etc.) only
> matters insofar as it helps answer that crucial question:
> "What's in it for me?"

If you do this, you have their attention and interest. If not? You don't have their attention, or their interest, and you most definitely are not going to communicate effectively. You most certainly won't move from starting state to finishing state.

Why? Because of the next two theories. I want you to remember this: All of these features are baked directly into our mental makeup as human beings. Evolution put them there. That's why these bedrock theories are so powerful and irrefutable.

1.10: PERCIEVED MARGINAL BENEFITS, PERCEIVED MARGINAL COSTS

Why must you follow theory nine (self-interest and WIIFM)? Because of this equation.

If you ever took a Microeconomics course, like the one I was skipping when I discovered structure theory way back in college, you're familiar with the marginal benefits versus marginal costs equation.

The adage of "energy in, energy out" is the same as marginal benefits versus marginal costs.

If someone perceives the marginal benefits of an activity to be greater than the marginal cost (including the value of the alternative activity forgone), all else equal, they will do that activity until the marginal benefits begin to be eclipsed by the marginal costs. If the costs exceed the benefits, they won't engage in an activity.

Energy in, energy out: If the energy someone has to put into an activity is greater than the rewards they get out of that activity, they won't engage in it.

Marginal benefits > marginal costs = activity engaged in until marginal costs > marginal benefits.

Marginal benefits < marginal costs = activity not engaged in until marginal costs < marginal benefits.

THE CRUCIAL ACTION-SELECTING COGNITIVE ALGORITHM

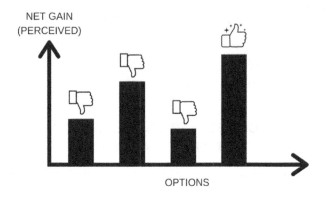

FIGURE 18: If an option has the highest perceived net gain of all the other options available, people select that option. Thus, a major sub-goal of your persuasive effort is to raise the perception of net gain associated with your proposal.

Keep in mind the essential key of applying this theory: This has nothing to do with actual benefits and actual costs, and everything to do with perceived benefits and perceived costs.

And this is exactly how this theory links to self-interest and WIIFM. When you speak in terms of self-interest – and answer the question "what's in it for me?" – perceived marginal benefits (or energy out) seem higher than perceived marginal costs (or energy in).

Now, you might be asking "What activity are they engaging in? What does this have to do with persuasive communication and applying persuasive communication patterns?" The activity they are engaging in (if you properly balance this equation by addressing self-interest and WIIFM) is listening to you; it is opting-in to give you their attention and mental space. Those are resources – scarce resources – that you are implicitly asking them to give up to you. You must ensure they think what they get by giving up the resources to you is greater in value than the resources themselves.

As for question number two – "what does this have to do with persuasive communication and persuasive communication patterns?" – the answer is *everything*. If you don't get them to opt-in to receiving your communication with enthusiasm by showing them, implicitly and explicitly, that marginal benefits far exceed marginal costs, then you don't get their attention, which means you can't persuade, because you can't truly communicate. Sure, you can try, but nobody will really be there to receive your message. They will be running through a to-do list, day-dreaming, or thinking about a totally unrelated subject, all while pretending to listen to you.

And this links perfectly to our next theory of eight seconds and the mental checklist, which then links to structure theory.

Before we get into that, know this: The further benefits exceed costs, the more enthused and attentive your audience will be. On the contrary, the further costs exceed benefits, the less enthused and attentive your audience will be. Yes, there is a threshold where marginal benefits are greater than marginal costs, but there is also a spectrum: The more marginal benefits exceed marginal costs, the more attention you get.

1.11: EIGHT SECONDS AND THE MENTAL CHECKLIST

To communicate persuasively and achieve a purpose you're your communication, you must make sure that your audience perceives the benefits of listening to you to be higher than the costs of listening to you. And to do that, you must speak in terms of their self-interest and answer the "WIIFM" question.

How do people decide if benefits of listening exceed costs of listening? By running through a mental checklist. How quickly do they run through the mental checklist after you begin speaking? In about eight seconds.

So not only do you have to express that energy out is greater than energy in by invoking self-interest, but you also have to do it quickly. In this book, you learn structures acting as templates for meeting the mental checklist, balancing the energy equation, portraying immense value, and doing so quickly.

WHY SOME INSTANTLY LOSE WHILE OTHERS INSTANTLY WIN

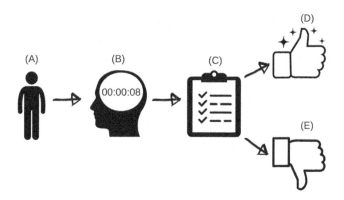

FIGURE 19: When a new speaker (A) appears to the audience, in about eight seconds (B) they run through a mental checklist (C) to decide if they approve (D) or disapprove (E); trust or distrust; like or dislike.

All you have to do to instantly get almost anyone's attention is to take one of these proven language patterns, plug in your words, and say it.

1.12: BENEFITS, FEATURES, AND CONFUSION

Benefits are the positive outcomes your audience will experience as a result of listening to you and taking your suggested action.

Features are what create the benefits. What aspects of your suggested action will produce those benefits? Those elements are the features.

When you want to speak in terms of self-interest and tip the energy equation in your favor, what do present? Benefits, or features?

This is a deeply divisive question in marketing and advertising, although a consensus has begun to emerge. What sells more? The benefits of a product, or the features that produce those benefits?

And in reference to persuasive communication, what appeals to self-interest more? What raises perceived energy out? Benefits, or features?

Speaking in terms of just features is the worst, and speaking in terms of just benefits is okay. But luckily for you, you don't have to pick one. It's a false dilemma.

The best case is to speak in terms of both features and benefits. Either describe a feature and then explain the benefits of that feature, or start with benefits, and then explain the features that create them.

And ideas are products. The algorithm people use to judge and "buy" ideas is the same as that they use to buy products. And I revealed the algorithm. It's called the "marketplace of ideas" for a reason.

An example of features-only communication: "This healthcare plan will decentralize the planning of aggregate treatments, and instead use blockchain and feedback infrastructure to determine what treatments to enact and when to enact them." *(What does that soup of big complicated words even mean? I have no idea what this politician is trying to say. Can't he just tell me how this will impact my life? I really don't trust him anymore, and I have no* faith in this healthcare plan because I don't know what it means for my life).

An **example of benefits-only communication**: "This healthcare plan will make you pay less money and receive better treatment." *(Woah! That sounds great. I see how that will impact my life. I definitely would love to pay less money. That's a huge plus. And I need better treatment. But it's just a promise. Can I trust it? It sounds good, but will it really happen? I'm doubting this. I'm intrigued, but not fully on board).*

An **example of benefit- and feature-oriented communication**: "This healthcare plan will decentralize the planning of aggregate treatments, and instead use blockchain and feedback infrastructure to determine what treatments to enact and when to enact them, which will make the whole system less wasteful and more efficient *(a bridge statement, which we'll discuss shortly)*, and therefore make you pay less money and receive better treatment." *(I'm blown away! I definitely would love to pay less money and receive better treatment. This is perfect. And what a well-thought-out plan! It makes perfect sense. I know exactly how this will impact my life, and exactly how it's going to work. I trust this guy and his plan. I'm going to donate to his campaign and vote for him!)*

When you are promising benefits to someone, they want to believe you. But without explaining the features that create those benefits, they can't. And if your features are particularly complex, throw in a bridge statement to connect your features to your benefits in a believable and understandable way.

1.13: THE WIND AND THE SUN

The principle of effective influences comes to us in the form of a parable passed down over thousands of years. The North Wind and the Sun had a quarrel about which of them was the stronger. While they were disputing with much heat and bluster, a Traveler passed along the road wrapped in a cloak. "Let us agree," said the Sun, "that he is the stronger who can strip that Traveler of his cloak."

"Very well," growled the North Wind, and at once sent a cold, howling blast against the Traveler. With the first gust of wind the ends of the cloak whipped about the Traveler's body. But he immediately wrapped it closely around him, and the harder the Wind blew, the tighter he held it to him. The North Wind tore angrily at the cloak, but all his efforts were in vain. Then the Sun began to shine. At first his beams were gentle, and in the pleasant warmth after the bitter cold of the North Wind, the Traveler unfastened his cloak and let it hang loosely from his shoulders. The Sun's rays grew warmer and warmer. The man took off his cap and mopped his brow. At last he became so heated that he pulled off his cloak, and, to escape the blazing sunshine, threw himself down in the welcome shade of a tree by the roadside. The moral? Gentleness and kind persuasion win where force and bluster fail.

THE LITTLE-KNOWN PROCESS OF COGNITIVE SUBSTITUTION

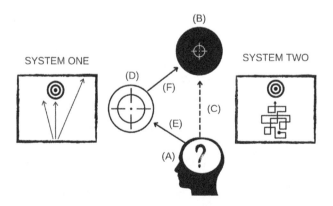

FIGURE 20: Cognitive substitution is foundational to many of these cognitive processes, both producing them and flowing from them. We cover it more deeply in a later

section. When someone is prompted (A) to form an evaluation about a "target question" (B), they can either approach it logically, deliberately, and slowly with system two (C) or perform "attribute substitution," which is a system one process. They "substitute" a "substitute question" (D) for the target question, evaluate this substitute question (E), and transfer the answer to the target question (F). This occurs in part because the substituted question is easier to evaluate than the target question.

THE WISDOM OF THE FABLE OF THE WIND AND THE SUN

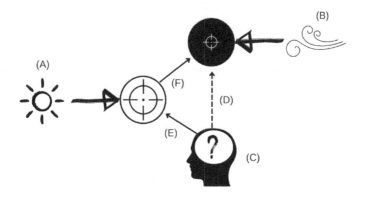

FIGURE 21: The sun (A) targets the heuristic variable; the wind (B) tries to influence the prospect (C) by targeting the target variable (D). The sun relies on the backdoor of substitution, evaluation (E), and transference (F).

KEY INSIGHT:

Learn Truth by Reason, Persuade the Reasonable by Reason, and Persuade the Unreasonable by Eloquence.

THE KEY TO CHARISMA ON COMMAND

FIGURE 22: In a room full of people adopting the approach of the wind, adopt the approach of the sun. Be the nicest, warmest person in the room. You can do this while being assertive. Be genuine with it. Try it. See how powerful it is.

KEY INSIGHT:

Be a Lighthouse of Warmth in a Cold Raging Sea of Indifference.

Be a Beacon of Appreciation in the Fog of Ingratitude.

Be a Light in the Dark.

1.14: MENTAL MALLEABILITY

This is something you must understand if any of the techniques, persuasive patterns, and strategies in this book will work for you.

Remember when we talked about purposeful communication? Remember how we talked about a starting state and a finishing state?

Persuasive communication, by its very nature, revolves around creating a desired finishing state in the world, which has to do with your audience taking some action. It might be buying a product, implementing a plan, thinking a new way, or doing anything that creates your desired finishing state in the real world.

At this point, this theory comes into play. For every single finishing state that revolves around your audience taking some action, there is a particular mental state which will immediately make them more likely to take that action. For every action X, there is a mental state Y which will make people more likely to take action X. But this is just part one of the theory.

Part two is this: People are prone to mental malleability. Outside influences and inputs will change their mental state.

In summary: For every action you want your audience to take, there is a particular mental state which will make taking that action more likely, and that mental state can be induced by outside inputs, including your communication.

First, identify what action you want your audience to take. Second, identify what mental state will make them most likely to actually take that action. Third, use the principle of mental malleability, and communicate the persuasive inputs to your audience that will mold their mental state to the one most likely to create your desired action.

Step three is difficult, unless you prepare yourself with the knowledge of your public speaking toolbox. Step three becomes easy only if you understand this: "If I use my [word / body / vocal] language in [insert way], then that input will produce the following impact on my audience's mental state: [insert impact]."

That's tough, but as you begin to unlock your public speaking and communication toolbox and understand persuasive cause and effect, it becomes much easier.

1.15: BRIDGE THEORY

All communication (at least, all communication worth engaging in) must have a purpose. Communication is effective if it fulfills that purpose. Communication is ineffective if it does not fulfill that purpose. There is a "starting state," which describes the world before your communication. There is a "finishing state," which describes the world after your communication if its purpose has been fulfilled. In truly purposeful communication, every single word, sentence, paragraph, structural component, pause, vocal intonation, gesture – every single use of your three languages – must be specifically, strategically, and deliberately designed to move in a straight line from the starting state to the finishing state.

Doesn't it follow logically that, if all effective communication must have an overarching goal, this overarching goal can be broken down into sub-goals that all add up to the total goal?

And here's the truth: If you are truly communicating efficiently (which is engaging, persuasive, and captivating), then you must be able to point to each and every statement you make, and identify a clear purpose for that statement, and not only a clear purpose, but a clear purpose that moves the communication toward accomplishing your overall goal.

But you need to connect these "purpose statements" in some way. How? With bridges, or transitions.

So, following from this theory, if you are speaking from a script, you should be able to point to every single statement and say "this statement accomplishes a clear purpose, and that clear purpose moves the world from my starting state to my desired finishing state, thereby completing my ultimate purpose" or "this statement or clump of words is there to connect and transition from one purpose statement to another."

If you can't say either of those two things about part of your communication, you should carefully consider removing it.

1.16: THE HUMAN DESIRE PYRAMID

Remember the cone of attention? Remember self-interest and WIIFM? This theory relates to those. Well, in truth, all these theories relate to all these theories. These just connect more immediately.

All humans have a set of core, innate desires; we desire other desires to satisfy our core desires; we desire other desires to satisfy the desires that satisfy our core desires; we desire other desires to... continued endlessly.

We have thousands of desires. Some of those desires are core, and other desires are manifestations of those core desires.

We have desire X, and then because of desire X, we have desire Y, because desire Y satisfies desire X. And then because desire Z satisfies desire Y, we want that too. And so on and so forth.

In summary: We have a set of core desires, and from those core desires emanates a massive pyramid of desires which are all linked because they satisfy other desires. Let's revisit our financier who wants the next hot stock: A financier wants to hit the next hot stock. Why? To make money. Why do they want more money? To afford nicer things, and to feel financial security. Here, we branch.

The "nicer-things" branch: Why do they want to afford nicer things? To have a more attractive outward appearance. Why do they want that? For social status and prestige. You have isolated two core motivating desires of that financier.

The "financial security" branch: Why do they want financial security? To be safe no matter what happens. Why do they want that? To be free to do whatever they want, and free from fear. You have isolated two more.

Core desires: Social status and freedom.

Level one derived desires: A more attractive outward appearance, and to be safe no matter what happens.

Level two derived desires: Affording nicer things, and financial security.

Level three derived desires: More money.

Level four derived desires: Hitting the next hot stock.

The core desires at the top of the pyramid are more likely to be shared by others. Almost everyone shares the desires of high social status and freedom. Not everyone shares the desires of hitting the next hot stock. As you move further down the pyramid, into tertiary desires (and even further), you begin to reach a place where the set of desires is more and more unique to your audience.

And we branch into "affording nicer things," and "financial security" at level two of the desire pyramid. The more you satisfy the "nicer things" desire, the less you can satisfy the "financial security" desire. A great deal of human indecision and internal conflict has to do with having two conflicting desires (as this financier does) and not knowing the degree to which to satisfy each. Further, much human motivation derives from having conflicting desires and seeking to reach a point of abundance where the sheer magnitude of resources renders the conflict meaningless.

And here's a key lesson: Every person has different derived desires, similar core desires, and a different value hierarchy; in other words, they place their desires in different hierarchies of value. This flows directly into the next few theories of persuasive communication.

1.17: AUDIENCE UNIQUENESS, AUDIENCE PERSONAS, LIMITS OF THEORIES, AND CETERIS PARIBUS

Part one, audience uniqueness: No audience is the same. They all have different human desire pyramids and value hierarchies. They all come with their own needs, beliefs, values, objections, pain-points, preconceptions about you, hierarchy of values, past experiences with similar ideas, speakers, and situations, and much more. To quote again from *The Way of the Wolf*: "We all arrive at any particular moment in time with a history of beliefs and values and opinions and experiences and victories and defeats and insecurities and decision-making strategies – and then based on all of that stuff, our brain, working at near light speed, will instantly relate it to whatever scenario lies before it. Then, based on the result, it will place us at whatever point on the certainty scale it deems appropriate for each of the three tens, and it's from that starting point that we can then be influenced."

Part two, audience personas: Based on your pre-existing intelligence, and the intelligence you can gather, you can develop a "persona" that includes the previously mentioned characteristics and describes at least two-thirds of your audience. Now you know who you're speaking to. Let's say you are having trouble creating an audience persona; let's say you have a broad audience, with a wide variety of people. What do you do then? Build your persona around what unites them. Speak in terms of core human desires, engaging with their self-interest as it exists at the top of the human desire pyramid, where most people have similar desires. Remember the diverse cones with overlapping vertices?

But what if you're speaking to a group of people that you can identify as relatively homogenous? What if you can build a clear and compelling audience persona that is distinct, specific, and in-depth? What if you can clearly identify audience needs, beliefs, values, objections, pain-points, preconceptions about you, hierarchy of values, past experiences with similar ideas, speakers, and situations? Then make that the audience persona. In this case, you can engage with your audience's self-interest at all stages of the human desire pyramid. If you're speaking to financiers, you know they all are likely to share a human desire pyramid that looks at least something like what we identified earlier.

Core desires: Social status and freedom.

Level one derived desires: A more attractive outward appearance, and to be safe no matter what happens.

Level two derived desires: Affording nicer things, and financial security.

Level three derived desires: More money.

Level four derived desires: Hitting the next hot stock.

And, in this case, you can safely engage with them at all five levels of desires.

Part three, limits of theories: No communication theory is bullet-proof in every situation. No communication theory works for every audience, under every circumstance, for every speaker, for every situation, for every subject. The real world is too messy. We can't predict every lurking variable. Now, we know this: In the vast majority of cases, these theories work. But these theories, due to the infinite variety of human psychological state, and the infinite variety of possible externalities, are only effective if our assumptions about human psychology and externalities are correct. But here's the good news: The vast majority of the time, our assumptions about these two things are correct. That said, we inevitably, arrive at a necessary caveat to this (and all) social theories. We discuss it now, in part four of this theory.

Part four, the *ceteris paribus* assumption: If you have explored any social science, like economics, politics, or psychology, you have knowingly or unknowingly stumbled across this assumption. *Ceteris paribus* is Latin for "other things equal." And all of these theories are bullet-proof only under this assumption. For example, Monroe's Motivated Sequence (which we will discuss shortly) is a proven speech structure that, other things equal, makes you much more likely to persuade your audience.

Now, you might be wondering, "what use are these theories if we have to apply that assumption?" Here's my answer: Think about gravity. If we drop a feather and a brick from the same height, according to the law of gravity, they should arrive at the ground at the same time. Go ahead and try it. You'll see that the feather falls much slower than the brick. Is the law of gravity broken? No, that is just air resistance. But here's my point: The law of gravity requires the *ceteris paribus* assumption too. It requires removing all external variables and isolating the relationship between the two variables you want to study. If the law of gravity requires this assumption, we can safely say it's reasonable to apply it for social theories as well.

These theories, if you remove all external variables, will make you infinitely more persuasive, basically instantly. But if are speaking to a room of ten people who all hate you on a deep, personal level, are these theories going to work? They'll make you more persuasive than you would have otherwise been, but they won't outweigh that external variable of deep hatred toward you and create an easily measurable difference in outcome.

In what we traditionally think of as science, you can isolate the relationship between two variables easily with a test-tube. You can't do the same with the social sciences. That's why this assumption is necessary. With gravity, you can remove the impact of air resistance by creating a vacuum.

1.18: SALIENCY, INTENSITY, STABILITY

Here's how this theory connects to audience uniqueness and the idea of audience personas: first, build an audience persona; second, identify the subjects that are salient, intense, and stable to that audience persona; third, speak in terms of those subjects.

Every single statement has three qualities: saliency, intensity, and stability. Every statement has these qualities in varying amounts, and the most compelling statements have the most of all of them.

Saliency: How many people care about a given subject, or in other words, how important a given subject is. It is the portion of the population that cares about something.

Intensity: How strongly people care about a subject; a measure of how much energy people are willing to devote to the subject.

Stability: How long people are willing to continue caring about a given subject, or how easy it is to switch the opinions of those who do care about a given subject.

ENSURING YOUR MESSAGE ENGAGES THE AUDIENCE

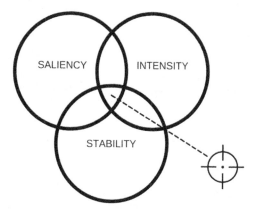

FIGURE 23: Conceive of saliency, intensity, and stability as a three-way Venn-diagram. Ensure your message is salient, intense, and stable; ensure it occupies the central position of the diagram.

HOW TO HOOK AND KEEP AUDIENCE ATTENTION

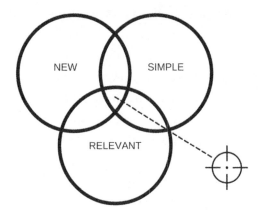

FIGURE 24: Conceive of the new, simple, and relevant triad as a three-way Venn-diagram. Ensure your message is new, simple, and relevant; ensure it occupies the central position of the diagram.

NEW, SIMPLE, RELEVANT; SALIENT, INTENSE, STABLE

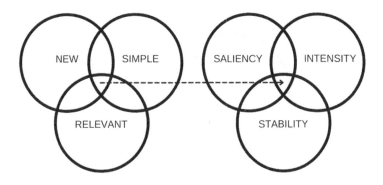

FIGURE 25: Satisfying the new, simple, relevant triad significantly improves your likelihood of achieving saliency, intensity, and stability.

In summary, saliency is how many people care, intensity is how much they care, and stability is for how long they will care.

Because saliency, intensity, and stability are not intuitive concepts, here's another helpful way to think about them: saliency is how important a topic is, intensity is how important it is to those who think it's important, and stability is for how long it will be important to those who think it's important.

Every compelling subject or statement is salient, intense, and stable: by combining these three qualities, you can maximize the chance that what you're saying will have an impact on your audience and that they will tune in. In many cases, however, your topic might not be salient, intense, or stable. In this case, the best strategy is to find the most salient, intense, and stable consequences of what you're speaking about and deliberately connect them to your subject.

Everything of impact occurring in the real world has consequences and is connected to other occurrences. Many topics are part of an interconnected consequence web of second, third, and fourth order effects, in which everything impacts everything else in one way or another.

By tapping into and connecting your subject to another one which is more salient, intense, and stable, you gain the very useful benefit of speaking in terms of something which most people in your audience will care about, which they will care about strongly, and which they will continue caring about long after you finish your speech. Stability is particularly important: stability is essentially the longevity of concern, interest, or relevance your ideas have to your audience. If they only care about what you're saying when you're saying it, and not after or even before you've said it, that's obviously not a good situation. Avoid this by connecting your idea to something you know your audience will care about in the long run.

As any career politician will vehemently assert, the economy is the most salient, intense, and stable issue. People will vote for a candidate who has a disappointing personal track record if they believe that he or she will lower their taxes. People love money. It's that simple. In order for our climatologist to tap into the salient, intense, and stable nature of how the general population thinks about the economy, money, and personal finance, they can say something like this: 'To my understanding, people usually don't realize how expensive climate change will be. It's not their fault, of course, but let me illuminate some numbers. The federal government, as well as state governments across the country, will have to increase taxes in order to deal with the consequences of climate change, so the average increase in taxes per person can be up to $1,000 annually. Similarly, if you live close to a coast, lake, or major river, you might have to pay up to $10,000 to protect your house from flooding caused by climate change.'

It might make you cynical to think that money is high on the list of what people care about, but it shouldn't. It makes sense that it is, so use it to your advantage.

Think of these three qualities as a three-way Venn diagram. In other words, think of them as three circles that each overlap each other. Something can be in only one circle, in two circles, or in the center where they all overlap, and it is enclosed by all three circles. The more circles your subject and theme are enclosed by, the more interested in your speech your audience will be. If your subject either ends up in the middle of that diagram, or you can find a logical connection that brings it there, then your persuasive power will be maximized."

This strategy of aligning your subject to something your audience cares about – something salient, intense, and stable to them – is the essence of backing the entire process with a powerful motive.

1.19: ONE VERSUS MANY

This theory directly addresses the specific techniques you learn in this book, and the thousands of techniques that are all different ways of using your three languages.

Remember what these techniques really are. When I tell you to "do X with your body language," or "do X with your voice," or in the case of this book, "do X with your words," it's me telling you to "provide input X to your audience, *to create result Y.*"

And here's the tricky part: The causation relationship between X and Y is not always clear, for two reasons: incomplete feedback and external variables.

When I tell you to use one of these speech structures, you are not going to have people walking up to you saying "Oh wow! Great structure, the reason I'm buying this product you're selling is because of that structure. Great use of your word language! It really persuaded me." You just don't get that type of instant feedback. And it gets trickier: Your audience doesn't even always know what persuaded them. Sometimes they do. But even if you did get people making these kinds of statements, there would be no reason to believe them with certainty. They don't always know how the techniques impacted them, and in what ways. The more subtle the technique, the less likely the audience detected it, and vice-versa. For example, if they tell you about a particular piece of information they valued highly in their judgement, or a particular logical argument you made, you have more reason to trust that this was in fact the persuasive factor that influenced them (or one of the persuasive factors, at least).

When I tell you to "provide input X to create impact Y on your audience," that doesn't mean that you aren't also providing thousands of other inputs which all tip the scale in one of two ways. No one technique will make the key difference; instead, persuasive communication succeeds because the aggregate, summed-up total of your inputs persuade. It's possible that one technique brings you over the edge, but only because it's standing on the shoulders of thousands of other inputs. I guarantee that these structures you will learn are incredibly powerful, proven persuasive language patterns. I do not guarantee that these structures will outweigh 200 other wrong inputs you might provide to your audience. I guarantee that they will tip the scale in your favor, but not so much that they will outweigh anything tipping the scale against you.

Because persuasion is not the result of a single input, but the result of the summation of all your inputs, the impact of a single technique is not going to guarantee persuasive success. One does not outweigh many.

But rejoice: 20% of the actions are particularly powerful, and produce 80% of the results. In other words, 20% of your persuasive inputs in communication produce 80% of the persuasion. The structure of persuasive communication is a big part of that 20%, which acts as a powerful lever with serious impact on the persuasive scale.

1.20: PSYCHOLOGICAL PERSUASION

Persuasion occurs in the mind, not outside of it. Persuasive communication is trying to influence a mind to believe something. You do not convince anyone; you simply apply the theory of mental malleability to get them to convince themselves. It all occurs in their minds.

Thus, we turn to the theory of psychological persuasion. Since persuasion occurs in the mind of the receiver of communication, this means that the environment of the receiving mind – or its psychology – is inherent to persuasion. And now we arrive at the final principle of this theory: Things are persuasive because of human psychology.

THE LITTLE-KNOWN SECRET OF IRRESISTIBLE INFLUENCE

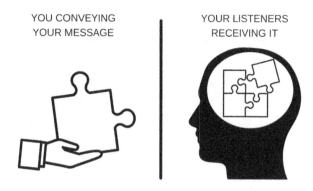

YOU CONVEYING
YOUR MESSAGE

YOUR LISTENERS
RECEIVING IT

FIGURE 26: All effective influence relies on conveying a message that conforms to (and / or minimizes the clash with) the contents, processes, biases, heuristics, and functions of the mind receiving it. Or, put simply, all effective influence relies on conveying information how the human mind is wired to receive it.

Effective persuasive communication is effective because it uses the characteristics of human psychology in its favor.

Remember the APP opening structure from the three-part-communication theory? Why does it work? What makes it effective? What makes it persuasive? What makes it move the world from starting state to finishing state? Why is it different from other communication beginnings? It uses the characteristics of human psychology in its favor. The APP opening, in one of its forms, is starting your persuasive communication by agreeing to an audience pain point, promising a solution, and previewing that solution.

Think about the characteristics of human psychology that these opening uses to grab attention and set the stage for successful persuasive communication. Agreeing portrays empathy, and empathy is the foundation for trust. We will be persuaded by those we trust. Why? Psychology. Agreeing to a pain-point will draw attention to and emphasize the struggle and pain related to it, which is the precursor to action, because we want to escape from and relieve pain. We will be persuaded when our struggles are top-of-mind. Why? Psychology. Promising benefits portrays value, and high perceived value is the foundation for receiving attention (which you need if you're going to persuade). We will be persuaded by someone who we see as valuable to us. Why? Psychology. (Remember energy in, energy out?) Promising also portrays benefits and a solution to a problem. This appeals to self-interest and whichever core human desires are harmed by the problem. We will be persuaded by someone who appeals to our self-interest, because we think they can help us get what we want. Why? Psychology. Previewing creates a giant mental open-loop. Curiosity tantalizes us, particularly in the context of the APP method (because of the empathy, trust, and high value portrayed so far). A giant mental open-loop – a massive unanswered question – grabs our attention and makes us want the answer. We will be persuaded when we are captivated by curiosity. Why? Psychology.

The same holds true for every single structure and persuasive pattern you learn in this book. If you are ever wondering "why does this strategy work?" remember the answer: psychology.

1.21: SPEAKING FOR ACTION

Why do we speak? What does it mean to try to persuade someone? How do you know if you have succeeded? We speak to get people to take action. When we persuade successfully, people take that action.

But it's not that black and white. If you want someone to buy something you're selling, and they don't, that doesn't mean you've totally failed at persuasive communication. Why not? Consider this possibility: What if they go on to talk about your product to twenty friends, who then buy it? Maybe you didn't persuade them to buy it themselves, but you persuaded them to have faith in your idea and to see it as something that will serve some of the people they know.

Remember that persuasion is not binary. Influence is a spectrum. If you move closer to your desired finishing state, even if you don't get all the way there, or if you accomplish a related purpose, even if it wasn't your primary goal, then the persuasion made your reality better. Thus, it can be considered a success.

And one more key principle: Energy in versus energy out applies not only to the action of listening to your communication, but to the action you seek to motivate. There are two times when you most need to maximize the energy out and minimize the energy in: At the start, and when you call your audience to action. Why? Because these are the two major points where you are actually asking you audience to do something. And they will only cooperate if you properly balance that equation.

1.22: THE 7C (OR 14C) COMMUNICATION MODEL

It's funny: Business schools love applauding this concept and teaching it to their students as the 7Cs of communication. According to me, they leave out seven additional Cs. There are 14Cs.

What are the original 7Cs? Clear, concise, concrete, correct, coherent, complete, and courteous.

And the second 7Cs? Creative, contextual, cogent, credible, compelling, consistent, and connected.

Creative: Are you using metaphors and similes to illustrate points? Are you expressing an old idea in new, creative ways? Are you presenting new, exciting, creative ideas? Are you being original, presenting ideas that you created (or familiar ideas in innovative ways)?

Contextual: Are you clearly explaining how your information fits into a bigger picture? Are you expressing the significance of your information? Are you giving the full picture, discussing all impacts and consequences worth noting? Are you using analogies to bring unfamiliar concepts into a familiar context?

Cogent: Are you presenting a main message that everything else neatly falls under? (As you've noticed, this one is a recurring theme). Are your sentences progressing in a logical line from beginning to end, with no stutters or accidental intrusions? Are you using simple language that everybody can easily understand, and that keeps cognitive load down? Are you connecting everything you say to one big central idea?

Credible: Are you experienced enough to speak about the subject? Are you authoritative enough to give advice about a subject? Are you credentialed enough to be trusted on the subject? Are you well-researched enough to talk about the subject?

Compelling: Are you using persuasive methods to compel your listeners? Are you speaking in an assertive way? Are you trying to create action with your communication? Are you speaking in a way that motivates people?

Consistent: Are you contradicting yourself? Are you giving a message that is consistent with itself? Are you giving a message that is consistent with who you are? Are you giving a message that is consistent with reality and your values as well as the values of your audience?

Connected: Are you connecting to your audience? Are you connecting to the subject? Are you connecting the audience to the subject? Are you connecting to your message?

Complete: Am I giving complete information? Am I using examples? Am I using quantitative examples? Am I using qualitative examples? Am I deliberately and effectively unifying everything I say under one main message? Am I avoiding the omission of any key details?

Concrete: Am I giving concrete details? Am I tying abstract concepts back to concrete, physical, tangible things? Am I being as specific as possible? Am I avoiding generalizations? Am I answering the big five questions?

Courteous: Am I being courteous and respectful? Am I speaking in terms of the audience's interests? Am I creating alignment between my interests and the audience's? Am I giving credit and praise where it is due? Am I being humble and grateful?

Correct: Am I correct about what I'm saying? Am I qualifying my statements properly? Am I prioritizing accuracy over kindness? Am I sourcing my facts and statistics? Am I avoiding exaggerations?

Clear: Am I being clear? Am I avoiding tangents and parentheticals? Am I saying short, crisp, commanding sentences? Am I using transitions? Am I applying "less is more?"

Considerate: Am I being considerate? Am I using inclusive pronouns? Am I talking about my own mistakes first? Am I avoiding criticizing, condemning, or complaining? Am I drawing attention to my own mistakes first?

Concise: Am I speaking in a concise way? Am I using verbal lists? Am I avoiding repetition? Am I cutting out unnecessary words?

1.23: NOVELTY AND SIMPLICITY

This ties to the energy in energy out theory. Effective communication has two key characteristics: novelty and simplicity. You must provide rapid-fire new information in a simple way.

Let's start with novelty. As Donald Draper, the main character of the highly acclaimed show *Mad Men* once said, "the most important word in advertising is *new.*" In public speaking, a powerful gift from you to your audience is something new: something unfamiliar to them, and something you haven't already told them. Everyone appreciates the speaker who gives them the most comprehensive information, especially if it is new and can give them a competitive advantage in life.

Our attention spans (on a micro-scale) have apparently dropped from 12 seconds to eight since the dawn of the internet age. So, if there's one lesson public speakers can gain from electronic media such as YouTube videos and Instagram feeds, which have experienced astounding success at gaining the attention of a global audience, let it be this: present new and exciting information rapidly.

As for simplicity: there's beauty in simplicity. An idea presented simply is an idea long remembered by your audience. Focus on the big picture before getting into specifics, and make sure that your audience is following the progression of your speech.

Oftentimes, experts forget that they are speaking to an audience that isn't made up of other experts. What ensues is a situation in which the speaker describes things in the complex jargon of his or her trade, while the audience is left helplessly trying to follow along. If you are presenting a complex topic, don't make your audience feel like they are "mentally running" to keep up with you. Hold their hands and take them for a nice, gentle walk through the information instead.

Break down your speech until it is simple and easy to follow. Unless you are aiming for evocative, flowing, beautiful language, don't say more than you need to. Furthermore, don't say it in more complex words than you need to. Always keep it simple.

Why does it link to the energy equation? Because receiving simple information is perceived as lower-cost. It truly is lower-cost: Less mental energy is required to receive simple communication than complex communication. As for novelty, while simple information decreases energy in, rapid-fire information increases energy out. Rapid-fire simple information seems more valuable than slow information, and it also reduces the energy expense.

1.24: UNCERTAINTY VERSUS CERTAINTY, EMOTIONAL VERSUS LOGICAL, SPECTRUMS, ATTENTION, AND COUNTERFACTUAL SIMULATION (AKA MENTAL MOVIES)

Remember the theory of mental malleability? Remember how there is one particular mental state that will almost force your audience to take your suggested action? Remember how, through strategic persuasive inputs, you can induce that mental state in your audience? This theory links to those theories (more immediately than the other theories).

Part one, the idea of spectrums: If you want to successfully apply the theory of mental malleability, you have to take one extra step and boil down mental states into spectrums. Your desired mental state, the one you want to induce in your audience through inputs, can be broken down into a series of qualities, each of which with its own spectrum of magnitude. Thus, with your persuasive inputs, or your action-levers, you can move people up and down these spectrums to achieve the desired mental state.

For example, let's say you're a politician campaigning for votes. What is the mental state that will most likely make your audience take the action you want them to, and bring about your desired finishing state?

Let's think about it. It goes much deeper than this, but for the sake of example, here are the qualities of that ideal mental state: Anger toward the other party, belief in personal gain as a result of voting for you, connection and agreement on values, and connection and agreement on policy.

Now, think of it this way: For each of these qualities, your audience can be at a one level or at a ten level. At ten, they completely have the quality. At one, they completely lack it. So, to achieve persuasive communication, your communication must be geared toward moving your audience from wherever they start on these spectrums to wherever you want them to be. Your statements should be geared toward making them angry toward the other party (moving them toward a ten – the highest possible amount of anger), showing them their personal benefit of voting for you (moving them toward a ten – the highest possible perception of benefit), and connecting on values and policy (moving them toward a ten – the deepest possible connection). And this is just one simple example of a mental state broken down into a set of qualities. The examples are infinite. I can't possibly predict what yours will be, but I can equip you with the tools to figure it out and use the theory for yourself. And think about the theory of purposeful communication: How do you know if a statement is contributing to or diluting from your persuasive communication? Ask yourself if it manipulates one of these spectrums in your favor or not.

VISUALIZING THE SPECTRUM MODEL OF COMMUNICATION

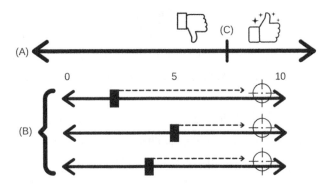

FIGURE 27: The overall spectrum between "success" and "failure" in communication (A) breaks down into a set of more specific spectrums (B). Your audience members occupy "starting states" along these spectrums. Your goal is to move them from these starting states to 10 positions using your communication. You can conceive of your position on the spectrum between success and failure as

the average of the positions the audience occupies on the sub-spectrums. There is some theoretical threshold signifying the communication as sufficiently successful (C).

Part two, attention and certainty: While each ideal audience mental state can be broken down into a vastly unique set of qualities, every single ideal mental state must have some basic ingredients. Your audience must be close to a ten on the attention spectrum, close to a ten on the trust in you spectrum, close to ten on the trust in your idea spectrum, and close to ten on the trust in the group you represent spectrum. So, let's update your ideal audience mental state, most likely to result in action: They must be close to a ten on whatever spectrums you believe define that mental state, in addition to those we just outlined.

Part three, emotion versus logic: If you do not fully understand parts one and two, go ahead and reread them, because it only gets more complicated. Every spectrum exists on both a logical plane and an emotional plane. They are both required. You can't ignore one of them. Even Aristotle knew this, with his theories of "logos" (logic) and "pathos" (emotion) as two-thirds of his rhetorical model. You must satisfy the logical spectrum, because while people make decisions based on emotional certainty, they only do so if they feel like they have logic's permission.

To persuade your audience to take an action, you must open the gate to their hearts. But to get to that gate in the first place, you must open the gate to their logical minds, so that they feel safe giving way to their emotion. If asked, they will say they took your suggested action because of their logical certainty. That's not true at all. In truth, they took it because of their emotional certainty, and rationalized it with their logical certainty. No rationalization? No decision. That's why the logical spectrums are important; because they supply a logical rationalization that makes emotional decision-making feel more justifiable.

Part four, counterfactual simulation: This is an explanation of why the ideal mental state is so important. When your audience is considering taking your action, here's how they will decide: They will run a mental movie in their minds of how the future will probably look if they take your action. If that mental movie is positive, they will take your suggested action. If it is negative? They won't. What determines the nature of this mental movie? Their positions on the emotional and logical quality spectrums that make up your ideal audience mindset.

1.25: MEANING THROUGH SEQUENCE

Compared to the last multi-part theory, this one is relatively simple. And it (like all these theories) it explains structure theory. But it does so in a particularly fundamental way.

This theory of persuasive communication states that sequence matters, and that the order of your communication adds meaning to your communication.

If we revisit the APP method, we see that the agree, then promise, then preview sequence is arranged that way because, due to that specific order and organization, it becomes more meaningful. Would the preview, promise, agree method work as well? Or the promise, preview, agree method? Or the preview, agree, promise method? Probably not. We already talked about why APP works. The agree phase establishes empathy, gains trust, grabs attention, and highlights a problem. This foundation adds meaning and power to the promise phase, because promising a solution doesn't work as well if the person promising it is not empathetic, trusted, and doesn't have attention or clearly exposes the problem the solution solves. It's like a step-ladder. Finally, the preview phase should come after the agree and promise phases because without the context of the promise, it doesn't make much sense at all. See how sequence matters?

So, remember this: Structure theory yields specific, compelling, step-by-step language structures and communication patterns that build up meaning through their specific sequence of statements.

1.26: FRAMES

Much communication revolves around frames. Frames are relationships between things and actions. Frames define our universe. We can boil down our realities into a list of frames. Frames often take the form of "X [verb] Y," or "X [verb clump]." For example, "climate change is bad," (X verb Y), or "war should stop" (X verb clump). Sub-frames support top-level frames. "War should stop (X verb clump, top-level frame) because war is bad (X verb Y, supportive sub-frame one), because war is expensive (X verb Y, supportive sub-frame two), and because war is unnecessary (X verb Y, supportive sub-frame three)."

The structures you're going to learn are all designed to implicitly or explicitly reframe the world to your advantage. That's what you need to know about this theory.

Frame reversal, a type of frame escalation, is a particularly elegant way to reframe. In its simplest form, this means reversing an opposing frame; not just countering with a new frame, but completely inverting the opposing frame and cancelling it out in totality. For example, if someone says that X contradicts Y, an elegant, persuasive, erudite, and compelling reframe is responding with, "actually, X does not only not contradict Y, but (new frame) X justifies Y." To justify is the opposite of to contradict. One particular structure uses reframing as its core foundation.

1.27: UNSPOKEN WORDS

When you are attempting persuasive communication, you can't just come right out and say, "Trust me! I have empathy for you! Here's your problem, which is what I'm trying to sell you a solution to. I promise that this solution is worth-your-while! You should be curious about it. Be curious this instant!"

That sounds crazy. But there's no way around it: You want your audience to feel that way, don't you? Indeed, you can't come right out and say those things. But you can use your three languages in such a way that your audience subconsciously receives that meaning; that they hear those words subconsciously; that they hear additional words that you have not actually said.

So, while you cannot come right out and say those things, you can use these structures, like the APP method, to convey unspoken words. In the case of the APP method, the additional words are these: "Trust me! I have empathy for you (agree)! Here's your problem, which is what I'm trying to sell you a solution to. I promise that this solution is worth-your-while (promise)! You should be curious about it. Be curious this instant (preview)!"

Because you're implicitly communicating these words directly to the subconscious mind, you can get away with it. In other words, you are embedding this meaning in the elegant face of the APP method. You wouldn't be able to come right out and just say those words, but you can impart them with this structure in an elegant and implicit but unmistakable way.

Email Peter D. Andrei, the author of the Speak for Success collection and the President of Speak Truth Well LLC directly.

pandreibusiness@gmail.com

EXPLICIT AND IMPLICIT; SPOKEN AND UNSPOKEN

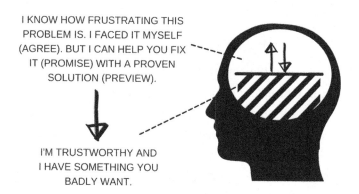

FIGURE 28: All words carry subtext, implication, and a subtle script of meaning layered a level under the literal language. For example, the script above drives directly to the conscious minds of the audience in its literal form, but also has a subtext of "unspoken speech" that hits at the subconscious mind. What cannot be said in "spoken speech" can often be (and often is) layered a level under at the level of "unspoken speech."

So, to summarize, many of these structures and techniques are designed to communicate additional, unspoken words, which you would never be able to say out loud, but which you must communicate somehow.

1.28: PERSUASIVE PATTERNS

Combine the theories of additional words, frames, and meaning through sequence, and what do you get? You get the theory of persuasive patterns. What is this theory? That there are particular sequences of statements that establish the correct frames and make your audience hear specific additional unspoken words that work for any subject. There are specific language templates, which are persuasive patterns you can plug any specific nouns, verbs, and subjects into, and which work for all subjects.

1.29: STRUCTURE THEORY

These previous 28 theories characterize persuasive communication that works. Structure theory is summarized by this next sentence: there are specific patterns of communication that satisfy the conditions of all of these theories, and that can be adapted to any subject and any speaker.

These patterns complete the public speaking triad as quickly as possible, with minimum effort and proven steps you can instantly apply to any subject.

These patterns maximize the power of your word language so that your words actually influence people and make them think and act the way you want them to, without coercion or cringe-inducing and forceful persuasion.

These patterns activate new layers of your word language, and control it by aligning it with your purpose, so that your words don't go unnoticed and actually impact the people and world around you for the better.

These patterns satisfy the ingredients for the persuasive public speaking triad to guarantee more successful persuasion without manipulative or forceful methods.

These patterns move the world from starting-state to finishing-state and fulfill the purpose of your communication which gives you the power of influencing reality with nothing but your words and some straightforward but little-known communication steps.

These patterns break down into structures for the beginning, middle, and end of your communication, so that the only simple, fast, and easy task remaining for you is to match a starting structure with a middle structure and an ending structure.

These patterns target subjects that bring you to the narrow top of the cone of attention and use language patterns that keep you there, which guarantees that people are going to be sitting on the edge of their seats listening to you, and that they are actually going to care about what you have to say.

These patterns convey the right words in the right way, so that you don't fail at persuasive communication by bungling the words, the way they are arranged, or both.

These patterns appeal to self-interest and immediately answer the question "what's in it for me?" so that people will instantly respect you, instantly give you their undivided attention, and instantly take the actions you want them to take.

These patterns convince your audience that marginal benefits far exceed marginal costs of paying you attention so that you can immediately balance the key persuasive equation and get people to act with a series of simple, easy, step-by-step language patterns.

These patterns satisfy the mental checklist in the first eight seconds to guarantee that your audience sees you as someone with authority, as someone worth listening to, as someone who understands them, as someone who can help them get what they want, and as someone they are going to give undivided attention to for however long you ask for it.

These patterns incorporate benefits and features so that your communication immediately highlights why your audience will benefit and how they will benefit, which *ceteris paribus*, guarantees, at the very least, immense interest.

These patterns follow the moral of the wind and the sun and use gentle persuasion so that you don't have to barge into your audience's mental space, but instead can earn entry with gentle, subtle, professional persuasion that doesn't put anyone on edge or sacrifice your self-respect and image.

These patterns create the proper mental state in your audience's mind so that they are willing – and enthusiastic – to do what you ask them to do, without you or them feeling like anyone got the better end of the deal.

These patterns include only purpose statements and bridges, so that every single word you speak is important, meaningful, and powerful, which in turn grants you infinite respect in the eyes of your listeners who will not be able to resist completely tuning in.

These patterns target the right parts of the human desire pyramid so that you immediately captivate your audience.

These patterns accommodate audience uniqueness and audience personas to guarantee that you are saying the right things to the right people, and that you don't bungle important moments by saying the wrong things to the wrong people.

These patterns focus on salient, intense, and stable subjects to guarantee that you are speaking about the subjects that your audience wants to hear about, and that they will then give you the attention you need to persuade them.

These patterns influence the outcome of your persuasion more than any other technique, and will be the 20% of your communication that will make 80% of the difference in outcome, which you only need to be moderately competent with to improve your communication and its results.

These patterns wield inherent elements of psychological persuasion to directly target the characteristics of human psychology that will give you unparalleled influence in communication.

These patterns speak for action and use the proven principles of calling your audience to action to essentially guarantee that people do what you ask them to do, not feeling like they're doing you a favor, but feeling like they're taking action to help themselves.

These patterns satisfy the 14Cs of communication so that your communication is worth listening to and easy to receive and retain.

These patterns apply the principles of novelty and simplicity, which will ensure that your audience is tuned in and enthusiastic about listening to you.

These patterns produce emotional and logical certainty with counterfactual simulation and move your mental-state spectrums the way you want to move them, with a set of proven, reliable templates that are easy and straightforward to use.

These patterns create meaning through sequence so that formulating your communication is much easier and much more organized, which will make speech writing, presentation preparation, and any communication much faster to compose.

These patterns produce compelling and persuasive frame effects that are designed to make your audience see things your way, making you a deeply influential communicator.

These patterns convey additional, implicit words to your audience which will bypass their conscious filters and punch straight to their subconscious minds, where real persuasion happens.

These patterns incorporate persuasive patterns that are strategically designed to play upon human psychology for maximum persuasion, and that do not involve hard-sell aggressive persuasion tactics.

These patterns, *ceteris paribus*, make your life better, more fulfilling, and more rewarding by giving you the one tool that makes the biggest, most impactful, most positive, and most enduring professional difference: effective communication.

Now, I by no means claim to have all of the patterns and structures. In theory, there are thousands, if not an infinite number of them. But the structures you learn in this book are more than enough. I have looked, and I have not found something like this anywhere else. I bought 100 books on this subject, and found nothing like this. I have read every article that might be related: nothing. I have bought courses and online training programs: nothing. You hold, in your lucky hands, the single key to the single theory of communication that will make the single important difference in your life by granting you the power of easy and effective persuasion.

Where have I seen these patterns? Good question. I have used them myself, time and time again. I have seen my audiences actually lean forward in their seats as I would conclude one of these structures. When I was a competitive public speaker, competing in front of audiences of hundreds, I actually had people come up to me and say "when you start talking, I feel like time stops and I get carried into another world listening to you." That is a direct quote. And I've heard it, in different forms, more times than I can remember. Another common occurrence for me, specifically when I use these exact structures, is this: I'm speaking in a loud, crowded room, whether it is a conference, competitive public speaking practice, or the preliminary stages of a competition, and these structures work their magic. I'm there, practicing my speech, along with 20 to 30 other people. Then, I jump into one of these structures, and by the time I've finished it, everyone else has stopped their own practice, their own conversations, or whatever else they were doing across the room on their own, and immediately tuned in.

If my experience is not enough, I have also seen these structures used by business leaders, political leaders, and famous speakers. Remember: I first discovered structure theory listening to Bill Clinton. And then I confirmed what I saw in him in hundreds of other speeches.

These structures are woven directly into almost all effective communication you hear, whether on purpose or by accident.

Why not yours, and why not on purpose?

...........................Chapter Summary..............................

- There are foundational theories of communication that allow you unparalleled insight.
- Understanding these theories allows you to effortlessly decode any communication situation.
- While these are only mental models for a complex reality, they describe that reality exceedingly well.
- Understanding these theories alone puts you head and shoulders above the communication skills of most people.
- Discovering the proven structures appealing to these theories allows you to communicate with easy influence.
- Many structures are accompanied by historical examples that illustrate the basic principles if not the exact steps.

KEY INSIGHT:

Rhetorical Strategy Liberates Truth from Languishing in the Swamp of Human Indifference.

Rhetorical Strategy Is Supposed to Be Virtue's Sword, Reason's Spear, and Truth's Shield.

THE IRREFUTABLE PERSUASIVE SYNTAX (PART ONE)

1	Master the Foundational Theories
1.1	Apply the Public Speaking Triad
1.2	Master the Communication Toolbox and the Three Layers
1.3	Activate, Control, and Align Your Three Languages
1.4	Satisfy the Triad Ingredients
1.5	Understand and Apply Purposeful Communication
1.6	Don't Forget the Three-Part Model of Communication
1.7	Speak to the Top of the Cone of Attention
1.8	Say the Right Things, But Also in the Right Way
1.9	Appeal to Self-Interest and "WIIFM?"
1.10	Raise Perceived Marginal Benefits, Drop Perceived Marginal Costs
1.11	Satisfy the Mental Checklist in Eight Seconds
1.12	Speak in terms of Benefits and Features
1.13	Remember the Wisdom of the Fable of the Wind and the Sun
1.14	Understand the Underlying Fact of Mental Malleability
1.15	Apply Bridge Theory to Keep Things Flowing Smoothly
1.16	Recognize the Pyramid of Human Desires
1.17	Remember Uniqueness, Personas, Ceteris Paribus and Limitations
1.18	Satisfy the Saliency, Intensity, and Stability Framework
1.19	Understand the Dilemma of One Versus Many

NO STRUCTURE VERSUS STRUCTURE

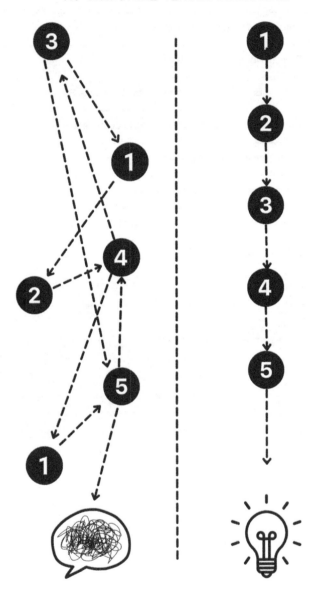

Claim These Free Resources that Will Help You Unleash the Power of Your Words and Speak with Confidence. Visit www.speakforsuccesshub.com/toolkit for Access.

18 Free PDF Resources

12 Iron Rules for Captivating Story, 21 Speeches that Changed the World, 341-Point Influence Checklist, 143 Persuasive Cognitive Biases, 17 Ways to Think On Your Feet, 18 Lies About Speaking Well, 137 Deadly Logical Fallacies, 12 Iron Rules For Captivating Slides, 371 Words that Persuade, 63 Truths of Speaking Well, 27 Laws of Empathy, 21 Secrets of Legendary Speeches, 19 Scripts that Persuade, 12 Iron Rules For Captivating Speech, 33 Laws of Charisma, 11 Influence Formulas, 219-Point Speech-Writing Checklist, 21 Eloquence Formulas

Claim These Free Resources that Will Help You Unleash the Power of Your Words and Speak with Confidence. Visit www.speakforsuccesshub.com/toolkit for Access.

30 Free Video Lessons

We'll send you one free video lesson every day for 30 days, written and recorded by Peter D. Andrei. Days 1-10 cover authenticity, the prerequisite to confidence and persuasive power. Days 11-20 cover building self-belief and defeating communication anxiety. Days 21-30 cover how to speak with impact and influence, ensuring your words change minds instead of falling flat. Authenticity, self-belief, and impact – this course helps you master three components of confidence, turning even the most high-stakes presentations from obstacles into opportunities.

Claim These Free Resources that Will Help You Unleash the Power of Your Words and Speak with Confidence. Visit <ins>www.speakforsuccesshub.com/toolkit</ins> for Access.

2 Free Workbooks

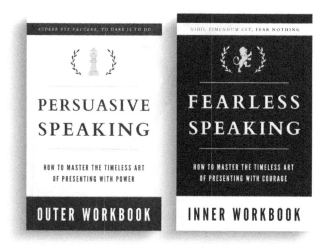

We'll send you two free workbooks, including long-lost excerpts by Dale Carnegie, the mega-bestselling author of *How to Win Friends and Influence People* (5,000,000 copies sold). *Fearless Speaking* guides you in the proven principles of mastering your inner game as a speaker. *Persuasive Speaking* guides you in the time-tested tactics of mastering your outer game by maximizing the power of your words. All of these resources complement the Speak for Success collection.

SPEAK FOR SUCCESS COLLECTION BOOK

THE PSYCHOLOGY OF PERSUASION CHAPTER

DIGGING DEEPER:

Breaking Down the Secret of Easy Influence

BUILDING OUT STRUCTURE THEORY

B EFORE WE GET INTO THE STRUCTURES THEMSELVES, we must define some basic principles of effective structure.

WHY THESE BASIC PRINCIPLES MATTER

Even professional public speakers get these wrong. Chances are you might too. And no matter how compelling your speech structure is, if the basics aren't there, it is liable to fall apart. Some of these might be repetitive: that's intentional. It is my duty to hammer them into your mind. You can't forget them.

THE CRUCIAL TRUTH ABOUT SPEECH STRUCTURE

Information is great. But if is thrown at you in a random, disorganized sequence, it becomes useless. And you don't want to be useless when you are communicating, whether you are giving a public speech, speaking in a meeting, writing, selling, running for office, or if you haven't gotten this by now, doing any type of persuasive communication.

Speech structure is the solution. This is the crucial truth about speech structure: A brilliant speaker, speaking brilliant words, with brilliant vocal modulation and brilliant body language, will fail if the speech has no structure. A less experienced speaker, who is good but not great, will easily exceed the brilliant speaker if he has one thing: speech structure.

WHY SPEECH STRUCTURE IS SO IMPORTANT

Structure is so important because it organizes your information. The same information placed in a different order can become vastly more powerful. The information doesn't change, but the sequence of the information does. It becomes structured, organized, and impactful.

SIMPLICITY

I repeat: If you can say the same information in fewer words, do it. If you can use more simple, direct, and short words and sentences, do it. If you can structure your speech in a simpler way, do it.

NOVELTY

I repeat: People crave new information. You must give a rapid-fire barrage of new information to your audience. Move from point to point quickly. This will keep them engaged and project your high value (as someone who knows a lot of information and conveys it quickly).

KEY INSIGHT:

We Are Cognitively Wired to Attend to the Opportune, the Dangerous, and the New.

New Means Opportunity. Or Danger. Or Nothing. We Must Discern, Decide, and Categorize.

This Is Reflexive and Constant.

SIMPLICITY AND NOVELTY

Yes, they work together. You can provide rapid pieces of new information in a simple way.

COGNITIVE LOAD

Too much information equals a high cognitive load, which equals a loss of attention. Don't overload your audience and increase their cognitive loads. Don't try to pack too much information in one chunk of communication. That said, another reason structure is so desirable in communication is because, by organizing your information according to one of these structures, you can increase the information per chunk of communication, but keep cognitive load down. Does this contradict novelty? Not necessarily. Novelty doesn't mean packing an excessive amount of information into your communication; it means conveying one idea fully, and then moving onto another instead of continuing to convey the first idea further.

ENGINEERED PERSUASION

The best persuasive communication is made persuasive not only by its content, but by its structure too. Two common methods of engineered persuasion (that are baked into the structure of the speech as opposed to its content) are contrast persuasion and aspirational persuasion. Contrast persuasion and aspirational persuasion often work together.

Contrast persuasion refers to speech structures that use strategic contrasts between situations, solutions, or paths. These contrasts are deeply persuasive. Aspirational persuasion refers to speech structures that appeal to the aspirations of the audience. These aspirations drive people to action.

TANGENTS OR PARANTHETICALS

These diminish the clarity of your message. They blur an otherwise clear, compelling, and commanding speech structure. They make you appear confused while confusing your audience (if they don't confuse you as well). One layer of tangents or parentheticals is okay, but not great. Two is not. Move in a logical, straight line from beginning to end.

TRANSITIONS

You must use transitions to smooth the changes between parts of your speech. You must use transitions to provide context. These are the "bridges" we talked about. Why are transitions so powerful? Because they tell your audience information about the upcoming information. For example, if you say "on the contrary," it primes your audience to look for the differences between what you just said and what you're about to say. And that keeps them intellectually engaged with your speech. How do you determine your transitions? The simplest heuristic is to ask yourself this: "how does what I'm about to say relate to what I just said?"

SIMILARITY OF STRUCTURE

All structures have three elements in common: the opening, the body, and the conclusion. The body usually takes up 80% of the allotted time and does 80% of the persuading, inspiring, or informing. As a result, we focus on body structures in this book.

OPENINGS

Openings must grab attention in a way that is relevant to your message, act as a gateway into your content, set the expectations for the rest of your speech, and show people the benefits of listening.

COMMUNICATION BODY

You should be able to summarize the communication body in a sentence. You can summarize all of these vastly powerful structures in a sentence. For example, "this is why you are facing the problem that is causing these disastrous side effects, and this is how I can help you solve it (diagnosis, problem, solution trifecta)."

SPEECH CLOSINGS

Closings must include a call to action. After you have given your speech, if you have done it well, your audience will be thinking, "What do I do now?" "How can I help?" "What's the next step?" And if you don't answer them, the entire speech becomes useless because you throw away all the persuasive momentum you built. You might as well have not given the speech. No real-world impact will happen.

HOW WE VISUALIZE STRUCTURES

YOUR ACTION	THEIR REACTION
WHAT YOU SAY, A STEP IN THE STRUCTURE, YOUR PERSUASIVE INPUTS	THEIR RESPONSE, INTERNAL DIALOGUE FEELING, ACTION, REALIZATION, BELIEF, THOUGHT, STATE, ETC.

FIGURE 29: This reveals the framework we will use to visualize the forthcoming structures.

...........................Chapter Summary.................................

- Information presented in a random sequence falls short. Structure provides a frame for your message.
- A speech (in fact, any message) demands an opening, body, and closing. There are structures for each of these steps.
- Keep cognitive load down, present information that is new and simple, and use transitions to smooth information flow.
- These speech structure engineer elements of persuasion into your communication. They are inherent to the structures.
- Aspirational persuasion is persuading by way of calling people to leap toward their aspirations.
- Contrast persuasion is persuading by way of using contrasts to emphasize your message, and the best path forward.

KEY INSIGHT:

A Structure Can Seal the Fate of Your Message. A Good Structure Can Sharpen It. A Bad Structure Can Blunt It Into Irrelevancy. A Good Structure Makes It Easy to Listen, Easy to Follow, and Easy to Agree. A Bad One, Impossible.

THE IRREFUTABLE PERSUASIVE SYNTAX (PART TWO)

1	Master the Foundational Theories
1.1	Apply the Public Speaking Triad
1.2	Master the Communication Toolbox and the Three Layers
1.3	Activate, Control, and Align Your Three Languages
1.4	Satisfy the Triad Ingredients
1.5	Understand and Apply Purposeful Communication
1.6	Don't Forget the Three-Part Model of Communication
1.7	Speak to the Top of the Cone of Attention
1.8	Say the Right Things, But Also in the Right Way
1.9	Appeal to Self-Interest and "WIIFM?"
1.10	Raise Perceived Marginal Benefits, Drop Perceived Marginal Costs
1.11	Satisfy the Mental Checklist in Eight Seconds
1.12	Speak in terms of Benefits and Features
1.13	Remember the Wisdom of the Fable of the Wind and the Sun
1.14	Understand the Underlying Fact of Mental Malleability
1.15	Apply Bridge Theory to Keep Things Flowing Smoothly
1.16	Recognize the Pyramid of Human Desires
1.17	Remember Uniqueness, Personas, Ceteris Paribus and Limitations
1.18	Satisfy the Saliency, Intensity, and Stability Framework
1.19	Understand the Dilemma of One Versus Many

2.10	Avoid Tangents and Parentheticals
2.11	Use Transitions to Maintain Audience Attention
2.12	Remember the Similarities of Structure
2.13	Engineer Your Openings
2.14	Complete Your Communication Body
2.15	Engineer Your Closing
3	**Master the Persuasive Structures**
4	**Master the Informative Structures**
5	**Master the Inspirational Structures**
6	**Master the Advanced Principles of Structure**

Email Peter D. Andrei, the author of the Speak for Success collection and the President of Speak Truth Well LLC directly.

pandreibusiness@gmail.com

KEY INSIGHT:

A Good Speaker Is Not Merely an Artist, But Also a Scientist and Engineer.

PERSUASIVE STUCTURES CREATE TENSION

What we have, how things are, the problems of the present, the obstacles we face, our actuality

What we want / what we could have, how things could be, the solutions of the future, the opportunities we face, our potentiality to succeed and to move forward

PERSUASIVE STRUCTURES OFTEN EMBODY THE ARCHETYPAL "MORAL MAP" / "MAP OF MEANING"

Where we could be... "Heaven"

Why it's great...

How we get here...

Why this plan will get us here...

Where we are...

Where we could be... "Hell"

Why it's awful...

How we get here...

Why these actions will get us here...

Access your 18 free PDF resources, 30 free video lessons, and 2 free workbooks from this link: www.speakforsuccesshub.com/toolkit

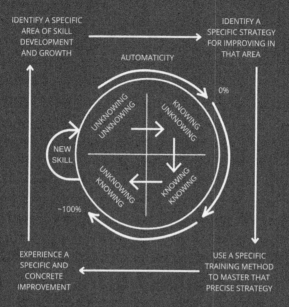

How do anxious speakers turn into articulate masters of the craft? Here's how: With the bulletproof, scientifically-proven, 2,500-year-old (but mostly forgotten) process pictured above.

First, we identify a specific area of improvement. Perhaps your body language weakens your connection with the audience. At this point, you experience "unknowing unknowing." You don't know you don't know the strategy you will soon learn for improving in this area.

Second, we choose a specific strategy for improving in this area. Perhaps we choose "open gestures," a type of gesturing that draws the audience in and holds attention.

At this point, you experience "knowing unknowing." You know you don't know the strategy. Your automaticity, or how automatically you perform the strategy when speaking, is 0%.

Third, we choose a specific drill or training method to help you practice open gestures. Perhaps you give practice speeches and perform the gestures. At this point, you experience "knowing knowing." You know you know the strategy.

And through practice, you formed a weak habit, so your automaticity is somewhere between 0% and 100%.

Fourth, you continue practicing the technique. You shift into "unknowing knowing." You forgot you use this type of gesture, because it became a matter of automatic habit. Your automaticity is 100%.

And just like that, you've experienced a significant and concrete improvement. You've left behind a weakness in communication and gained a strength. Forever. Every time you speak, you use this type of gesture, and you do it without even thinking about it. This alone can make the difference between a successful and unsuccessful speech.

Now repeat. Master a new skill. Create a new habit. Improve in a new area. How else could we improve your body language? What about the structure of your communication? Your persuasive strategy? Your debate skill? Your vocal modulation? With this process, people gain measurable and significant improvements in as little as one hour. Imagine if you stuck with it over time. This is the path to mastery. This is the path to unleashing the power of your words.

Access your 18 free PDF resources, 30 free video lessons, and 2 free workbooks from this link: www.speakforsuccesshub.com/toolkit

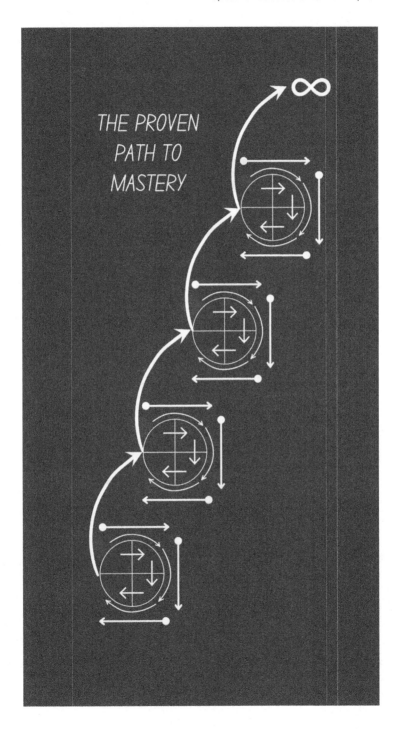

SPEAK FOR SUCCESS COLLECTION BOOK

THE PSYCHOLOGY OF PERSUASION CHAPTER

HOW TO PERSUADE:

Revealing Proven, Step-by-Step Persuasive Structures

MY PROMISE TO YOU

THIS CHAPTER WILL TEACH YOU EXACTLY HOW to persuade your audience by applying proven, step-by-step persuasive structures like the "objection-prediction model." These persuasive speech structures will make writing a persuasive message easy, persuading an audience easy, and delivering a speech easy.

3.1: MONROE'S MOTIVATED SEQUENCE

What is it? A proven persuasive process that has worked since the 1930s; five simple steps to persuading your audience.

Why does it work? It forms a "yes-ladder" of positive persuasive momentum. It focuses on the problem before the proposed solution, so the solution makes more sense in context. It empowers the audience by focusing on their capacity for creating change through personal action.

When do you use it? When you want to persuade, motivate, or influence an audience. When you want to make a sales pitch. When you want to use a gentle, proven method of persuasion.

What is the step-by-step process? Attention: "Hey! Listen to me, you have a problem!" Need: "Let me explain the problem." Satisfaction: "But, I have a solution!" Visualization: "If we implement my solution, this is what will happen. Or, if we don't implement my solution, this is what will happen." Action: "You can help me, and you, in this specific way. Will you do it?"

KEY INSIGHT:

Strategies Motivated by Motivating Motivate. It's Intelligent Design.

MONROE'S MOTIVATED SEQUENCE VISUALIZED

YOUR ACTION		THEIR REACTION
ATTENTION	- - →	INTEREST
↓		↓
NEED	- - →	DESIRE
↓		↓
SATISFACTION	- - →	DESIRE
↓		↓
VISUALIZATION	- - →	DESIRE
↓		↓
ACTION	- - →	ACTION

FIGURE 30: Monroe's Motivated Sequence is highly effective at instigating audience desire.

Historical Example: "(Attention) And so today, we pledge an end to the era of deadlock and drift; a new season of American renewal has begun. To renew America, we must be bold. We must do what no generation has had to do before. (Need) We must invest more in our own people, in their jobs, in their future, and at the same time cut our massive debt. And we must do so in a world in which we must compete for every opportunity. It will not be easy; it will require sacrifice. But it can be done, and done fairly, not choosing sacrifice for its own sake, but for our own sake. We must provide for our nation the way a family provides for its children. Our Founders saw themselves in the light of posterity. We can do no less. Anyone who has ever watched a child's eyes wander into sleep knows what posterity is. Posterity is the world to come; the world for whom we hold our ideals, from whom we have borrowed our planet, and to whom we bear sacred responsibility. We must do what America does best: offer more opportunity to all and demand responsibility from all. It is time to break the bad habit of expecting something for nothing, from our government or from each other. Let us all take more responsibility, not only for ourselves and our families but for our communities and our country. (Satisfaction) To renew America, we must revitalize our democracy. This beautiful capital, like every capital since the dawn of civilization, is often a place of intrigue and calculation. Powerful people maneuver for position and worry endlessly about who is in and who is out, who is up and who is down, forgetting those people whose toil and sweat sends us here and pays our way. Americans deserve better, and in this city today, there are people who want to do better. And so I say to all of us here, let us resolve to reform our politics, so that power and privilege no longer shout down the voice of the people. Let us put aside personal advantage so that we can feel the pain and see the promise of America. Let us resolve to make our government a place for what Franklin Roosevelt called 'bold, persistent experimentation,' a government for our tomorrows, not our yesterdays. Let us give this capital back to the people to whom it belongs. To renew America, we must meet challenges abroad as well at home. There is no longer division between what is foreign and what is domestic; the world economy, the world environment, the world AIDS crisis, the world arms race; they affect us all. Today, as an old order passes, the new world is more free but less stable. Communism's collapse has called forth old animosities and new dangers. Clearly America must continue to lead the world we did so much to make. While America rebuilds at home, we will not shrink from the challenges, nor fail to seize the opportunities, of this new world. Together with our friends and allies, we will work to shape change, lest it engulf us. When our vital interests are challenged, or the will and conscience of the international community is defied, we will act; with peaceful diplomacy whenever possible, with force when necessary. The brave Americans serving our nation today in the Persian Gulf, in Somalia, and wherever else they stand are testament to our resolve. But our greatest strength is the power of our ideas, which are still new in many lands. Across the world, we see them embraced, and we rejoice. Our hopes, our hearts, our hands, are with those on every continent who are building democracy and freedom. Their cause is America's cause. The American people have summoned the change we celebrate today. (Visualization) You have raised your voices in an unmistakable chorus. You have cast your votes in historic numbers. And you have changed the face of Congress, the presidency and the political process itself. Yes, you, my fellow Americans have forced the spring. (Action) Now, we must do the work the season demands. To that work I now turn, with all the authority of my office. I ask the Congress to join with me. But no president, no Congress, no government, can undertake this mission alone. My fellow Americans, you, too, must play your part in our renewal. I challenge a new generation of young Americans to a season of service; to act on your idealism by helping troubled children, keeping company with those in need, reconnecting our torn communities. There is so much to be done; enough indeed for millions of others who are still young in spirit to give of themselves in service, too." – Bill Clinton

This is one of my favorites. It has been studied, stress-tested, and proven to work. Additionally, it emphasizes three things: the problem, the solution, and the audience action. This makes your audience feel like they have power over the situation; like their personal actions can influence the outcome. The result is that they are more likely to act.

3.2: THE OBJECTION MODEL

What is it? Predicting the reasons your audience might object to your offer, then structuring your speech around addressing those objections.

Why does it work? It removes all the reasons your audience wouldn't accept your call to action. It clears the most common barriers to action. It leaves your audience no logical reason to not do what you ask of them.

When do you use it? When you have to persuade an audience. When you have to make a sales pitch. When you predict opposition to your proposal.

What is the step-by-step process? Discovery phase: Discover the most common, probable objections to your proposal. Invalidation phase: Invalidate the objections. Construction phase: Construct your speech around the reasons why those objections are invalid. Presentation phase: Present a speech constructed around invalidating the objections you've discovered.

THE OBJECTION-PREDICTION MODEL VISUALIZED

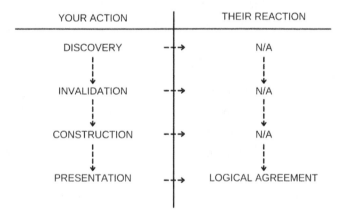

FIGURE 31: The objection-prediction model is highly effective at achieving logical agreement, and convincing the audience logically.

Historical Example: "Socialism is a scare word they have hurled at every advance the people have made in the last 20 years. Socialism is what they called public power. Socialism is what they called social security. Socialism is what they called farm price supports. Socialism is what they called bank deposit insurance. Socialism is what they called the growth of free and independent labor organizations. Socialism is their name for almost anything that helps all the people. When the Republican candidate inscribes the slogan 'Down With Socialism' on the banner of his 'great crusade,' that is really not what he means at all. What he really means is 'Down with Progress – down with Franklin Roosevelt's New Deal,' and 'down with Harry Truman's Fair Deal.' That's all he means." – Harry Truman

This one removes all the reasons your audience won't do what you want. When you are persuading someone, you will be met with persuasion resistance. Persuasion resistance often takes the form of specific objections to your offer, idea, or proposal. Here are some common examples: "I don't want to give anything up for it (which is a form of loss aversion: spending feels like a loss). I don't believe it can work. I don't think it can work for me. I can wait. I think it's too difficult. I don't understand it. I don't understand why I need it. I don't believe it will do what is promised. I don't know if it fits into my life. I don't trust the speaker." And with this speech structure, you quickly remove all the audience objections.

Counter each objection at the exact moment you think your audience might be thinking it. Counter the right objections: Don't counter objections that people don't have. If you are a trustworthy authority, then trusting you isn't a common objection. In this case, don't talk about your credentials over and over. You would be countering an objection that doesn't exist. Do not directly state the objections. Only say your counters. Don't say, "Now you might be thinking it costs too much, but it's $3,000 less than our competitors." Instead, just say "It's $3,000 less than our competitors." Stating the objection puts it in their heads if they weren't thinking about it.

This structure is four steps that remove all barriers your audience has to accepting your offer (assuming you do it right).

3.3: PATH CONTRAST

What is it? Structuring your speech by contrasting two different paths. Contrasting a "good" proposed path with a "bad" alternative.

Why does it work? It frames the contrast between the two paths, which allows you to control the narrative. It uses contrast persuasion, one of the most effective persuasive methods. It makes your proposed path seem like the obvious choice.

When do you use it? When you want to persuade, motivate, or inspire your audience to take one path instead of another. When there is uncertainty about how to proceed. When the future is unclear and you want to lead the way.

What is the step-by-step process? Good path: "Here's the good path we should take." Good outcome: "Here are the good things that will happen if we do." Alternative path: "Or, here's a bad alternative path we could take." Alternative outcome: "And here are the bad outcomes that will happen if we do." Back-and-forth: Jump back and forth between describing the good path and the alternative.

THE PATH-CONTRAST STRUCTURE VISUALIZED

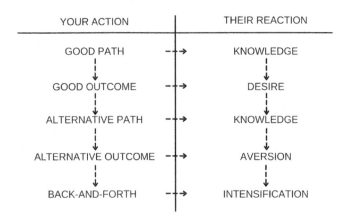

FIGURE 32: The path-contrast structure uses both contrast persuasion and aspirational persuasion. It persuades

people to move both away from an alternative to your
position and toward your position.

Historical Example: "Not too long ago, two friends of mine
were talking to a Cuban refugee, a businessman who had escaped
from Castro, and in the midst of his story one of my friends turned to
the other and said, 'We don't know how lucky we are.' And the Cuban
stopped and said, 'How lucky you are? I had someplace to escape to.'
And in that sentence he told us the entire story. If we lose freedom
here, there's no place to escape to. This is the last stand on earth. And
this idea that government is beholden to the people, that it has no
other source of power except the sovereign people, is still the newest
and the most unique idea in all the long history of man's relation to
man. This is the issue of this election: Whether we believe in our
capacity for self-government or whether we abandon the
American revolution and confess that a little intellectual elite in a far-
distant capitol can plan our lives for us better than we can plan them
ourselves. You and I are told increasingly we have to choose between
a left or right. Well I'd like to suggest there is no such thing as a left
or right. There's only an up or down – [up] man's old-aged dream,
the ultimate in individual freedom consistent with law and order, or
down to the ant heap of totalitarianism. And regardless of their
sincerity, their humanitarian motives, those who would trade our
freedom for security have embarked on this downward course." –
Ronald Reagan

Persuasion is more powerful when it has contrast. In other
words, if you want people to take a path, don't only talk about the
benefits of that path. Contrast the "good" path with an alternative
"bad" path.

So, don't only say "Imagine our lives when we take [good path].
We will [insert benefit one], [insert benefit two], and [insert benefit
three]." You must also say "Imagine our lives when we take [bad

path]. We will [insert consequence one], [insert consequence two], and [insert consequence three]." And then jump back and forth between them. Hit the contrast button over and over again. Make it a glaring, obvious, clear answer that they should take the good path by repeatedly and vividly contrasting it with a bad one.

Why is this such a powerful strategy? The contrast between the "good" and "bad" outcome is more persuasive than either of them alone. Presenting a "good" option that you want and a "bad" alternative makes doing what you want the obvious action. I repeat: Making it seem like a contrast between two options allows you to control the narrative.

3.4: PAST, PRESENT, MEANS

What is it? Presenting the problems of a difficult past, shifting to the easy, successful present, and explaining how you (or the "main character" of this story) made the transition.

Why does it work? It builds audience relatability by resonating emotionally. It shows the contrast between having unsolved problems and solved problems. It makes the "means" extremely desirable and builds immense suspense.

When do you use it? When you want to influence or persuade your audience to do something (whatever your "means" are). When your proposed action worked personally for you in your life, or you have a compelling and clear case study. When your life before taking the proposed action matches the lives of your audience now.

What is the step-by-step process? Past: "Here's how my life was difficult in the past. Here were my unsolved problems. I was suffering in the ways you are suffering." Present: "Here's how my life is successful now. Here's what it's like to have the problems solved. Here's how I'm no longer suffering, and life is easy." Means: "Here's the exact solution I personally used to get from the difficult past to the successful present."

THE PAST, PRESENT, MEANS STRUCTURE VISUALIZED

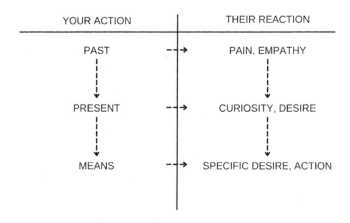

FIGURE 33: The past, present, means structure arouses immense curiosity, instigating the pressing, urgent question of "how did you make the change?"

Historical Example: "The South Bend I grew up in was still recovering from economic disasters that played out before I was even born. Once in this city, we housed companies that helped power America into the 20th century. Think of the forces that built the building we're standing in now, and countless others like it now long gone. Think of the wealth created here. Think of the thousands of workers who came here every day, and the thousands of families they provided for. And think of what it must have been like in 1963 when the great Studebaker auto company collapsed and the shock brought this city to its knees. Buildings like this one fell quiet, and acres of land around us slowly became a rust-scape of industrial decline, collapsing factories everywhere. Houses, once full with life and love and hope, stood crumbling and vacant. For the next half-century it took heroic efforts just to keep our city running, while our population shrank, and young people like me grew up believing the only way to a good life was to get out. Many of us did. But then some of us came back. We wanted things to change around here. And when the national press called us a dying city at the beginning of this decade, we took it as a call to arms. I ran for mayor in 2011 knowing that nothing like Studebaker would ever come back – but believing that we would, our city would, if we had the courage to reimagine our future. And now, I can confidently say that South Bend is back. More people are moving into South Bend than we've seen in a generation. Thousands of new jobs have been added in our area, and billions in investment. There's a long way for us to go. Life here is far from perfect. But we've changed our trajectory, and shown a path forward for communities like ours. And that's why I'm here today. To tell a different story than 'Make America Great Again.' Because there is a myth being sold to industrial and rural communities: the myth that we can stop the clock and turn it back. It comes from people who think the only way to reach communities like ours is through resentment and nostalgia, selling an impossible promise of returning to a bygone era that was never as great as advertised to begin with. The problem is, they're telling us to look for greatness in all the wrong places. Because if there is one thing the city of South Bend has shown, it's that there is no such thing as an honest politics that revolves around the word 'again.' It's time to walk away from the politics of the past, and toward something totally different." – Pete Buttigieg

This speech structure is so powerful. The entire time you're in the past and present stages, your audience is viscously curious, wondering: "How did you do it? How did you solve the problem? Help me! Can you please show me the solution? I need this in my life! I want to do what you did!"

And then you hit them with the solution. At this point, there's almost nothing that can stop them from adopting it (whether it's something they buy, or something they simply do). The curiosity, suspense, and intrigue built up during the two phases of your personal story (past and present) are too strong.

Maintain humility: Yes, you solved the problem they are struggling with. Yes, you still have to be humble about it.

Maintain honesty: Don't make your past and present seem like anything other than what they are.

Maintain relatability: Is your past really similar to the current lives of your audience members? Can they read themselves into you story (or the story of your "main character?")

Maintain emotional resonance: Can you accurately depict the emotions you felt during the difficult past? Can you convey them to your audience? If you do, will they think "wow, that's exactly how I feel right now?"

Don't present the solution until step three. Don't let step two and three blend. In step two, only explain the relief from the problem. Don't explain how it happened. This builds curiosity and suspense. Show vulnerability in step one: Be open, honest, and willing to expose parts of your past. In step three, describe the solution at length. Emphasize how it worked for you. Imply that if it worked for you, it can work for them.

3.5: PROBLEM-SOLUTION FORMULA

What is it? Presenting a clear problem your audience has, and then presenting a solution to that problem.

Why does it work? It ensures that your audience understands why your solution matters. It educates your audience and provides value. It points out a problem which your audience might not have known about.

When do you use it? When you want to persuade your audience to solve a problem. When they might not be aware of the problem, or how serious it is. When you are selling a solution.

What is the step-by-step process? Problem presentation: "Here's a problem you face." Problem consequences: "Here's why this problem is worse than you think." Solution presentation: "But there's a solution." Solution outcome: "Here's what it will feel like when you solve the problem."

THE PROBLEM-SOLUTION FORMULA VISUALIZED

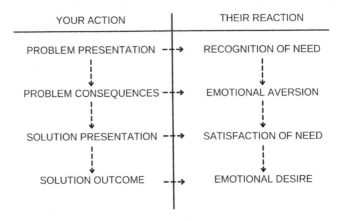

FIGURE 34: The ubiquitous problem-solution structure is foundational. Almost all structures incorporate problems and solution to some extent.

THE PROBLEM, AGITATE, SOLUTION, AGITATE STRUCTURE

STRUCTURE	"PASA" Structure			
BEHAVIORAL DUALITY	Escape		Approach	
SEMANTIC DUALITY	Problem		Solution	
EMOTIONAL DUALITY	Pain		Pleasure	
TEMPORAL DUALITY	Now		Later	
EXISTENTIAL DUALITY	Here		There	
DESIRE DUALITY	Aversion		Desire	
MODAL DUALITY	Chaos		Order	
STATE DUALITY	Actual		Potential	
KAIROS DUALITY	Conflict		Resolution	
THE SEQUENCE	**Problem**	**Agitate**	**Solution**	**Agitate**

Historical Example: "In such a spirit on my part and on yours we face our common difficulties. They concern, thank God, only material things. Values have shrunken to fantastic levels; taxes have risen; our ability to pay has fallen; government of all kinds is faced by serious curtailment of income; the means of exchange are frozen in the currents of trade; the withered leaves of industrial enterprise lie on every side; farmers find no markets for their produce; the savings of many years in thousands of families are gone. More important, a host of unemployed citizens face the grim problem of existence, and an equally great number toil with little return. Only a foolish optimist can deny the dark realities of the moment. Yet our distress comes from no failure of substance. We are stricken by no plague of locusts. Compared with the perils which our forefathers conquered because they believed and were not afraid, we have still much to be thankful for. Nature still offers her bounty and human efforts have multiplied it. Plenty is at our doorstep, but a generous use of it languishes in the very sight of the supply. Primarily this is because the rulers of the exchange of mankind's goods have failed, through their own stubbornness and their own incompetence, have admitted their failure, and abdicated. Practices of the unscrupulous money changers stand indicted in the court of public opinion, rejected by the hearts and minds of men. True they have tried, but their efforts have been cast in the pattern of an outworn tradition. Faced by failure of credit they have proposed only the lending of more money. Stripped of the lure of profit by which to induce our people to follow their false leadership, they have resorted to exhortations, pleading tearfully for restored confidence. They know only the rules of a generation of self-seekers. They have no vision, and when there is no vision the people perish. The money changers have fled from their high seats in the temple of our civilization. We may now restore that temple to the ancient truths. The measure of the restoration lies in the extent to which we apply social values more noble than mere monetary profit.

Happiness lies not in the mere possession of money; it lies in the joy of achievement, in the thrill of creative effort. The joy and moral stimulation of work no longer must be forgotten in the mad chase of evanescent profits. These dark days will be worth all they cost us if they teach us that our true destiny is not to be ministered unto but to minister to ourselves and to our fellow men. Recognition of the falsity of material wealth as the standard of success goes hand in hand with the abandonment of the false belief that public office and high political position are to be valued only by the standards of pride of place and personal profit; and there must be an end to a conduct in banking and in business which too often has given to a sacred trust the likeness of callous and selfish wrongdoing. Small wonder that confidence languishes, for it thrives only on honesty, on honor, on the sacredness of obligations, on faithful protection, on unselfish performance; without them it cannot live. Restoration calls, however, not for changes in ethics alone. This Nation asks for action, and action now. Our greatest primary task is to put people to work. This is no unsolvable problem if we face it wisely and courageously. It can be accomplished in part by direct recruiting by the Government itself, treating the task as we would treat the emergency of a war, but at the same time, through this employment, accomplishing greatly needed projects to stimulate and reorganize the use of our natural resources." – Franklin Delano Roosevelt

This persuasive speech structure is so simple but so powerful. Most people make the mistake of only talking about their solution, which is weak. A solution only makes sense in the context of a problem. So, expound on the problem. Magnify the perceived scope of the problem, and it validates a bigger, bolder, and broader solution.

3.6: DIAGNOSE, PROBLEM, SOLUTION

What is it? Diagnosing a problem that people know they have but don't understand the cause of, then providing a solution.

Why does it work? It implies you know how to solve the problem you diagnosed. It uses contrast persuasion (problem versus solution). It gives you authority as the "diagnoser."

When do you use it? When you want to persuade your audience to solve a problem. When they are aware of the problem, but don't understand it. When you know why a problem exists, but your audience doesn't.

What is the step-by-step process? Diagnose: "You already know you have this problem. But here's exactly why you have this problem. Here's what causes it." Problem: "Here's why this problem is worse than you think." Solution: "Now that I've diagnosed this problem, let me tell you how to solve it."

THE DIAGNOSE, PROBLEM, SOLUTION METHOD VISUALIZED

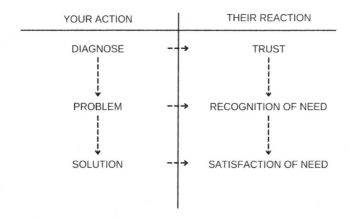

FIGURE 35: The diagnosis earns trust. Expanding the diagnosis of a problem – or rediagnosing it – makes you appear as the person with the most comprehensive understanding of the problem. This earns trust.

Historical Example: "What I want you to understand is, the national debt is not the only cause of that. It is because America has not invested in its people; it is because we have not grown; it is because we've had twelve years of trickle-down economics. We've gone from first to twelfth in the world in wages, we've had four years when we produced no private sector jobs, most people are working harder for less money than they were making ten years ago. It is because we are in the grip of a failed economic theory. And this decision you're about to make better be about what kind of economic theory you want; not just people saying I wanna go fix it, but what are we going to do! What I think we have to do is invest in American jobs, American education, control American healthcare costs, and bring the American people together again." – Bill Clinton

If you're wondering how this is different from the problem-solution structure, here's how: The problem-solution structure is for audiences who aren't fully aware of a problem. The diagnose-problem-solution structure is for audiences who are aware of a problem, but not why it exists.

Why diagnose the problem at all? Because it builds trust and presents your authority. The audience thinks that the person who understands why a problem exists is the one best equipped to fix it. And the person who is best equipped to fix a problem is probably the best person from which to buy the solution.

And another captivating rhetorical structure is this: The diagnose phase can consist of not only properly diagnosing what the problem is, but telling the audience what it is not. "The problem is not [insert superficial problem one], it is not [insert superficial problem two], it is not [insert superficial problem three], [repeat as many as you want]. The problem is [insert deep problem that causes the previous superficial problems; the underlying root cause that causes the symptoms that are those superficial problems]."

3.7: CRITERIA MATCHING

What is it? Presenting the criteria which define the best option, and then proving that your proposal meets them.

Why does it work? It focuses on establishing agreement first. It builds speaker to audience rapport. It builds a two-step "yes-ladder" by first agreeing on what criteria matter and only then presenting an option that meets them.

When do you use it? When you want to persuade your audience to choose your option out of many options. When there are generally agreed-upon criteria for judging what makes this type of thing the best, or when it is easy to establish such criteria.

What is the step-by-step process? Criteria establishment: "Here's what makes this type of thing good. Can we agree on that? We agree, so far, on what this type of thing would need to be good, right?" Criteria satisfaction: "As you can see, my proposed option fills the criteria we just agreed on."

THE CRITERIA-MATCHING MODEL VISUALIZED

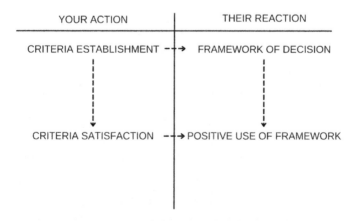

FIGURE 36: It is easier to gain agreement to a framework of evaluation that you then apply to your proposal than it is to try to barge in through the front door and speak of your proposal directly.

Like many of these persuasive speech structures, this one is a yes-ladder. Instead of getting right into the hard sell, it slowly builds up to it. Along the way, it gets a series of "yes" responses.

"Yes, those are definitely the criteria I'm looking to fill for this type of solution." "Yes, that checklist seems reasonable." "Yes, I guess your option does fill the checklist." "Yes, that means your option fills the criteria." "Yes, that means your option is the best." "Yes, since it is the best, I should buy it or agree with your point of view."

Due to the principle of persuasive consistency (people want to be consistent with their previous actions), with every additional "yes," the chances of hearing a "no" decrease. In other words, you gain "yes-momentum." Compare that to jumping straight to it: "No, I don't think your option is the best. What are the criteria you're using to judge that? I bet you have none. No, since it's not the best, I won't take it. Go away."

3.8: CRITERIA MATCHING AND DEMATCHING

What is it? Presenting the criteria which define the best option. Proving that all other options don't meet them (criteria de-matching). Proving that your option does (criteria matching).

Why does it work? It has all the benefits of criteria matching. It adds another persuasive layer to the equation. It turns "mine is good" to "mine is good, the others aren't." It makes your audience think twice about considering another option.

When do you use it? When criteria matching fits. When there are multiple options in fierce competition. When you aren't concerned about discrediting an opponent's position.

What is the step-by-step process? Criteria establishment: "Here's what makes this type of thing good. Can we agree on that? We agree, so far, on what this type of thing would need to be good, right?" Criteria satisfaction: "As you can see, my proposed option fills the criteria we just agreed on." Criteria dissatisfaction: "As you can see, the other options clearly don't fit the checklist. Thus, the other options aren't the best."

THE MATCHING AND DEMATCHING MODEL VISUALIZED

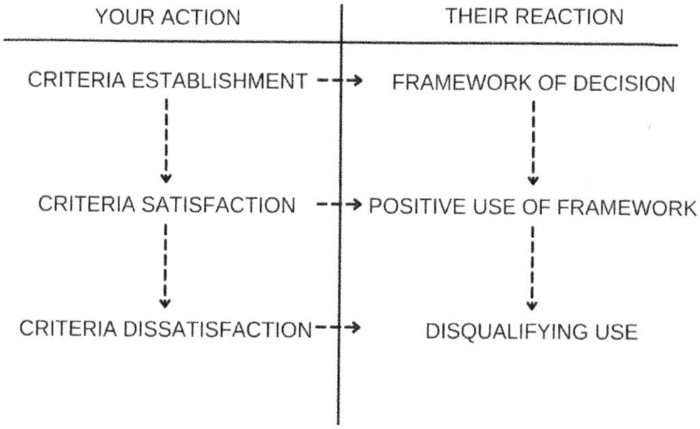

YOUR ACTION	THEIR REACTION
CRITERIA ESTABLISHMENT --→	FRAMEWORK OF DECISION
↓	↓
CRITERIA SATISFACTION --→	POSITIVE USE OF FRAMEWORK
↓	↓
CRITERIA DISSATISFACTION--→	DISQUALIFYING USE

FIGURE 37: This is also a sort of path-contrast structure. Ensure the framework of evaluation actually excludes the alternatives and promotes your proposal.

3.9: THE SIX-POINT PUNCH

What is it? A quick, assertive, hard-sell approach for fast sales pitches (which works even if you are selling an idea).

Why does it work? It is designed to pack the most persuasion into the smallest amount of time. It is designed to convince people as quickly as possible. It is brief, but psychologically persuasive.

When do you use it? When you don't have a lot of time. When you aren't trying to pitch a big commitment. When you are trying to persuade an audience to buy (instead of another action), although it does work for persuading the adoption of ideas.

What is the step-by-step process? Unique value proposition and headline statement: "Here's why this product offers unique value to you. Here's why you should pay attention." Supporting statement: "Normally, this type of product causes [insert pain point or inconvenience]. But this model offers [repeat unique value] without [insert pain point or inconvenience]." Physical description (if applicable): "Here's what it looks like. Here's what it feels like." Benefit statements: "It will [insert benefit one], [insert benefit two], [insert benefit three]." Call-to-action: "Do this to get it." Trust indicators and social proof: "These people bought it too, and here's what they have to say about it."

THE SIX-POINT PUNCH VISUALIZED

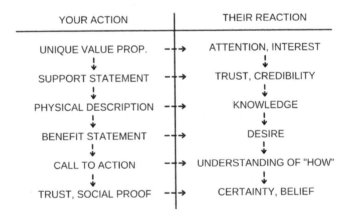

FIGURE 38: This structure is fast and effective. It balances earning trust with building desire. Desire without trust that a proposal can satisfy it lacks persuasive force.

Humans have a central processing route and a peripheral processing route. The peripheral route controls mental processes dictating impulsive, emotional decisions, and the central route controls mental processes dictating big commitments. The central route is careful, slow, and logical.

The six-point-punch targets the peripheral route. This next structure is for selling people on big commitments, targeting the central route.

3.10: ECONOMIC VALUES STRUCTURE

What is it? Presenting a product, and then showing how it satisfies the nine economic values.

Why does it work? It is designed to give potential customers as much information as possible. It is designed to convince people to make big commitments. It is designed to earn trust.

When do you use it? When you are selling a complex, expensive product. When you are trying to get people to make a big financial commitment. When you are selling via the central processing route.

What is the step-by-step process? Product presentation: "Here's what it is, what it does, and how it does it." Efficacy: "Here's how well it does what it's supposed to do. Speed: "Here's how quickly you'll get results." Reliability: "Here's how reliable it is." Ease of Use: "Here's how easy it is to use." Flexibility: "Here's how many things it can do." Status: "Here's how it will make others see you." Aesthetic Appeal: "Here's how aesthetically pleasing it is." Emotion: "Here's how it makes you feel." Cost: "Here's how much it costs."

KEY INSIGHT:

Imagine: Your Idea Is Exactly What They Want and Need, But You Didn't Know What They Wanted and Needed, So You Didn't Tell Them.

THE ECONOMIC VALUES STRUCTURE VISUALIZED

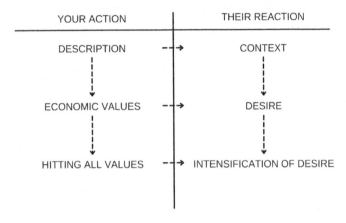

FIGURE 39: As you hit upon the economic desires, you intensify the desire of the audience for your proposal or product, *ceteris paribus*.

This speech structure is perfect for selling big, expensive things. Why? Because it builds trust. Because it is education-based selling (teaching about a product rather than trying to sell it from the start). Because it speaks in terms of the economic values people use to evaluate products.

And if you are thinking "it seems a little too long," you can leave out certain economic values. You can also reorder them to put the important ones first. But persuasion via the central route demands a higher degree of deliberate information-exchange and time-commitment.

3.11: SHORT-FORM RHETORICAL THREE-POINT PUNCH

What is it? Structuring a speech by making a claim, and supporting that claim with an emotional subpoint, an evidence-driven subpoint, and a logical subpoint.

Why does it work? Because it uses the three proven rhetorical methods (evidence, logic, and emotion). Because it is memorable. Because it is flexible.

When do you use it? When you want to give a brief persuasive speech. When you want to change someone's point-of-view.

What is the step-by-step process? Main claim: "X should Y because [emotional reason], [logical reason], and [evidence-driven reason]. Emotional reason: "X should Y because it hurts people. Here's how..." Logical reason: "X should Y because it is inherently self-contradictory. Here's how..." Evidence-driven reason: "X should Y because 9/10 doctors say so. Here's why..."

THE SHORT-FORM THREE-POINT PUNCH VISUALIZED

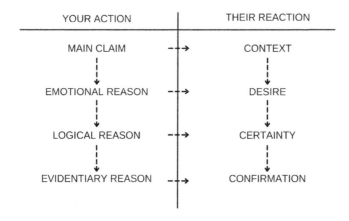

FIGURE 40: This structure is simple and straightforward, and it appeals to the three essential elements of persuasive communication.

Centuries ago, Aristotle boiled down all of persuasion to three things: emotion (pathos), logic (logos), and evidence (ethos), which includes evidence creating the perception that the speaker is trustworthy and has the best interests of the audience at heart. And with this structure, you are using each of them to support a main claim.

If you have to give a brief persuasive speech, just answer these questions: What do I want to persuade people of? What's an emotional reason they should agree with me? What's a logical reason they should agree with me? What's the evidence that should make them agree with me?

And once you do that, you have your brief persuasive speech. But let's say you want to give a longer persuasive speech using these principles. For that, we have this next structure. Like an accordion, it stretches out the short-form three-point-punch.

3.12: LONG-FORM RHETORICAL THREE-POINT PUNCH

What is it? Structuring a speech by making one claim, and supporting that claim with three sub-points, each of which have ethos, pathos, and logos within them.

Why does it work? It extends the short-form rhetorical three-point-punch. It is more substantial. It uses three times as much emotion, three times as much logic, and three times as much evidence as the short-form version.

When do you use it? When you want to give a longer persuasive speech. When you want to change someone's point-of-view, but they are particularly entrenched. When you need extra persuasive power.

What is the step-by-step process? Main claim: "X should Y because [reason one], [reason two], and [reason three]. Reason one: "[Reason one] [emotional details], [logical details], [evidence]." Reason two: "[Reason two] [emotional details], [logical details], [evidence]." Reason three: "[Reason three] [emotional details], [logical details], [evidence]."

THE LONG-FORM THREE-POINT PUNCH VISUALIZED

YOUR ACTION		THEIR REACTION
MAIN CLAIM	- -→	CONTEXT
↓		↓
SHORT-FORM ONE	- -→	DESIRE, CERTAINTY, CONFIRM.
↓		↓
SHORT-FORM TWO	- -→	DESIRE, CERTAINTY, CONFIRM.
↓		↓
SHORT-FORM THREE	- -→	DESIRE, CERTAINTY, CONFIRM.

FIGURE 41: This structure extends the short-form three-point punch, achieving more desire, certainty, and confirmation.

I know exactly what you're thinking: "what's the difference between this and the last one?" The short-form version is essentially just one third of the long-form version. The long-form version is basically three of the short-form versions stacked together, in support of one broader claim.

Now, let's move away from the three-point, six-point, and extended-three-point punches. Enough punches. Time for a series of persuasive trifectas. These are some of my favorite structures. They are easy, simple, and powerful.

3.13: GAIN, LOGIC, FEAR TRIFECTA

What is it? Structuring a persuasive speech around an audience gain, logical justifications of the gain, and then fear of missing the gain.

Why does it work? It uses tantalizing benefits to get audience attention. It plays on the "fear of missing out." It combines gain and fear with logic, to make the whole structure appeal properly to reason instead of just emotion.

When do you use it? When you want to persuade the audience to do something that will help them. When the thing that the audience gains from also helps you. When your offer expires soon, or there is a time limit, or there is some scarcity involved, like limited availability.

What is the step-by-step process? Present the subject: "Here's what I want you to do." Present gain: "Here are all the benefits you'll gain from doing it. Aren't they great?" Justify with logic: "Here's the logical proof of the gain." Instill fear: "But act fast! The offer expires in 24 hours. Then, you won't be able to gain anything!"

THE GAIN, LOGIC, FEAR TRIFECTA VISUALIZED

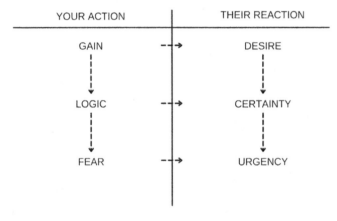

FIGURE 42: This structure is particularly effective at motivating enthusiastic action because it doesn't only answer the question "why should I do this?" but the more important question "why should I do this now?"

Historical Example: "(Gain) I think there's a better way. It's true, the American people are ready. There's a historic majority right now, even broader than what was available to President Obama a decade ago. There is now a majority ready to act to make sure there is no such thing as an uninsured American and no such thing as an unaffordable prescription. (Logic) Just so long as we don't command people to accept a public plan if they don't want to. That's the idea of Medicare for All Who Want It. My point is, what I am offering is campaigning for all of these things that America wants. Yes, higher wages, doubling the rate of unionization in this country, making corporations and the wealthy pay their fair share, delivering healthcare and college affordability. (Fear) But also offering a way to do these game changing transformations that will actually galvanize and energize, not polarize the American people. That is not only what we need in order to win, it's what we need in order to govern and actually get these things done." – Pete Buttigieg

The gain-logic-fear trifecta can convince almost anyone of anything. It is so powerful because of that final step, when you make people fear missing out. Why? Because of loss aversion: People hate losing opportunities, and generally anticipate the pain of loss to feel twice as intense as the pleasure of gain.

And when you use this structure, here's what your audience will be thinking: "I would hate to figure out later that I really needed this. I don't want to miss this opportunity to take action now. I'm afraid I'll pass the offer, and then regret it."

3.14: TENSION, DESIRE, ACTION TRIFECTA

What is it? Structuring a persuasive speech around creating tension in the audience's minds, building desire through tension, and then providing an action by which to escape the tension.

Why does it work? It uses cognitive dissonance in the audience to motivate action. It uses aspirational persuasion. It captures attention through tension.

When do you use it? When your audience has a clear and unfulfilled area of improvement. When your audience isn't living in the best way or fulfilling their highest potential. When you have a solution for these two problems.

What is the step-by-step process? Create tension: "You aren't living your best life. Here's what you want to be: [insert aspirations]. Do your actions line up with who you want to be? No. You could be better." Build desire: "Imagine what it would feel like to finally be on the path you want to be on. Imagine how relaxed you would feel, knowing that you are acting in alignment with your desires and values." Propose action: "Here's a way you can be on that path."

THE TENSION, DESIRE, ACTION TRIFECTA VISUALIZED

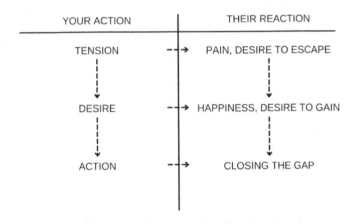

FIGURE 43: People move for three reasons: to escape pain, to attain pleasure, or both. This structure takes advantage of our core motivational impulses.

This structure creates cognitive dissonance, or "the state of having inconsistent thoughts, beliefs, or attitudes, especially as relating to behavioral decisions and attitude change."

You are pointing out the gaping gaps between who your audience members want to be, or even think they already are, and who they actually are.

At this point, because of the tension created by the cognitive dissonance, the desire is huge. They crave a way to close the gap you just pointed out between "who I want to be or who I think I already am" and "who I actually am." They probably want an easy, quick, and simple way to close the gap. And that's exactly what you'll give them in the action step.

3.15: PERSUASIVE STACK STRUCTURE

What is it? Structuring a persuasive speech around Dr. Robert Cialdini's six proven principles of psychological persuasion outlined in his book *Influence*.

Why does it work? It uses proven, scientific methods of persuasion. It uses all six of the persuasive principles in sequence. It is flexible.

When do you use it? When you want to make your audience like you. When you want to use a gentle, subtle form of persuasion. When you want to give a conversational speech.

What is the step-by-step process? Use likeability: "I am trying to [insert common goal with your audience]. You guys are [insert compliment]. I also [insert similarity]." Use reciprocity: "Normally I don't do this, but here's this free report that covers more than I can cover in this speech. People usually pay $200 for it, but it's free for you guys." Use authority: "Here's why I'm an expert on this subject. Here's why you should trust me. Here are my credentials." Use consensus: "Not a lot of people used to agree with me. Now, 86% of people do." Use scarcity: "But time is running out. We have to take action fast, or else we won't be able to." Use consistency: "Do you all agree with [small claim]? What about [slightly larger claim]? Maybe also [medium claim]? Do you also agree with [large, primary claim]?"

THE PERSUASIVE STACK VISUALIZED

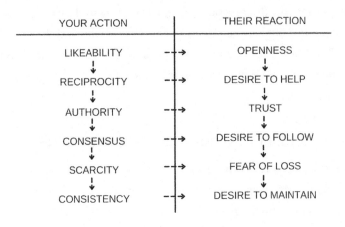

FIGURE 44: This structure incorporates six powerful forms of influence into a simple, step-by-step process.

People like those who have common goals as them, who compliment them, and who are similar to them. And if your audience likes you, they are more likely to accept your persuasion.

You are more likely to persuade your audience if you give them something. Why? They feel the need to reciprocate that action.

You are more likely to persuade people if they see you as an authority. This is psychologically programmed.

People follow those around them. They look to others to decide how to act. So, when you tell them that "86% of people believe this," they are more likely to believe it too. This is consensus.

We talked about scarcity already. Remember? It is the "fear of missing out" in the Tension-Desire-Action structure.

Last but not least: If you get people to agree to smaller claims, that "yes momentum" will carry over to larger claims. This is part of a "yes-ladder." Why? People want to be consistent with their actions.

Reciprocity: People tend to feel the need to repay any kind behavior they receive. If a friend buys you lunch, there's an obligation to buy them lunch in the future to return the favor. If you give another speaker a standing ovation, they are likely to reciprocate this behavior back to you later on. If you want to persuade the audience to buy a product from you, giving them a discount on it will make them more likely to buy it because you are essentially giving up money you would have earned for them to give up money in return.

Interestingly enough, how you give the discount is just as important as the discount itself. If you say "there's a 10% discount on my product," that may only attract a few buyers from the audience. However, if you say "now I normally only offer a 5% discount on my product at the end of these speeches, but because you were such a great audience, I'll give a 10% discount. Make sure you don't tell anyone!" the results will be much more profitable. You are giving the same discount in both cases, but in one situation you are doing it in a much more personal way. Additionally, by including the "don't tell anyone!" you are entering into a lighthearted, friendly conspiracy with the audience.

To appear more genuine, you can even announce the 5% discount, leave the microphone, but then turn back and say "actually, I think such a great audience deserves a 10% discount." By exchanging this kindness with the audience, they are much more likely to buy the product because they will be supporting someone they like. People will never admit the reason they bought it is because they like you; they will form a logical rationalization to use as an explanation of their purchase. If you recall, most decisions are made on emotion, not logic, and yet most decisions are consciously rationalized by logic after they are made on an emotional impulse.

Scarcity: People want things that other people don't have. That is why people buy expensive jewels. They serve no real function, but are desirable because of their rarity. An example of scarcity in action is when a consumer product in the market decreases in availability, and the prices go up. The product itself is the same, but because there is less of it available on the market, people are willing to pay more for it.

The underlying subconscious assumption behind this behavioral phenomenon is that a rare resource will run out faster, and that more people are competing for the same resource.

You can use the principle of persuasive scarcity in a speech by portraying your idea or product as one your audience should adopt soon, because if they do not, they will soon regret losing the opportunity as it will be sold out or too late. Loss aversion is a very powerful motivator: people typically don't play to win, just not to lose. Losing out on the opportunity to buy or do something, even if one hasn't already, triggers loss aversion as well.

Many online stores use scarcity to spur purchases, which is a highly effective strategy. They do so by putting a timed discount, or a decreasing stock number. Just as scarcity can work on an online store, it can work in your speech. Don't create fake scarcity: if fake scarcity is detected by your audience, which it likely will be, then they will feel manipulated or lied to. If there is even a small amount of scarcity, then expose it. Don't make it up, just express it if it already exists.

Authority: Ethos and the persuasive principle of authority are very similar. They are using what people of authority on a subject have said about it to help validate your point. The principle of personal authority is when you try to generate the appearance of being an authority on a subject, and thereby ethos is automatically generated whenever you say something. You can create this appearance by explaining complex aspects of an idea, problem, or product to your audience. Additionally, you can briefly mention the amount of research that supports what you are saying, or briefly allude to your credentials. Anything that makes you appear as an expert on a subject generates personal ethos. Personal ethos is a very powerful tool for persuading an audience. Harnessing this principle of persuasion can go a long way; you are making use of the reason why patients defer to the judgements of doctors, and athletes listen to their coaches.

An interesting example of the principle of authority is the Milgram experiment, which showed that people would willingly shock what they believed to be a real person in another room at higher and higher voltages, and even at lethal voltages. They did so because an authority figure told them to. Nobody was actually shocked; the test participant was just made to believe that someone was being shocked. Why did they do this? Why did they willingly shock another human being, despite having clear reservations about it? Because an authority figure told them to.

Determining what people are willing to do just because an authority figure told them to was the purpose of the famous Milgram experiment, and it found that authority is an incredibly powerful quality. Just make sure you use it for good.

Consistency: People want to be consistent with themselves. The principle of persuasive consistency suggests that it is easier to get someone to agree to something substantial if you've gotten them to agree to something smaller in the past.

If you approach someone and ask them directly for a donation to a nonprofit, they will likely say no, but if you approach someone and first ask them to verbally endorse a nonprofit, and then ask for a donation later on, they are much more likely to say yes to making the donation if they previously agreed to a verbal endorsement.

People like to be consistent with themselves. If you've gotten someone to agree to something small, they are more likely to agree to something bigger later on. If you try to get someone to agree to something big immediately, they are far more likely to turn you down than if you ease them into it by first getting them to make smaller commitments. Doing so is essentially forming a "ladder" in which each rung of the ladder represents a slightly larger commitment than the last. Whether the commitment is to purchase something or to agree with someone, the principle of consistency applies. If your audience agrees first to a small claim you make, and then to a slightly more controversial claim, and then to your most contentious point, you are more likely to get them to agree to your most contentious point than if you started with it.

Likability: The fable of the Wind and the Sun is instructive here. There is a lot to learn from this fable. In some cases, it is better to be gentle when persuading. Some people grow defensive when faced with aggressive persuasion tactics, and instead of getting anything out of them, they tighten their metaphorical coats. The sun gently shined its warmth on the traveler, and the traveler took off the coat on his own.

In many cases, subtle and gentle persuasion beats obvious persuasion. The coat represents an inherent aversion to be persuaded that many carry like a shield. Indeed, persuasion resistance is a well-documented psychological phenomenon. Many assume that if you try to persuade them of something, it must be beneficial for you at their expense. Do not try to rip the shield from people for that will surely fail. On the other hand, get them to willingly give up their shield just as the traveler took off his coat.

The principle of likeability embodies the moral of Aesop's fable. People prefer to help those who they like. People tend to like those who are similar to them, have complimented them, or who are working toward similar goals as them. Employ these to get people to like you before trying to persuade them to your cause.

It is well known that in business, if you want to convince someone to make a big purchase or commitment, you don't want to get right to business. Take them to a business dinner, ask about their day, exchange pleasantries, see how their family is doing, and ignore the business for the first half hour or so. During this time set aside the business and focus on establishing similarity, complimenting them, and looking for common goals. Only after establishing a bond of friendship with the prospective buyer is it time to bring up business.

At this point, because they view you as a friend, they will subconsciously not want to turn you down in fear that they might lose the connection. Humans are inherently social creatures, and we are genetically predisposed to value a large social network. Many businessmen say that it is better to "get right into it," but it has been proven time and time again that the approach of fostering likeability for a few minutes and then getting into the business is much more effective and results in more profitable agreements for both parties.

Use the principle of likability often in your speech. It can often make the difference between people following your call to action or ignoring it. You can use the principle of likability in your speech by establishing common goals with your audience, expressing similarity, and complimenting them. Specifically how to do this will be answered in the Audience Interaction section.

A last word on the principle of likability and soft persuasion is this: you cannot force anyone to listen to your speech. They may be sitting there, but it is up to you to persuade them to listen. Just because you have an audience doesn't mean your audience is listening. How do you make them listen? By making them *choose* to listen. They cannot be forced. This evokes the same truth as the fable of the wind and the sun. Be so valuable as a speaker, with such important ideas and such an engaging presence, that they almost have to choose to listen.

Consensus: The herd mindset is an interesting phenomenon. A study conducted by researchers at Leeds University concluded that ten confident people who pretended to know what they were doing in an unfamiliar situation were able to influence 190 people to follow them. The principle of consensus plays off of the tendency people have to follow the crowd, or a few particularly confident people from the crowd. This principle applies especially in times of uncertainty.

You can use this principle to your advantage by asking a group of friends who you know will be attending your speech to give a standing ovation after you finish. Upon seeing five or six people stand, others will begin to follow their lead. This is simply how human beings are wired.

3.16: LAST METHOD

What is it? Structuring a persuasive speech around discrediting all other methods, and then presenting one final "remaining" method.

Why does it work? It waits to propose a solution, which builds trust. It makes your proposal seem like the only possible option. It makes the audience think twice about doing anything other than what you want.

When do you use it? When you want to persuade your audience to take a specific action. When there are multiple options to choose from. When the other options have problems that your option doesn't have.

What is the step-by-step process? Option presentation: "Here's another option we could take." Option invalidation: "Here's what's wrong with that option." Repetition: Repeat steps one and two for all other options. Last method presentation: "Here's the final remaining method." Last method validation: "Here's why the final method works."

Email Peter D. Andrei, the author of the Speak for Success collection and the President of Speak Truth Well LLC directly.

pandreibusiness@gmail.com

THE LAST METHOD STRATEGY VISUALIZED

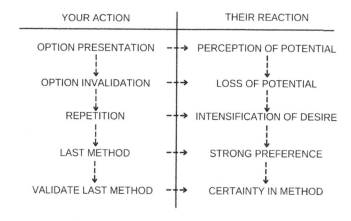

FIGURE 45: This structure is particularly effective for situations in which the need for action is clear, but there is little clarity on which action to take.

Historical Example: "I have but one lamp by which my feet are guided, and that is the lamp of experience. I know of no way of judging of the future but by the past. And judging by the past, I wish to know what there has been in the conduct of the British ministry for the last ten years to justify those hopes with which gentlemen have been pleased to solace themselves and the House. Is it that insidious smile with which our petition has been lately received? Trust it not, sir; it will prove a snare to your feet. Suffer not yourselves to be betrayed with a kiss. Ask yourselves how this gracious reception of our petition comports with those warlike preparations which cover our waters and darken our land. Are fleets and armies necessary to a work of love and reconciliation? Have we shown ourselves so unwilling to be reconciled that force must be called in to win back our love? Let us not deceive ourselves, sir. These are the implements of war and subjugation; the last arguments to which kings resort. I ask gentlemen, sir, what means this martial array, if its purpose be not to force us to submission? Can gentlemen assign any other possible motive for it? Has Great Britain any enemy, in this quarter of the world, to call for all this accumulation of navies and armies? No, sir, she has none. They are meant for us: they can be meant for no other. They are sent over to bind and rivet upon us those chains which the British ministry have been so long forging. And what have we to oppose to them? Shall we try argument? Sir, we have been trying that for the last ten years. Have we anything new to offer upon the subject? Nothing. We have held the subject up in every light of which it is capable; but it has been all in vain. Shall we resort to entreaty and humble supplication? What terms shall we find which have not been already exhausted? Let us not, I beseech you, sir, deceive ourselves. Sir, we have done everything that could be done to avert the storm which is now coming on. We have petitioned; we have remonstrated; we have supplicated; we have prostrated ourselves before the throne, and have implored its interposition to arrest the tyrannical hands of the ministry and Parliament. Our petitions have been slighted; our remonstrances have produced additional violence and insult; our supplications have been disregarded; and we have been spurned, with contempt, from the foot of the throne! In vain, after these things, may we indulge the fond hope of peace and reconciliation. There is no longer any room for hope. If we wish to be free – if we mean to preserve inviolate those inestimable privileges for which we have been so long contending – if we mean not basely to abandon the noble struggle in which we have been so long engaged, and which we have pledged ourselves never to abandon until the glorious object of our contest shall be obtained – we must fight! I repeat it, sir, we must fight! An appeal to arms and to the God of hosts is all that is left us! They tell us, sir, that we are weak; unable to cope with so formidable an adversary. But when shall we be stronger? Will it be the next week, or the next year? Will it be when we are totally disarmed, and when a British guard shall be stationed in every house? Shall we gather strength by irresolution and inaction? Shall we acquire the means of effectual resistance by lying supinely on our backs and hugging the delusive phantom of hope, until our enemies shall have bound us hand and foot? Sir, we are not weak if we make a proper use of those means which the God of nature hath placed in our power. The millions of people, armed in the holy cause of liberty, and in such a country as that which we possess, are invincible by any force which our enemy can send against us. Besides, sir, we shall not fight our battles alone. There is a just God who presides over the destinies of nations, and who will raise up friends to fight our battles for us. The battle, sir, is not to the strong alone; it is to the vigilant, the active, the brave. Besides, sir, we have no election. If we were base enough to desire it, it is now too late to retire from the contest. There is no retreat but in submission and slavery! Our chains are forged! Their clanking may be heard on the plains of Boston! The war is inevitable – and let it come! I repeat it, sir, let it come. It is in vain, sir, to extenuate the matter. Gentlemen may cry, Peace, Peace – but there is no peace. The war is actually begun! The next gale that sweeps from the north will bring to our ears the clash of resounding arms! Our brethren are already in the field! Why stand we here idle? What is it that gentlemen wish? What would they have? Is life so dear, or peace so sweet, as to be purchased at the price of chains and slavery? Forbid it, Almighty God! I know not what course others may take; but as for me, give me liberty or give me death!" – Patrick Henry

Don't be too derisive of the other options. That makes it seem personal. Try your best to seem objective and logical. This is an objective and logical structure, isn't it? Go through all the other options, if possible. If not? Go through the most popular ones. Don't present your method until you've invalidated all the other options. Try to make your method seem good in the ways that the others are bad, achieving contrast persuasion.

3.17: PAST, PRESENT, FUTURE

What is it? Structuring a persuasive speech around the past, present, and future. Showing how a solution works not only in the present, but the past and future too.

Why does it work? It makes your proposed solution seem timeless. It builds belief in your solution. It removes the common objection "it won't work in the future," and the common objection "it hasn't worked in the past."

When do you use it? When you want to persuade your audience to accept a solution to a consequential problem that you can't afford attempting to treat with an ineffective solution. When there is history related to your solution from which you can draw a past example. When the solution will be used for a long time, and people need to be particularly certain that it is valuable, proven, and effective over the long term, not just the short term.

What is the step-by-step process? Solution presentation: "Here's what we should do." The past: "Here's how this solution worked in the past, or here's how this solution would have been better than what was done." The present: "Here's why this solution is the best right now." The future: "Here's why this solution will continue to work in the future."

KEY INSIGHT:

This Strategy Works If Your Solution Is Anti-Fragile, If You Are Thinking Long-Term, If You Expect the Unexpected.

THE PAST, PRESENT, FUTURE STRATEGY VISUALIZED

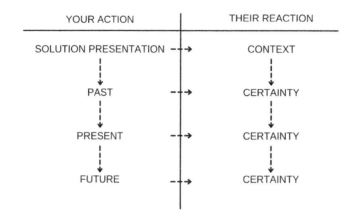

FIGURE 46: This structure is particularly effective at creating certainty. This is best-suited for situations in which the need for a solution or action is clear, but the question remains open as to what solution or action is best.

With this structure, you are asserting yourself over three dimensions of time. Many speakers make a common mistake; the mistake of only speaking in terms of the present; of only answering the question "why does this solution work now?" With this structure, you are answering these three questions: "Why does this solution work now?" "Has this solution worked in the past?" "Will this solution work in the future?"

3.18: DESIRE, DISSONANCE, DECISION TRIFECTA

What is it? Structuring a persuasive speech around an unfulfilled desire. Showing your audience how they can satisfy the desire.

Why does it work? It puts people in a state of cognitive dissonance, and they will do anything to close the gap. It hits the pain-points of the audience over and over, and then provides an action to relieve those pain-points. It uses emotion, a powerful motivator, and it focuses on directly addressing the "WIIFM" question.

When do you use it? When you want to persuade your audience to make a particular decision. When your proposed action fills a desire. When your audience has an unfilled desire that you can hit upon over and over again to create powerful cognitive dissonance.

What is the step-by-step process? Desire: "Don't you want to [insert desire]?" Dissonance: "Right now, [insert desire] isn't real. You're missing it." Decision "Here's what you have to do to fulfill that desire."

THE DESIRE, DISSONANCE, DECISION TRIFECTA VISUALIZED

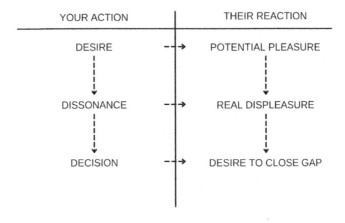

FIGURE 47: This strategy creates a gap between what people want and what they have before inspiring them to make a decision to close the gap. Like many of these structures, it combines contrast and aspirational influence.

...............................Chapter Summary...............................

- Persuasive structures are deeply powerful processes for motivating patterns of action and thought.

- All persuasive structures, to some extent, rely on problems and solutions. Problems validate the need for solutions.
- Persuasive structures rely heavily on contrast and aspirational persuasion to motivate action.
- Some persuasive structures rely on negative reasoning; on eliminating alternatives to your proposal.
- Other persuasive structures rely on positive reasoning; on maximizing the desirability of your proposal.
- And some persuasive structures combine both positive and negative reasoning.

KEY INSIGHT:

Persuade By Connecting Their Aspirations to Truth and then Contrasting Truth with Mistruth.

Reveal the Principles of the Upward Path and then Contrast Them with the Temptations That Drag them Downward.

THREE POWERFUL MODES OF INFLUENCE

ASPIRATIONAL INFLUENCE

We could be here.

We are here.

CONTRAST INFLUENCE

This is way better...

...than this.

CROSSROADS INFLUENCE

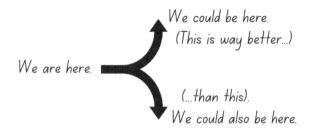

We could be here.
(This is way better...)

We are here.

(...than this).
We could also be here.

THE IRREFUTABLE PERSUASIVE SYNTAX (PART THREE)

1	Master the Foundational Theories
1.1	Apply the Public Speaking Triad
1.2	Master the Communication Toolbox and the Three Layers
1.3	Activate, Control, and Align Your Three Languages
1.4	Satisfy the Triad Ingredients
1.5	Understand and Apply Purposeful Communication
1.6	Don't Forget the Three-Part Model of Communication
1.7	Speak to the Top of the Cone of Attention
1.8	Say the Right Things, But Also in the Right Way
1.9	Appeal to Self-Interest and "WIIFM?"
1.10	Raise Perceived Marginal Benefits, Drop Perceived Marginal Costs
1.11	Satisfy the Mental Checklist in Eight Seconds
1.12	Speak in terms of Benefits and Features
1.13	Remember the Wisdom of the Fable of the Wind and the Sun
1.14	Understand the Underlying Fact of Mental Malleability
1.15	Apply Bridge Theory to Keep Things Flowing Smoothly
1.16	Recognize the Pyramid of Human Desires
1.17	Remember Uniqueness, Personas, Ceteris Paribus and Limitations
1.18	Satisfy the Saliency, Intensity, and Stability Framework
1.19	Understand the Dilemma of One Versus Many

3.14	Use the Tension, Desire, Action Trifecta
3.15	Use the Persuasive Stack Sequence
3.16	Use the Last Method Strategy
3.17	Use the Past, Present, Future Method
3.18	Use the Desire, Dissonance, Decision Trifecta
4	**Master the Informative Structures**
5	**Master the Inspirational Structures**
6	**Master the Advanced Principles of Structure**

Email Peter D. Andrei, the author of the Speak for Success collection and the President of Speak Truth Well LLC directly.

pandreibusiness@gmail.com

KEY INSIGHT:

Persuading Is an Act of Sculpting People's Relationship to Truth. As Such, It Is of a Moral Character, Good or Bad

Claim These Free Resources that Will Help You Unleash the Power of Your Words and Speak with Confidence. Visit www.speakforsuccesshub.com/toolkit for Access.

18 Free PDF Resources

12 Iron Rules for Captivating Story, 21 Speeches that Changed the World, 341-Point Influence Checklist, 143 Persuasive Cognitive Biases, 17 Ways to Think On Your Feet, 18 Lies About Speaking Well, 137 Deadly Logical Fallacies, 12 Iron Rules For Captivating Slides, 371 Words that Persuade, 63 Truths of Speaking Well, 27 Laws of Empathy, 21 Secrets of Legendary Speeches, 19 Scripts that Persuade, 12 Iron Rules For Captivating Speech, 33 Laws of Charisma, 11 Influence Formulas, 219-Point Speech-Writing Checklist, 21 Eloquence Formulas

Claim These Free Resources that Will Help You Unleash the Power of Your Words and Speak with Confidence. Visit www.speakforsuccesshub.com/toolkit for Access.

30 Free Video Lessons

We'll send you one free video lesson every day for 30 days, written and recorded by Peter D. Andrei. Days 1-10 cover authenticity, the prerequisite to confidence and persuasive power. Days 11-20 cover building self-belief and defeating communication anxiety. Days 21-30 cover how to speak with impact and influence, ensuring your words change minds instead of falling flat. Authenticity, self-belief, and impact – this course helps you master three components of confidence, turning even the most high-stakes presentations from obstacles into opportunities.

Claim These Free Resources that Will Help You Unleash the Power of Your Words and Speak with Confidence. Visit www.speakforsuccesshub.com/toolkit for Access.

2 Free Workbooks

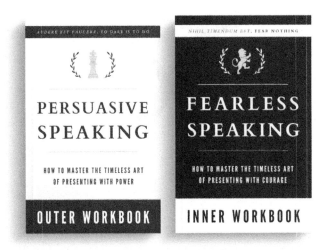

We'll send you two free workbooks, including long-lost excerpts by Dale Carnegie, the mega-bestselling author of *How to Win Friends and Influence People* (5,000,000 copies sold). *Fearless Speaking* guides you in the proven principles of mastering your inner game as a speaker. *Persuasive Speaking* guides you in the time-tested tactics of mastering your outer game by maximizing the power of your words. All of these resources complement the Speak for Success collection.

SPEAK FOR SUCCESS COLLECTION BOOK

THE PSYCHOLOGY OF PERSUASION CHAPTER

HOW TO INFORM:

Uncovering the Patterns of
Effective Presentation

DON'T MAKE THIS MISTAKE

H AVE YOU EVER LISTENED TO A SPEAKER THAT HAS BORED you for what seemed like hours? These informational structures ensure that you are not that speaker.

But before we jump into them let me answer this question you might be asking yourself: "this is a book about the psychology of communication and the persuasive patterns that appeal to it – what does informing people have to do with persuasion?"

And here's my answer: Informing demands persuading. You need to persuade people to opt-in and buy-in with their mental energy and attention. You need to persuade people to listen to your information and trust you. And much of effective persuasion demands effectively informing your audience as well. Information and persuasion are inextricably tied together. A predominantly persuasive endeavor often calls for moments of predominantly informative communication.

4.1: THE INFORMATIONAL MOTIVATED SEQUENCE

What is it? Shortening Monroe's Motivated Sequence so that each step is one sentence or a handful of sentences. Putting that before an informational speech to persuade your audience to listen to the information.

Why does it work? It provides clear, obvious benefits of listening to the speech. It avoids the mistake of forgetting to make the audience care about the information before sharing it. It guarantees that the audience knows why the information is important and worth their time.

When do you use it? When you want to inform, but you aren't sure if the audience cares about the information. When the benefits of listening to you are not already clear. When you want to guarantee audience interest before informing. And even if these things aren't true, most of the time that you need to inform, this structure works.

What is the step-by-step process? Attention: "Listen, you have a problem!" Need: "Here's why you need to solve this problem." Satisfaction: "This information will fix the problem. Desire: "Here's how great it will feel to know this, and the great things you can do with the information." Action: "So listen to this!" Information: Proceed with your informational speech.

THE INFORMATIONAL MOTIVATED SEQUENCE VISUALIZED

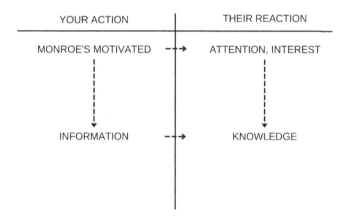

YOUR ACTION		THEIR REACTION
MONROE'S MOTIVATED	--→	ATTENTION, INTEREST
INFORMATION	--→	KNOWLEDGE

FIGURE 48: This structure is highly effective at conveying the value of your information, grabbing attention, and maintaining engagement throughout.

This structure instantly applies Monroe's Motivated Sequence to an informational speech. There are four types of speeches: those to inform, persuade, inspire, and entertain. And obviously, Monroe's Motivated Sequence is persuasive. The Informational Motivated Sequence is informational. And a simple three-step process turns Monroe's Motivated Sequence into an informational structure.

Squish Monroe's Motivated Sequence until each step is one or two sentences. Put it in front of an informational speech. Enjoy more interest, attention, and applause. It is the art of using Monroe's Motivated Sequence to persuade the action of listening to your information. Instead of getting right into your information – while your audience is wondering "What does this have to do with me? Why should I care? Why is this information important to me?" – first sell them the benefits of the information itself.

Sentence one (attention): "It's a problem if you don't know this information." Sentence two (need): "If you don't understand this, you will [insert bad consequence one], [insert bad consequence two], [insert bad consequence three]." Sentence three (satisfaction): "But I can teach you!" Sentence four (visualization): "When you learn this, you will [insert benefit one], [insert benefit two], [insert benefit three]." Sentence five (action): "So if you give me X minutes of your time, I'll teach you everything about [subject]."

Only then do you get into your information. Why is this useful? Because it makes your audience care. It shows them why they should listen.

4.2: STRAIGHT-LINE METHOD

What is it? A speech structured around a logical progression of points, from evidence to the main claim. A speech structured as a sequence of logical units that form a straight line of claims, justifications, and evidence.

Why does it work? It clearly and deliberately breaks down the logic of an argument. It moves through the logic with discipline, and produces a claim from evidence (instead of fitting evidence to a claim). It makes your audience understand your logic, which leads to them accepting your claim.

When do you use it? When you want to prove a point in the most clear, logical, and undeniable way. When you want to explain a complicated line of reasoning. When you want to inform your audience why something is true, or why something isn't true. When your audience is being driven by logic, and not emotion, or at least not too much emotion, or when you have supplied the emotional persuasion, and you need logic to give your audience permission to let their emotional hunch take the wheel.

What is the step-by-step process? Evidence presentation: "Here's what we know." Evidence explanation: "Here's why that evidence is significant. Here's what it really means." Logical connection: "Here's why it connects to a broader claim." Main claim presentation: "Here's the main claim. Here's the truth proven by the evidence." Use this moment: Explain the significance of your claim, of the truth you've discovered. You've proven it, but why does it matter? What does it mean? Why should your audience care? Now you can break away from pure reasoning and logic, and get into the personal and impactful interpretation.

THE STRAIGHT-LINE METHOD VISUALIZED

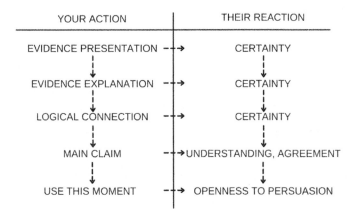

FIGURE 49: This structure is highly effective at conveying a claim with a crystal-clear logical progression that good-faith listeners can't deny.

Historical Example: "So, as we begin, let us take inventory. We are a nation that has a government – not the other way around. And this makes us special among the nations of the Earth. Our Government has no power except that granted it by the people. It is time to check and reverse the growth of government which shows signs of having grown beyond the consent of the governed. It is my intention to curb the size and influence of the Federal establishment and to demand recognition of the distinction between the powers granted to the Federal Government and those reserved to the States or to the people. All of us need to be reminded that the Federal Government did not create the States; the States created the Federal Government. Now, so there will be no misunderstanding, it is not my intention to do away with government. It is, rather, to make it work-work with us, not over us; to stand by our side, not ride on our back. Government can and must provide opportunity, not smother it; foster productivity, not stifle it." – Ronald Reagan

The straight-line structure makes you seem sharp as a tack, well-researched, logical, sophisticated, direct, and assertive. So why shouldn't you love it? It pushes through the muck and uses logic to connect a claim to evidence. Now, most speakers do that anyway. But they usually do it inside their minds and nowhere else. This is essentially taking the mental, internal logical processes that probably already occurred in your mind, and deliberately stating the logic for your audience.

4.3: REVERSE LINE METHOD

What is it? A speech structured around a logical progression of points, starting with the claim, and then connecting it to evidence.

Why does it work? It starts with the claim, which provides context for the evidence. It makes the claim when audience attention is highest: at the start. It is still a series of disciplined, logical connections, just in reverse.

When do you use it? When you want to prove a claim in a bullet-proof way. When you don't want to wait until the end of the unit of meaning to present the claim. When it would seem dishonest to go from evidence to claim, because the audience already knows what you think.

What is the step-by-step process? Main claim presentation: "Here's the main claim. Here's the truth that I will prove with evidence." Logical connection: "Here's why this claim is proven by the evidence." Evidence presentation: "Here's the exact evidence that proves the claim. Here's what we know." Evidence explanation: "Here's why that evidence is significant. Here's what it really means." Use this moment: Explain the significance of your claim; of the truth you've discovered. You've proven it, but why does it matter? What does it mean? Why should your audience care?

THE REVERSE-LINE METHOD VISUALIZED

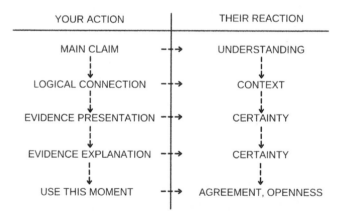

FIGURE 50: This structure frames the evidence with the claim instead of letting the claim emerge from the evidence. This lends context to the evidence.

4.4: STREAM OF CONSCIOUSNESS

What is it? Speaking in a loose stream of consciousness, structured around a particular story, theme, or idea.

Why does it work? It is engaging, and strengthens the speaker to audience connection. It requires much less planning than other structures. It creates a smooth flow of information.

When do you use it? When you want to speak in a more informal way. When you feel comfortable allowing your stream of consciousness to run free. When you understand the subject-matter well enough to speak without a more defined structure, or when you are the subject.

What is the step-by-step process? Overarching theme presentation: Present a central story, theme or idea. Connection presentation: Present how what you're going to be talking about connects to the central story, theme, or idea. Stream of consciousness: Start speaking. Connection repetition: As you speak, repeatedly tie what you're saying back to the overarching theme.

THE STREAM OF CONSCIOUSNESS METHOD VISUALIZED

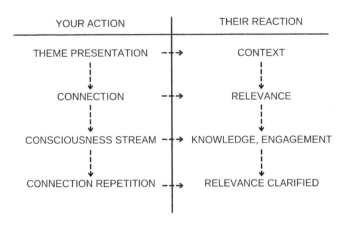

FIGURE 51: A stream of consciousness is highly engaging, drawing people in and boosting the connection between

speaker and audience. However, you must apply some structure and form to the stream of consciousness.

Historical Example: "Go back to Mississippi, go back to Alabama, go back to South Carolina, go back to Georgia, go back to Louisiana, go back to the slums and ghettos of our northern cities, knowing that somehow this situation can and will be changed. Let us not wallow in the valley of despair, I say to you today, my friends. And so even though we face the difficulties of today and tomorrow, I still have a dream. It is a dream deeply rooted in the American dream. I have a dream that one day this nation will rise up and live out the true meaning of its creed: 'We hold these truths to be self-evident, that all men are created equal.' I have a dream that one day on the red hills of Georgia, the sons of former slaves and the sons of former slave owners will be able to sit down together at the table of brotherhood. I have a dream that one day even the state of Mississippi, a state sweltering with the heat of injustice, sweltering with the heat of oppression, will be transformed into an oasis of freedom and justice. I have a dream that my four little children will one day live in a nation where they will not be judged by the color of their skin but by the content of their character. I have a dream today! I have a dream that one day, down in Alabama, with its vicious racists, with its governor having his lips dripping with the words of 'interposition' and 'nullification' – one day right there in Alabama little black boys and black girls will be able to join hands with little white boys and white girls as sisters and brothers. I have a dream today! I have a dream that one day every valley shall be exalted, and every hill and mountain shall be made low, the rough places will be made plain, and the crooked places will be made straight; 'and the glory of the Lord shall be revealed and all flesh shall see it together.'" – Martin Luther King (This was delivered relatively extemporaneously).

Is this even a structure? I debated that for a long time before deciding to put it in this book. Sometimes the lack of structure is, in a way, a structure, but only if you can do one thing: consistently connect what you're talking about to the central theme or idea. If you do this, it qualifies as a structure, just barely. For example, let's say that you are asked to speak about yourself. Maybe you're a role model for the audience. Maybe the audience is a room of interns who all want your job someday. So, the subject is your life and career. The theme is the lens through which you talk about yourself. Let's say that your theme is the qualities that led you to success: discipline, honesty, and confidence. As you're streaming out stories about your career, repeatedly connect them to that theme. Show how those qualities are a constant thread throughout your entire life.

4.5: MONTAGE STRUCTURE

What is it? A series of stories, events, or examples that are unrelated except for their connection to a central idea.

Why does it work? It provides rapid-fire novelty, which captivates audiences. It uses engaging narrative, which inherently grabs attention. It presents a subtle claim, and illustrates it, rather than stating it.

When do you use it? When you want to guarantee an engaged audience. When you want to use narratives throughout your speech. When you want to illustrate, rather than flat-out state, one big central idea, and create the sense that the idea emerges as an undeniable truth from the stories.

What is the step-by-step process? Theme presentation: Present your theme, central idea, or core message. Be brief – don't elaborate. Just state it eloquently and quickly. Montage presentation: Present your stories sequentially. After each story, briefly connect it to the theme. Montage elaboration: Elaborate on how the theme exists in all of the montage stories. Theme elaboration: Elaborate on the theme.

THE MONTAGE STRUCTURE VISUALIZED

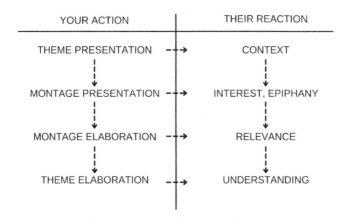

FIGURE 52: The persuasive magic of this structure is that you can hint at the theme and then allow the audience to come to the epiphany of the core message simply by hearing the components of the montage.

Historical Example: "We have every right to dream heroic dreams. Those who say that we are in a time when there are no heroes just don't know where to look. You can see heroes every day going in and out of factory gates. Others, a handful in number, produce enough food to feed all of us and then the world beyond. You meet heroes across a counter – and they are on both sides of that counter. There are entrepreneurs with faith in themselves and faith in an idea who create new jobs, new wealth and opportunity. They are individuals and families whose taxes support the Government and whose voluntary gifts support church, charity, culture, art, and education. Their patriotism is quiet but deep. Their values sustain our national life." – Ronald Reagan

This structure works for two reasons. First, stories are naturally engaging. Second, you illustrate a theme, rather than flatly stating it. When your audience leaves, they will deeply understand the theme on an intuitive level. Rather than telling them the theme, you show it. That is much more vivid and memorable. It prompts them to think about it and extract the theme from the stories. Thus, the main message is not sent into their minds from outside; rather, it emerges in their minds, from within. You give them the ingredients to come to the epiphany you desire instead of just hammering them with the epiphany.

This structure is also engineered for novelty. The "montage" of the different stories provides rapid-fire information. That too is naturally engaging.

4.6: ATTACHED LIST STRUCTURE

What is it? A claim followed by a list of pieces of supporting evidence, sub-claims, examples, etc. Any complete statement broken down into a list of parts. A list of statements supporting one big idea.

Why does it work? Because it is efficient, straightforward, and avoids misunderstanding. It minimizes the need for transitions. It uses a clear and memorable list structure.

When do you use it? When you want to make deliberate, technical points, in a sophisticated way. When clarity is your first priority. When you want to inform about a big idea that can be broken down into sub-points, or want to provide a superabundance of proof.

What is the step-by-step process? Main idea presentation: What do all of the informational sub-units fall under? What is the big heading? What is the main, central principle? Sub-unit list: What are the informational sub-points that express the main idea?

THE ATTACHED LIST STRUCTURE VISUALIZED

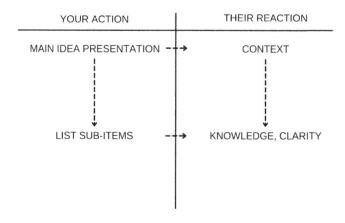

FIGURE 53: This is a straightforward, clear, and simple work-horse structure.

Historical Example: "It is in these five areas of concern – economic growth, unemployment, the business cycle, price stability, and our balance of payments – that I think we can do better, that I think we must do better. And I believe that most businessmen share my concern – and share my belief that we can do better. What changes are needed? What policies would be successful? First, a Democratic administration would use monetary policies more flexibly than the Republicans. The Republicans adopted the seemingly simple and easy policy of tightening interest rates when demand was strong and prices were rising – a principle that requires allowing rates to fall when the economy needed stimulation. But the facts of the matter are that each successive peak and each successive valley in the economy has ended with higher and higher interest rates – with the result that paradoxically high rates accompanied heavy unemployment, low production, and a slack economy. For this policy has not worked. By periodically cutting back on investment, it has held back on a normal, healthy rate of growth. By staying tight too long, as it did in the fall of 1957 when the storm signals were already flying for the recession of 1958 – by the Federal Reserve Board's tight credit – by the defense stretchout of 1958 – it helped to bring on that and other recessions. And, by penalizing most those who must borrow from banks for investment or homebuilding, it is weighted in favor of the larger corporations, which have access to the open market or which can invest from their own earnings. A Democratic administration would not rely upon lopsided monetary policy. It would maintain greater flexibility for investment, expansion and growth. It would not raise interest rates as an end in itself. Without rejecting monetary stringency as a potential method of curbing extravagant booms, we would make more use of other tools. Secondly, and in this connection, we would use the budget as an instrument of economic stabilization. I believe that the budget should normally be balanced. The exception apart from a serious or extraordinary threat to the national security is serious unemployment. In boom times we should run a surplus and retire the debt. When men and plant are unemployed in serious numbers, the opposite policies are in order. We should seek a balanced budget over the course of the business cycle with surpluses during good times more than offsetting the deficits which may be incurred during slumps. I submit that this is not a radical fiscal policy. It is a conservative policy. But we must have a flexible, balanced and, above all, coordinated monetary and fiscal policy. I do not, let me make clear, advocate any changes in the constitution of the Federal Reserve System. It is important to keep the day-to-day operations of the Federal Reserve removed from political pressures. The President's responsibility – if he is to lead – includes longer range coordination an a direction of economic policies, subject to our system of checks and balances. And I believe the Federal Reserve Board – which during the last 8 years has cooperated closely with this administration – would also cooperate with future strong and well considered Presidential leadership which expresses the responsible will of

Congress and the people. Third, I believe that the next administration must work sympathetically and closely with labor and management to develop wage and price policies that are consistent with stability. We can no longer afford the large erratic movements in prices which jeopardize domestic price stability and our balance of payments abroad. Nor is there a place for the kind of ad hoc last-minute intervention which settled the steel strike. Without resorting to the compulsion of wage or price controls, the President of the United States must actively use the powers of leadership in pursuit of well-defined goals of price stability. For those powers – of reason, moral suasion, and informed public opinion, influencing public opinion – have by no means been exhausted to date. Fourth, we must make certain that there is proper encouragement to plant modernization. Postwar Europe has a new and modern industrial plant. So has the Soviet Union. We cannot compete if our plants are out of date or second rate. Wherever we can be certain that tax revision, including accelerated depreciation, will encourage the modernization of our capital plant – and not be a disguise for tax avoidance – we should proceed with such revision. It is sound, liberal policy to see that our productive plant is the best and most modern in the world. And a combination of these policies with policies of full employment can help us realize the full promise of automation. Taxes affect not only revenue but also growth and a new administration must review carefully but with imagination our entire tax policy to see that these objectives are being met. Fifth, we must pay equal attention to the men that man the plant. Growth requires that we have the best trained and best educated labor force in the world. Investment in manpower is just as important as investment in facilities. Yet today we waste precious resources when the bright youngster, who should have been a skilled draftsman or able scientist or engineer must remain a pick-and-shovel worker because he never had a chance to develop his talents. It is time we geared our educational systems to meet the increased demand of modern industry – strengthening our public schools, our colleges, and our vocational programs for retraining unemployed workers. Finally, we must remember that, in the long run, the public development of natural resources too vast for private capital – and federally encouraged research, especially basic research – are both sources of tremendous economic progress." – John F. Kennedy

Your biggest, primary focus with this structure is placed on the information. Main idea: "The United States Government is designed to create checks and balances between branches." Sub-unit list: "First form of checks and balances... second... third... fourth... etc."

Main idea: "The minimum wage is..." Sub-unit list: "Study number one... study number two... study number three... etc."

If you're teaching and want to efficiently express a main idea, this is for you. If you want a little more "showmanship," perhaps another structure. But if you want to list out points that aren't attached to a central idea, then use this next method.

4.7: DETACHED LIST STRUCTURE

What is it? A list of thematically related but unlinked claims. A list of information units that don't relate to one bigger idea. A list of information units that are united by quality: "interesting," "funny," or "surprising," instead of connected to a central theme.

Why does it work? It allows you to make multiple claims that don't support one big idea. It allows you a lot more freedom to choose your information units. It provides fast-paced novelty.

When do you use it? When you want to make multiple detached points that don't support one idea. When you have certain pieces of knowledge that are useful, interesting, funny, etc., and you want to teach them. When you want to inform with more freedom.

What is the step-by-step process? Present unifying quality: "These are some particularly hilarious pieces of information from my studies of politics." List the items: "The first funny moment... the second funny moment... the third funny moment..."

THE DETACHED LIST STRUCTURE VISUALIZED

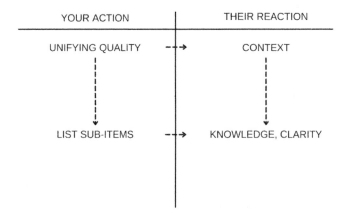

FIGURE 53: This is also a straightforward, clear, and simple work-horse structure.

Historical Example: "How did we get here, and how do we fix it? I want to make just four brief points. Number one: in our system, the legislative branch is supposed to be the center of our politics. Number two: it's not. Why not? Because for the last century, and increasing by the decade right now, more and more legislative authority is delegated to the executive branch every year. Both parties do it. The legislature is impotent. The legislature is weak. And most people here want their jobs more than they really want to do legislative work, and so they punt most of the work to the next branch. The third consequence is that this transfer of power means the people yearn for a place where politics can actually be done, and when we don't do a lot of big actual political debating here, we transfer it to the Supreme Court, and that's why the supreme court is increasingly a substitute political battleground in America. It is not healthy, but it is what happens and it's something that our founders wouldn't be able to make any sense of. And fourth and finally: we badly need to restore the proper duties and the balance of power from our constitutional system." – Ben Sasse

This is an entertaining structure. If you have a good command of the subject matter (which should always be true), this structure allows you the flexibility to put that deep, intuitive knowledge to good use.

4.8: INFORMATION STACK

What is it? Structuring your speech in a series of "information units," starting with the basic, leading to the complex and, if possible, presenting one complete concept, idea, process, etc., from beginning to end.

Why does it work? Because it is efficient. Because it guarantees that your audience understands the advanced information. Because it focuses on making your audience experts in one particular silo of information.

When do you use it? When you are teaching a complex subject to novices. When you want to give your audience a practical, working understanding of something. When you want the audience to synthesize how all the information fits together.

What is the step-by-step process? Promise the outcome: "Today, I'm going to teach you exactly how to do [insert process]." Present the stack order: "First, you'll learn the basics, like [insert sub-topic]. Then, we'll move into a few expert secrets, such as [insert sub-topic]. After that, you'll learn..." Present the stack items: Start presenting the items in the stack, from the easy to the complex.

THE INFORMATION STACK VISUALIZED

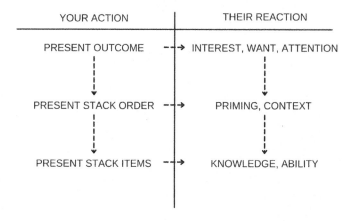

FIGURE 54: This structure grabs attention by promising a practical, real-world outcome. It is highly effective at helping the audience gain a new ability.

Almost all areas of study are like pyramids. They have a set of basic concepts, which lead to more and more advanced topics up the pyramid. And if you try to start at the top of the pyramid, it will be much harder to help your audience understand these difficult concepts. The information stack forms a gentle ladder of understanding not unlike a persuasive yes-ladder by first starting with the basic, easy concepts, and then stacking the advanced concepts on top of the basics. Stacking your information in this way guarantees your audience will understand the advanced concepts with greater ease and less frustration.

4.9: THE BIG ANSWER

What is it? Structuring your speech around a massive mental open loop. An informational speech that teases a big answer.

Why does it work? Because it is incredibly suspenseful and captivating. Because it creates curiosity, which grabs attention. Because it creates intrigue.

When do you use it? When you can work a "central question" into your speech. When you have a "big answer" to the central question. When you are informing an audience.

What is the step-by-step process? Present the subject: "Today, we're going to be talking about [insert subject]." Present the dilemma: "There's a dilemma. There's a problem with [insert subject]." Present the central question: "The big question nobody can answer is why does [the problem with your subject] keep happening? Why is [insert subject] so broken?" Tease the big answer: "I have the big answer to that big question. I'll tell you at the end of the speech." Inform: This is the bulk of your speech. Inform the audience. Give the big-answer: "Remember the big question? Well, here's the answer: [insert answer]."

THE BIG ANSWER STRATEGY VISUALIZED

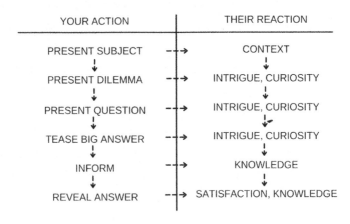

FIGURE 55: This structure is highly effective at maintaining a high level of intrigue and curiosity.

If you don't know what a mental "open loop" is, then you probably don't see why this structure is so powerful. A mental open loop emerges, in this case, when you present the question. A question demands an answer to close the mental loop. And if you don't close the open loop, people crave to close it. The open loop is strengthened when you tell them that you have the big answer. It's strengthened even more if you tease it, saying things like "it's the most simple, unexpected answer that even experts haven't found."

The open loop creates massive curiosity in your audience, it captivates their attention, and it makes them sit on the edge of their seats, thinking "what's the big answer?" And to strengthen the open loop even further, repeatedly present the big question during the speech, and repeatedly tease the big answer. I mentioned in the foreword of this book that the foreword itself was an example of structure theory in action. This was the structure I used.

4.10: THE BACK-AND-FORTH

What is it? Structuring your speech around a back-and-forth debate between two sides.

Why does it work? Because the back-and-forth structure builds an ongoing open loop: "who is right?" Because presenting both sides of an argument is engaging. Because the audience can decide for themselves who they agree with, and in doing so, intellectually engage themselves with the subject matter, while seeing you as an objective, logical, trustworthy person due to your impartiality.

When do you use it? When you are informing an audience about a subject that is divisive. When there are two distinct sides in argument about your subject that have clear arguments in favor of their opposing stances. When you are an objective "teacher" rather than someone on one of the two sides, and your goal is to accurately represent the debate or subject area as best as you can.

What is the step-by-step process? Subject presentation: "Here's what we're going to be talking about. Here's what you need to know about this subject." Side presentation: "Here are the two sides. Here's how they disagree about this subject." Side one argument presentation: "Here's the first main argument of one side." Side two rebuttal: "Here's how the second side responds." Side two argument presentation: "Here's the first main argument of the second side." Side one rebuttal: "Here's how the first side responds." Back-and-forth repetition: Repeat the argument presentation and rebuttal steps for as many arguments as you want.

THE BACK-AND-FORTH METHOD VISUALIZED

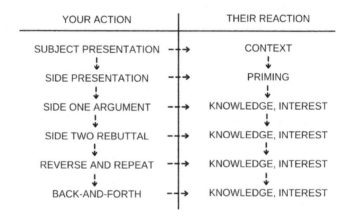

FIGURE 56: This structure is highly effective at meshing interest-inducing and captivating communication with knowledge-conveying and informative communication, and thus it holds attention.

Rather than just informing your audience, you're engaging them in an intellectual debate. This makes them more interested, helps them remember your information, gets them thinking, and informs them better than just laying out the information flatly would. You're informing through the lens of an engaging argument.

4.11: CHRONOLOGICAL

What is it? Structuring your informational speech along the lines of a chronological sequence of events. Telling a chronological story.

Why does it work? Because the structure is straightforward and mirrors the information. Because chronological stories are engaging and provide novelty. Because it is the best way to present a sequence of events, simply due to the mirror effect between subject matter and structure that it creates.

When do you use it? When you are informing an audience about history, or relaying a story. When you are relaying information about a sequence of events. When your information naturally fits into a chronological structure.

What is the step-by-step process? Subject presentation: "Here's what I'm going to teach you about today." Chronological presentation: "First, [insert event]. Then, [insert event]. After that, [insert event] happened, etc."

THE CHRONOLOGICAL SEQUENCE VISUALIZED

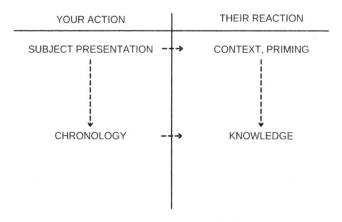

FIGURE 57: This structure is intuitive and natural, and as such, it captivates attention and conveys information in a straightforward and memorable way.

Historical Example: "To my fellow Americans: Eight years ago, America faced a moment of peril unlike any we'd seen in decades. A spiraling financial crisis threatened to plunge an economy in recession into a deep depression. The very heartbeat of American manufacturing – the American auto industry – was on the brink of collapse. In some communities, nearly one in five Americans were out of work. Nearly 180,000 American troops were serving in harm's way in Iraq and Afghanistan, and the mastermind of the worst terror attack on American soil remained at large. And on challenges from health care to climate change, we'd been kicking the can down the road for way too long. But in the depths of that winter, on January 20, 2009, I stood before you and swore a sacred oath. I told you that day that the challenges we faced would not be met easily or in a short span of time – but they would be met. And after eight busy years, we've met them – because of you. Eight years later, an economy that was shrinking at more than eight percent is now growing at more than three percent. Businesses that were bleeding jobs unleashed the longest streak of job creation on record. The auto industry has roared its way back, saving one million jobs across the country and fueling a manufacturing sector that, after a decade of decline, has added new jobs for the first time since the 1990s. And wages have grown faster over the past few years than at any time in the past forty. Today, thanks to the Affordable Care Act, another 20 million American adults know the financial security and peace of mind that comes with health insurance. Another three million children have gained health insurance. For the first time ever, more than ninety percent of Americans are insured – the highest rate ever. We've seen the slowest growth in the price of health care in fifty years, along with improvements in patient safety that have prevented an estimated 87,000 deaths. Every American with insurance is covered by the strongest set of consumer protections in history – a true Patients' Bill of Rights – and free from the fear that illness or accident will derail your dreams, because America is now a place where discrimination against preexisting conditions is a relic of the past. And the new health insurance marketplace means that if you lose your job, change your job, or start that new business, you'll finally be able to purchase quality, affordable care and the security and peace of mind that comes with it – and that's one reason why entrepreneurship is growing for the second straight year. Our dependence on foreign oil has been cut by more than half, and our production of renewable energy has more than doubled. In many places across the country, clean energy from the wind is now cheaper than dirtier sources of energy, and solar now employs more Americans than coal mining in jobs that pay better than average and can't be outsourced. We also enacted the most sweeping reforms since the Great Depression to protect consumers and prevent a crisis on Wall Street from punishing Main Street ever again. These actions didn't stifle growth, as critics predicted. Instead, the stock market has nearly tripled. Since I signed Obamacare into law, America's businesses have added more than 15 million new jobs. And the economy is undoubtedly more durable than it was in the days when we relied on oil from unstable nations and banks took risky bets with your money." – Barack Obama

The easy part of this structure is that your information is "pre-structured" for you. Only use this when the chronological aspect of the subject matter isn't contrived. Don't try to fit a square peg into a round hole.

4.12: CAUSE AND EFFECT

What is it? Structuring your speech around a prominent cause-and-effect relationship. Presenting the cause, and then what it causes.

Why does it work? Because it focuses on the relationship between the two things, building a narrative. Because the cause-and-effect frame helps the audience put the information in context. Because many subjects are, in reality, split into causes and effects. Because it speaks in terms of consequences, and consequences raise the stakes of the situation, which engages.

When do you use it? When your information can be split into a set of causes, and a set of effects. When your information is about current events. When you have a specific analysis of the cause-and-effect relationship.

What is the step-by-step process? Present the cause: "Here's what has been happening." Present the effect: "Here's what this has led to." Repetition: Repeat the previous two steps for a series of cause-and-effect relationships related to a subject.

THE CAUSE-AND-EFFECT METHOD VISUALIZED

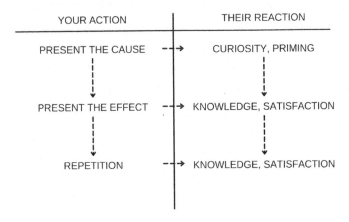

FIGURE 58: This structure is also intuitive and natural, and it is inherently compelling because the cause-and-effect relationship constitutes an open loop.

4.13: PRESENTATION, ESCALATION, CONTRAST TRIFECTA

What is it? Structuring your speech around a response to a common point of view. Structuring your speech around a "reframing" technique.

Why does it work? It uses reframing, which can be especially informative. It challenges an intellectual consensus. It responds to another point of view, which is engaging.

When do you use it? When you are informing about something, and there is another common opinion that happens to be wrong. When the information is primarily about the relationship between two things. When you can use frame escalation, a reframing technique.

What is the step-by-step process? Frame presentation: "Most people say that X [insert relationship] Y." Pre-escalation: "However, they're wrong. They're wrong because [insert reasons]." Frame escalation: "Actually, it turns out that X [insert different relationship] Y. Or, turns out that Y [insert original relationship] X. Or, turns out that X [opposite relationship] Y." Contrast: "While most people think, [original frame], they're actually wrong. The truth is that [escalated frame]."

THE PRESENTATION, ESCALATION, CONTRAST VISUALIZED

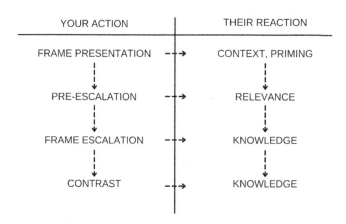

FIGURE 59: This structure is highly effective at challenging a preexisting intellectual status quo, and establishing a new frame as the dominant frame.

Historical Example: "There are some who question the reason for this conference. Let them listen to the voices of women in their homes, neighborhoods, and workplaces. There are some who wonder whether the lives of women and girls matter to economic and political progress around the globe... Let them look at the women gathered here and at Huairou... the homemakers, nurses, teachers, lawyers, policymakers, and women who run their own businesses." – Hillary Clinton

Reframing is changing the relationship between two subjects.

For example, these are some logical relationships: X causes Y. X happens because of Y. X happens despite Y. X is necessary for Y. X is disconnected from Y. X contradicts Y

Frame escalation is zooming out on a common frame and reversing it from a new perspective. Frame escalation is changing the perceived relationship between two things, controlling the narrative and the information in the process. For example, let's say most people criticize a public figure. They say X statement contradicts Y statement. If you object to this, there are a few options: You could say the contradiction doesn't matter, or find a way to say it isn't a contradiction. However, escalating the frame from an "X contradicts Y" statement to an "X is true because of Y" statement is the most powerful strategy, provided it represents reality. This is at once counterintuitive and intuitive. The world's most effective politicians, and the winners of political debates, have the speakers who have used frame escalation.

Frame escalation is especially effective if the new frame and the original frame seem to be at odds with one another. Frame escalation is particularly powerful, persuasive, and elegant if the new frame seems to undo, or totally reverse, the old frame, completely deflating its energy.

4.14: NARRATIVE STRUCTURE

What is it? Structuring your speech around a narrative story. Informing through storytelling.

Why does it work? It uses long-form narrative, which captivates audiences. It gets audiences wondering, "what comes next?" It builds a speaker-to-audience connection.

When do you use it? When you are informing about a philosophical concept, rather than set of facts. When you can illustrate the concept through a story. When you want to "show" not "tell" the concept.

What is the step-by-step process? Exposition: "These are the characters and setting." Rising action: "Here's when the conflict started. Tension stared building." Climax: "This is what happened in the peak of the conflict." Falling action: "Here's what happened after the conflict. Things started to relax." Resolution: "Here's how life was different after the whole thing happened." Thematic takeaway: "Here's the theme we learn from this story."

THE NARRATIVE STRUCTURE VISUALIZED

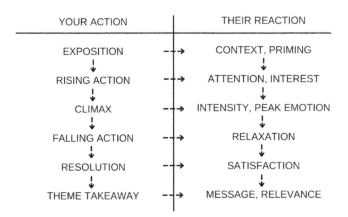

YOUR ACTION		THEIR REACTION
EXPOSITION	--→	CONTEXT, PRIMING
RISING ACTION	--→	ATTENTION, INTEREST
CLIMAX	--→	INTENSITY, PEAK EMOTION
FALLING ACTION	--→	RELAXATION
RESOLUTION	--→	SATISFACTION
THEME TAKEAWAY	--→	MESSAGE, RELEVANCE

FIGURE 60: This structure taps into our primordial, fundamental, and overpowering human tendency to love

stories. It captivates attention and conveys information more effectively than nearly anything else.

Historical Example: "Thank you so much. Thank you. Thank you. Thank you so much. Thank you so much. Thank you, Dick Durbin. You make us all proud. On behalf of the great state of Illinois crossroads of a nation, land of Lincoln, let me express my deep gratitude for the privilege of addressing this convention. Tonight is a particular honor for me because, let's face it, my presence on this stage is pretty unlikely. My father was a foreign student, born and raised in a small village in Kenya. He grew up herding goats, went to school in a tin-roof shack. His father, my grandfather, was a cook, a domestic servant to the British. But my grandfather had larger dreams for his son. Through hard work and perseverance my father got a scholarship to study in a magical place, America, that's shown as a beacon of freedom and opportunity to so many who had come before him. While studying here my father met my mother. She was born in a town on the other side of the world, in Kansas. Her father worked on oil rigs and farms through most of the Depression. The day after Pearl Harbor, my grandfather signed up for duty, joined Patton's army, marched across Europe. Back home my grandmother raised a baby and went to work on a bomber assembly line. After the war, they studied on the GI Bill, bought a house through FHA and later moved west, all the way to Hawaii, in search of opportunity. And they too had big dreams for their daughter, a common dream born of two continents. My parents shared not only an improbable love; they shared an abiding faith in the possibilities of this nation. They would give me an African name, Barack, or "blessed," believing that in a tolerant America, your name is no barrier to success. They imagined me going to the best schools in the land, even though they weren't rich, because in a generous America you don't have to be rich to achieve your potential. They're both passed away now. And yet I know that, on this night, they look down on me with great pride. And I stand here today grateful for the diversity of my heritage, aware that my parents' dreams live on in my two precious daughters. I stand here knowing that my story is part of the larger American story, that I owe a debt to all of those who came before me, and that in no other country on Earth is my story even possible." – Barack Obama

Why is this structure so effective? Because it is naturally captivating. People love stories. But there's another element to it: This structure "shows" and doesn't "tell" a central message. In other words, your audience comes to the thematic takeaway themselves rather than you telling them the thematic takeaway directly. So, they feel like they truly know it. It becomes part of them. It's a conclusion they have reached themselves.

4.15: DEMONSTRATIVE

What is it? Structuring your speech around demonstrating the qualities of a new thing.

Why does it work? It is a simple template to demonstrate a new innovation. It describes almost everything about a new creation. It inherently contains fast-paced novelty.

When do you use it? When you are informing about something new. When you want to give people a complete picture of a new innovation. When you are presenting a new product, idea, or creation.

What is the step-by-step process? What it is: "Here's what we created! Check it out!" What it does: "Here's exactly what it does." How it does it: "It does it in this way." Why it's needed: "This is the problem it solves." What its benefits are: "These are the benefits it has." How it's different: "It's different from older things of the same category in these ways." Proof of concept: "Here's the proof that something of this kind works." Proof of efficacy: "Here's the proof that this specific one works." Cost framing: "It's $3,000 less than the older model." Trust indicators: "It has X positive reviews. You can trust it because [insert trust indicators]."

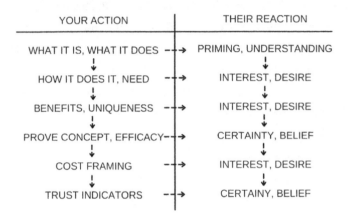

THE DEMONSTRATIVE METHOD VISUALIZED

YOUR ACTION	THEIR REACTION
WHAT IT IS, WHAT IT DOES	PRIMING, UNDERSTANDING
HOW IT DOES IT, NEED	INTEREST, DESIRE
BENEFITS, UNIQUENESS	INTEREST, DESIRE
PROVE CONCEPT, EFFICACY	CERTAINTY, BELIEF
COST FRAMING	INTEREST, DESIRE
TRUST INDICATORS	CERTAINY, BELIEF

FIGURE 61: This structure is highly effective at alternating between creating interest and desire and creating certainty and belief.

This structure is inherently filled with novelty. People love fast-paced, new information. This structure will always give new information quickly. For this structure, present each step as a new massive reveal. That will compound its power.

4.16: SHORT-FORM INFORMATIONAL THREE-POINT PUNCH

What is it? Structuring your speech around a main piece of information and three supporting examples.

Why does it work? It is a brief way to teach a complete concept. It uses three examples, and you usually don't need more. It can be used for almost any information.

When do you use it? When you are informing an audience about anything. When you have supporting examples. When you want to inform efficiently.

What is the step-by-step process? Main piece of information: "The big idea is..." Example one: "The first time this was seen was..." Example two: "Another example is..." Example three: "And another clear piece of evidence is..."

THE SHORT-FORM INFO. THREE-POINT PUNCH VISUALIZED

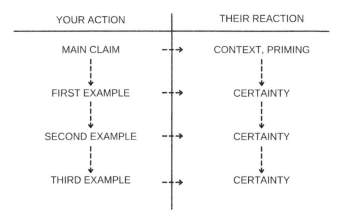

FIGURE 62: The core function of this structure is raising certainty. It is best suited for situations in which the biggest obstacle is a lack of certainty in an idea or knowledge about a given claim.

Historical Example: "The challenge of the next half-century is whether we have the wisdom to use that wealth to enrich and elevate our national life, and to advance the equality of our American civilization. Your imagination, your initiative, and your indignation will determine whether we build a society where progress is the servant of our needs, or a society where old values and new visions are buried under unbridled growth. For in your time we have the opportunity to move not only toward the rich society and the powerful society, but upward to the Great Society. The Great Society rests on abundance and liberty for all. It demands an end to poverty and racial injustice, to which we are totally committed in our time. But that is just the beginning. The Great Society is a place where every child can find knowledge to enrich his mind and to enlarge his talents. It is a place where leisure is a welcome chance to build and reflect, not a feared cause of boredom and restlessness. It is a place where the city of man serves not only the needs of the body and the demands of commerce but the desire for beauty and the hunger for community. It is a place where man can renew contact with nature. It is a place which honors creation for its own sake and for what it adds to the understanding of the race. It is a place where men are more concerned with the quality of their goals than the quantity of their goods. But most of all, the Great Society is not a safe harbor, a resting place, a final objective, a finished work. It is a challenge constantly renewed, beckoning us toward a destiny where the meaning of our lives matches the marvelous products of our labor. So I want to talk to you today about three places where we begin to build the Great Society — in our cities, in our countryside, and in our classrooms." – Lyndon B. Johnson

.................................Chapter Summary.................................

- Informing people does not have to make for dry and boring communication. It can be deeply engaging.
- Most speakers make a critical mistake when informing. They forget that informing calls for some persuading.
- To effectively inform people, you must first persuade them to listen; to see the value of the information.
- The combining principle (discussed more fully in the final section) states that you can combine structures.

- The lengthening and shortening principle states that you can lengthen and shorten structures.
- Thus, an effective strategy is shortening a persuasive structure and using it to open an informational speech.

KEY INSIGHT:

Our Nervous Systems Take in an Incalculable Number of Inputs, Consciously and Unconsciously.

Judgment is the Result of Reason Acting On These Inputs, As Well As Past (And Anticipated) Inputs.

It Is Also the Result of Instinct Acting On These Inputs. Persuasive Rhetoric, Then, Speaks to Both Reason and Instinct.

THE IRREFUTABLE PERSUASIVE SYNTAX (PART FOUR)

1	Master the Foundational Theories
1.1	Apply the Public Speaking Triad
1.2	Master the Communication Toolbox and the Three Layers
1.3	Activate, Control, and Align Your Three Languages
1.4	Satisfy the Triad Ingredients
1.5	Understand and Apply Purposeful Communication
1.6	Don't Forget the Three-Part Model of Communication
1.7	Speak to the Top of the Cone of Attention
1.8	Say the Right Things, But Also in the Right Way
1.9	Appeal to Self-Interest and "WIIFM?"
1.10	Raise Perceived Marginal Benefits, Drop Perceived Marginal Costs
1.11	Satisfy the Mental Checklist in Eight Seconds
1.12	Speak in terms of Benefits and Features
1.13	Remember the Wisdom of the Fable of the Wind and the Sun
1.14	Understand the Underlying Fact of Mental Malleability
1.15	Apply Bridge Theory to Keep Things Flowing Smoothly
1.16	Recognize the Pyramid of Human Desires
1.17	Remember Uniqueness, Personas, Ceteris Paribus and Limitations
1.18	Satisfy the Saliency, Intensity, and Stability Framework
1.19	Understand the Dilemma of One Versus Many

2.10	Avoid Tangents and Parentheticals
2.11	Use Transitions to Maintain Audience Attention
2.12	Remember the Similarities of Structure
2.13	Engineer Your Openings
2.14	Complete Your Communication Body
2.15	Engineer Your Closing
3	**Master the Persuasive Structures**
3.1	Use Monroe's Motivated Sequence
3.2	Use the Objection-Prediction Model
3.3	Use the Path-Contrast Method
3.4	Use the Past, Present, Means Structure
3.5	Use the Problem-Solution Formula
3.6	Use the Diagnose, Problem, Solution Triad
3.7	Use Criteria Matching
3.8	Use Criteria Matching and Dematching
3.9	Use the Six-Point Punch
3.10	Use the Economic Values Structure
3.11	Use the Short-Form Rhetorical Three-Point Punch
3.12	Use the Long-Form Rhetorical Three-Point Punch
3.13	Use the Gain, Logic, Fear Trifecta

3.14	Use the Tension, Desire, Action Trifecta
3.15	Use the Persuasive Stack Sequence
3.16	Use the Last Method Strategy
3.17	Use the Past, Present, Future Method
3.18	Use the Desire, Dissonance, Decision Trifecta
4	**Master the Informative Structures**
4.1	Use the Informational Motivated Sequence
4.2	Use the Straight-Line Method
4.3	Use the Reverse-Line Method
4.4	Use the Stream of Consciousness Principle
4.5	Use the Montage Structure
4.6	Use the Attached List Structure
4.7	Use the Detached List Structure
4.8	Use the Information Stack
4.9	Use the Big Answer Strategy
4.10	Use the Back-and-Forth Method
4.11	Use the Chronological Sequence
4.12	Use the Cause-and-Effect Method
4.13	Use the Presentation, Escalation, Contrast Trifecta
4.14	Use the Narrative Structure

| The Psychology of Persuasion

4.15	Use the Demonstrative Sequence
4.16	Use the Short-Form Informational Three-Point Punch
5	Master the Inspirational Structures
6	Master the Advanced Principles of Structure

Email Peter D. Andrei, the author of the Speak for Success collection and the President of Speak Truth Well LLC directly.

pandreibusiness@gmail.com

KEY INSIGHT:

We Are Wired to Feel Deep Compassion Toward People, Not Abstractions.

In Any Structure, You Can Choose to Complete a Step Not by Reciting a Set of Facts, But by Telling a Story.

Claim These Free Resources that Will Help You Unleash the Power of Your Words and Speak with Confidence. Visit www.speakforsuccesshub.com/toolkit for Access.

18 Free PDF Resources

12 Iron Rules for Captivating Story, 21 Speeches that Changed the World, 341-Point Influence Checklist, 143 Persuasive Cognitive Biases, 17 Ways to Think On Your Feet, 18 Lies About Speaking Well, 137 Deadly Logical Fallacies, 12 Iron Rules For Captivating Slides, 371 Words that Persuade, 63 Truths of Speaking Well, 27 Laws of Empathy, 21 Secrets of Legendary Speeches, 19 Scripts that Persuade, 12 Iron Rules For Captivating Speech, 33 Laws of Charisma, 11 Influence Formulas, 219-Point Speech-Writing Checklist, 21 Eloquence Formulas

SPEAK FOR SUCCESS COLLECTION BOOK

THE PSYCHOLOGY OF PERSUASION CHAPTER

HOW TO INSPIRE:

Revealing the Proven Steps to Instant Inspiration

THE SCIENCE OF INSPIRATION

T HIS CHAPTER WILL TEACH YOU EXACTLY HOW TO give speeches that will excite, inspire, and motivate your audiences. For example, the "want-got" structure can inspire almost any audience if you illustrate the persuasive gap correctly. We will discuss this structure shortly.

5.1: QUOTE PRESENTATION

What is it? Structuring a speech around the best quotes from the best experts in a subject area. Usually, the subject area is one of aspiration. The audience wants to be good at it.

Why does it work? It is an easy structure because the content is already given to you. The quotes from the experts provide authority. The structure is linear and straightforward.

When do you use it? When you are inspiring an audience. When the audience is particularly interested in a subject area. When you can compile a set of quotes from experts about the subject.

What is the step-by-step process? Present subject: "Today, we're going to be talking about [subject area]." Present structure: "Sure, I'm pretty good at [subject area]. But today, I'm going to bring you the wisdom from the top minds on [subject area]. They have a lot more wisdom than I do." Present first expert: "[Insert expert] once said something very important about [subject area]. Here's what you need to know about [insert expert]." Present quote: "Here's what [insert expert] said." Present analysis: "Here's what this means." Repeat steps three-five: Repeat the previous three steps for as many quotes as you want.

THE QUOTE PRESENTATION STRATEGY VISUALIZED

YOUR ACTION		THEIR REACTION
PRESENT SUBJECT	--→	PRIMING, CONTEXT
↓		↓
PRESENT STRUCTURE	--→	EXPECTATIONS, TIMELINE
↓		↓
PRESENT FIRST EXPERT	--→	TRUST, CREDIBILITY
↓		↓
PRESENT QUOTE	--→	KNOWLEDGE
↓		↓
PRESENT ANALYSIS	--→	KNOWLEDGE
↓		↓
REPEAT	--→	KNOWLEDGE

FIGURE 63: This structure is highly effective at establishing ethos and credibility, as some of the authority of the experts you cite transfers to you.

5.2: LONG-FORM ANAPHORA

What is it? Structuring an entire speech around the rhetorical device anaphora.

Why does it work? It uses anaphora, a rhetorical device of repetition that is incredibly eloquent. It has been proven by the inspirational speeches recorded in history. It cements a core message through repetition.

When do you use it? When you have a clear purpose you want to inspire your audience toward achieving. When your core message bears repetition. When you want to use a simple repetitive template that you can fill in.

What is the step-by-step process? Anaphora purpose phrase: "We will do [action]." Subsequent clause: "So that we can [result]" or another subsequent clause, like "to [group, person, institution]" Repetition: Repeat steps one and two until you have a full-length speech.

THE LONG-FORM ANAPHORA STRATEGY VISUALIZED

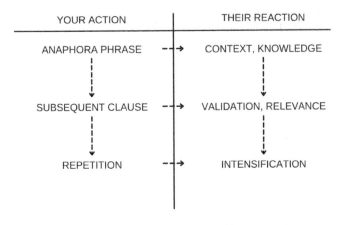

FIGURE 64: This structure uses repetition to create a massive flow of psychological inspiration and self-belief.

Historical Example: "I have, myself, full confidence that if all do their duty, if nothing is neglected, and if the best arrangements are made, as they are being made, we shall prove ourselves once again able to defend our Island home, to ride out the storm of war, and to outlive the menace of tyranny, if necessary for years, if necessary alone. At any rate, that is what we are going to try to do. That is the resolve of His Majesty's Government-every man of them. That is the will of Parliament and the nation. The British Empire and the French Republic, linked together in their cause and in their need, will defend to the death their native soil, aiding each other like good comrades to the utmost of their strength. Even though large tracts of Europe and many old and famous States have fallen or may fall into the grip of the Gestapo and all the odious apparatus of Nazi rule, we shall not flag or fail. We shall go on to the end, we shall fight in France, we shall fight on the seas and oceans, we shall fight with growing confidence and growing strength in the air, we shall defend our Island, whatever the cost may be, we shall fight on the beaches, we shall fight on the landing grounds, we shall fight in the fields and in the streets, we shall fight in the hills; we shall never surrender, and even if, which I do not for a moment believe, this Island or a large part of it were subjugated and starving, then our Empire beyond the seas, armed and guarded by the British Fleet, would carry on the struggle, until, in God's good time, the New World, with all its power and might, steps forth to the rescue and the liberation of the old." – Winston Churchill

Entire speeches, world-changing speeches, nation-moving speeches, have been constructed with this process: An anaphora phrase, a subsequent clause, repetition of steps one and two, and, if needed, a new anaphora purpose phrase, repeating steps two and three.

Want to see how powerful this structure is? Check it out: both Winston Churchill and Martin Luther King's most famous speeches are referred to by their anaphora purpose phrase. Churchill's is called his "we shall fight speech." MLK's is called his "I have a dream speech."

And consider how the anaphora purpose phrase lines up with the actual purpose of the speech. For Churchill, his purpose was to inspire the United Kingdom to fight. His anaphora purpose phrase was "we shall fight." For MLK, his purpose was to inspire the African American community and the civil rights movement to dream. His anaphora purpose phrase was "I have a dream." Bernie Sanders, in his candidacy announcement address, had multiple purposes: inspiring people to speak out against power, inspiring people to embrace where they came from, inspiring people to come together, and inspiring people to take the White House by voting for him. Look at his anaphora purpose phrases: "Today, we say to... I did not come from... Together... When we are in the White House..." Look at how they line up with his purposes: "Today, we say to... (inspiring people to speak out against power) I did not come from... (inspiring people to embrace where they came from) Together... (inspiring people to come together) When we are in the White House (inspiring people to take the White House by voting for him)..."

That's why I call it an "anaphora *purpose* phrase." It almost always lines up directly to the purpose of the speech.

5.3: WANT, GOT, EMPOWERMENT

What is it? Structuring a speech around presenting a gap between what people want and what they have. Then, inspiring them to close that gap.

Why does it work? It uses the aspirations of the audience. It creates cognitive dissonance. It makes the "empowerment" actually make sense in the context of the gap.

When do you use it? When your audience has a clear gap in their lives that could be filled. When you want to inspire your audience. When you want to empower them to close the "want-got" gap.

What is the step-by-step process? Want presentation: "Here's what you want to have in your life." Got presentation: "Instead, here's what you actually have. It's not what you want." Want-got repetitive contrast: Repeatedly jump back and forth, contrasting what they want with what they have. Empowerment: "But you can get what you want. You have what it takes."

KEY INSIGHT:

Inspiration Enters Our Souls Through the Gap Between What We Are and What We Could Be.

THE WANT, GOT, EMPOWERMENT TRIFECTA VISUALIZED

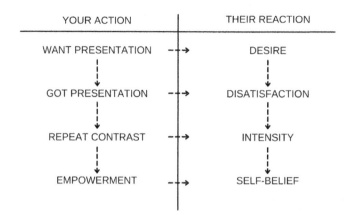

FIGURE 65: This structure points out a gap between what people want and what they have before empowering them to believe in their capability to close that gap.

I told you that there would be a lot of contrast persuasion and aspirational persuasion. This speech structure uses both. A common mistake speakers make when trying to inspire is just doing the empowerment. But the empowerment becomes a lot more useful in the context of a want-got gap. A solution only makes sense in the context of the problem it solves.

5.4: CURRENT PROBLEMS, FUTURE, EMPOWERMENT

What is it? Structuring a speech around the problems of the present, and then empowering the audience to fix them in the future.

Why does it work? It contrasts a problematic present with a better future. It puts the empowerment in context. It presents a vision for the future.

When do you use it? When you want to inspire your audience to work toward a better future. When there are problems in the present that your audience is struggling with. When you want to be a visionary or a leader.

What is the step-by-step process? Current problems: "Here's what's wrong right now." Future vision: "Here's how the future can look. Here's how it can feel to pass these obstacles." Empowerment: "You can do it. You can make this difference. You have the power."

THE NOW, FUTURE, EMPOWERMENT TRIFECTA VISUALIZED

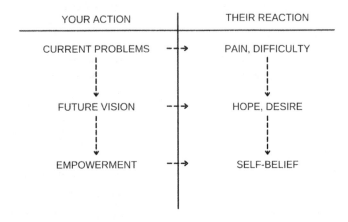

FIGURE 66: This structure presents the problems of the present to instigate pain, before offering a desirable vision for a better future, creating hope in the name of this vision, and giving the audience the self-belief to pursue it.

It is important to have specific, symmetric contrast. Here's a contrast between present and future that is neither specific nor symmetric: "Our business processes are inefficient and frustrating. We can have better management."

Here's why it satisfies neither of the two criteria: "business processes" is a vague phrase, and "business processes" and "better management" are not symmetric. In other words, the future must be good in the same way – along the same dimension – that the present is lacking.

Here's a contrast between present and future that is both specific and symmetric: "Our sales processes are inefficient and frustrating. We can have streamlined, satisfying, rewarding sales processes." In this example, the speaker is pointing out a specific problem in the present. In the future, it is this same specific problem that is fixed.

5.5: SHORT-FORM INSPIRATIONAL THREE-POINT PUNCH

What is it? Structuring a speech around examples of your audience having the qualities they need to have to do what they want.

Why does it work? It makes your audience feel like they are capable. It makes your audience confident in their abilities. It builds the speaker to audience connection.

When do you use it? When you have personal knowledge of your audience. When you know of examples of your audience expressing the necessary qualities. When you want to inspire a specific group of people to believe they can do a specific thing.

What is the step-by-step process? Limited frame presentation: "You might think that you aren't capable of achieving [goal]." Goal presentation: "Here's the specific goal you want to achieve. You think you can't." Qualities presentation "Here are the qualities you need to achieve that goal. You already have these qualities." Example one: "Here's the first time you showed me you have these qualities." Example two: "Here's the second time you showed me you have these qualities." Example three: "Here's the third time you showed me you have these qualities."

THE SHORT-FORM INSPIRING THREE-POINT VISUALIZED

YOUR ACTION		THEIR REACTION
LIMITED FRAME	--→	CONTEXT, PRIMING
↓		↓
GOAL PRESENTATION	--→	DESIRE, AIM
↓		↓
QUALITIES PRESENTATION	--→	AGREEMENT TO FRAMEWORK
↓		↓
EXAMPLE ONE	--→	SELF-BELIEF, CERTAINTY
↓		↓
EXAMPLE TWO	--→	SELF-BELIEF, CERTAINTY
↓		↓
EXAMPLE THREE	--→	SELF-BELIEF, CERTAINTY

FIGURE 67: This structure is particularly well-suited at maximizing the extent of the audience's self-belief.

To summarize this structure, you are essentially saying "you have everything you need to do what you want to do." In other words, you are taking a goal your audience thought was unreachable, and putting it within reach. How? By showing them extremely specific examples that prove how they already have exactly what it takes. In doing so, this structure removes a limiting belief (or multiple limiting beliefs).

5.6: LIMITING BELIEF PREDICTION

What is it? Structuring a speech around addressing and removing your audience's limiting beliefs.

Why does it work? It makes your audience realize their own potential. It destroys their excuses. It gets rid of all their barriers to motivation.

When do you use it? When you have a solid understanding of your audience's limiting beliefs. When you want to inspire people to do something difficult. When people have lots of excuses as to why they won't do it.

What is the step-by-step process? Present limiting belief or excuse: "You say you can't do it because [insert limiting belief or excuse]." Invalidate limiting belief or excuse: "Here's why that limiting belief makes no sense." Repetition: Repeat steps one and two for all limiting beliefs your audience has. Enumeration: "Clearly all of your excuses are invalid." Empowerment: "There's nothing holding you back. The reasons you tell yourself you can't do this don't apply. You can do this."

THE LIMITING-BELIEF PREDICTION STRATEGY VISUALIZED

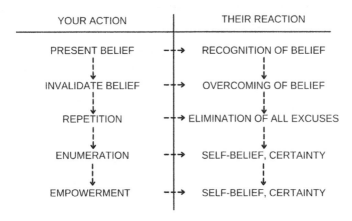

FIGURE 68: This structure is much like the objection-prediction model, turned to the goals of an inspirational speech or message.

Historical Example: "If there is anyone out there who still doubts that America is a place where all things are possible; who still wonders if the dream of our founders is alive in our time; who still questions the power of our democracy, tonight is your answer. It's the answer told by lines that stretched around schools and churches in numbers this nation has never seen; by people who waited three hours and four hours, many for the very first time in their lives, because they believed that this time must be different; that their voice could be that difference. It's the answer spoken by young and old, rich and poor, Democrat and Republican, black, white, Latino, Asian, Native American, gay, straight, disabled and not disabled – Americans who sent a message to the world that we have never been a collection of red states and blue states; we are, and always will be, the United States of America. It's the answer that led those who have been told for so long by so many to be cynical, and fearful, and doubtful of what we can achieve to put their hands on the arc of history and bend it once more toward the hope of a better day. It's been a long time coming, but tonight, because of what we did on this day, in this election, at this defining moment, change has come to America." – Barack Obama

You are systematically and repetitively invalidating your audience's limiting beliefs. You are calling them out. You are exposing their excuses. And this is often exactly what people need to be inspired.

5.7: VISIONARY STRUCTURE

What is it? Structuring a speech around a bright vision of the future.

Why does it work? It motivates people to strive toward that vision. It makes you a leader. It gives people a goal, and your audience can't be motivated or inspired without a goal.

When do you use it? When you have a bright, ambitious vision for the future. When you know your audience would appreciate your vision. When you want to inspire your audience to strive toward your vision.

What is the step-by-step process? Empowerment: "You are all brilliant, capable people. You all have what it takes to go after your goals." Accomplishment enumeration: "Look at all the amazing things you've already achieved. [Insert accomplishment one], [insert accomplishment two], [insert accomplishment three]." Pre-accomplishment recall: "Remember how we felt before those accomplishments? We thought we couldn't do it. But we kept working toward it, and we did it." Vision: "And now, we're turning to a new goal. [Insert your vision]." Empowerment: "We have everything it takes to go after this vision and get it." Accomplishment string: "Just like we achieved [insert accomplishment one], [insert accomplishment two], and [insert accomplishment three], we will also achieve [insert your vision]."

THE VISIONARY STRUCTURE VISUALIZED

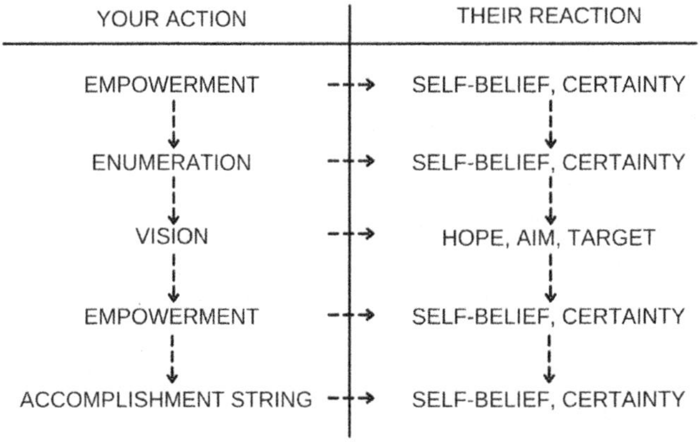

YOUR ACTION		THEIR REACTION
EMPOWERMENT	--→	SELF-BELIEF, CERTAINTY
ENUMERATION	--→	SELF-BELIEF, CERTAINTY
VISION	--→	HOPE, AIM, TARGET
EMPOWERMENT	--→	SELF-BELIEF, CERTAINTY
ACCOMPLISHMENT STRING	--→	SELF-BELIEF, CERTAINTY

FIGURE 69: This structure is highly effective at inspiring practical action by raising self-belief and certainty in the service of a well-defined hope, aim, or target.

Historical Example: "Through the Civil War, the Great Depression, World War, 9/11, through struggle, sacrifice, and setbacks, our "better angels" have always prevailed. In each of these moments, enough of us came together to carry all of us forward. And, we can do so now. History, faith, and reason show the way, the way of unity. We can see each other not as adversaries but as neighbors.

We can treat each other with dignity and respect. We can join forces, stop the shouting, and lower the temperature. For without unity, there is no peace, only bitterness and fury. No progress, only exhausting outrage. No nation, only a state of chaos. This is our historic moment of crisis and challenge, and unity is the path forward. And, we must meet this moment as the United States of America. If we do that, I guarantee you, we will not fail. We have never, ever, ever failed in America when we have acted together. And so today, at this time and in this place, let us start afresh. All of us. Let us listen to one another. Hear one another. See one another. Show respect to one another. Politics need not be a raging fire destroying everything in its path. Every disagreement doesn't have to be a cause for total war. And, we must reject a culture in which facts themselves are manipulated and even manufactured. My fellow Americans, we have to be different than this. America has to be better than this. And, I believe America is better than this." – Joe Biden

This structure doesn't just lay out your vision, leaving people wondering "how are we going to do it?" Instead, it makes the vision seem believable, and it does this because it empowers. It uses previous accomplishments to prove that the empowerment is more than just empty words. It uses the now-proven empowerment to inspire the audience to move toward the vision.

5.8: DRAMA STRUCTURE

What is it? Structuring a speech around an inspirational story.

Why does it work? It enthralls people. It uses narrative, which is naturally engaging. It helps people draw inspiration from another person's story.

When do you use it? When you want to inspire an audience. When you have an inspirational story related to the subject. When you have a personal background that is inspirational.

What is the step-by-step process? Exposition: "These are the characters and setting." Problem: "This the immense problem and the impassable obstacle the character faced." False-starts: "This is the series of failed attempts to solve the problem the character went through." Low-point: "This is the low point the character reached, when he was about to give up for good." Rising action: "Instead of giving up, he decides to try one more solution." Climax: "This was the crucial breaking point. This was when the solution either worked or failed." Success: "It worked! Here's how that felt, and what that meant for the characters." Falling action: "Here's what happened after the climax. Things started to relax." Resolution: "Here's how life was different after the whole thing happened." Inspirational takeaway: "Here are the inspirational lessons we can take from this story."

THE DRAMA STRUCTURE VISUALIZED

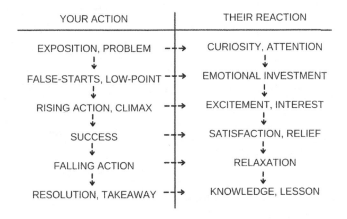

YOUR ACTION	THEIR REACTION
EXPOSITION, PROBLEM --→	CURIOSITY, ATTENTION
FALSE-STARTS, LOW-POINT --→	EMOTIONAL INVESTMENT
RISING ACTION, CLIMAX --→	EXCITEMENT, INTEREST
SUCCESS --→	SATISFACTION, RELIEF
FALLING ACTION --→	RELAXATION
RESOLUTION, TAKEAWAY --→	KNOWLEDGE, LESSON

FIGURE 70: This structure is deeply powerful. Humans love stories. Stories are vehicles we have used to passed down information for thousands of years.

Historical Example: "Each one of those markers is a monument to the kinds of hero I spoke of earlier. Their lives ended in places called Belleau Wood, The Argonne, Omaha Beach, Salerno and halfway around the world on Guadalcanal, Tarawa, Pork Chop Hill, the Chosin Reservoir, and in a hundred rice paddies and jungles of a place called Vietnam. Under one such marker lies a young man – Martin Treptow – who left his job in a small-town barber shop in 1917 to go to France with the famed Rainbow Division. There, on the western front, he was killed trying to carry a message between battalions under heavy artillery fire. We are told that on his body was found a diary. On the flyleaf under the heading, 'My Pledge,' he had written these words: 'America must win this war. Therefore, I will work, I will save, I will sacrifice, I will endure, I will fight cheerfully and do my utmost, as if the issue of the whole struggle depended on me alone.' The crisis we are facing today does not require of us the kind of sacrifice that Martin Treptow and so many thousands of others were called upon to make. It does require, however, our best effort, and our willingness to believe in ourselves and to believe in our capacity to perform great deeds; to believe that together, with God's help, we can and will resolve the problems which now confront us. And, after all, why shouldn't we believe that? We are Americans. God bless you, and thank you." – Ronald Reagans

The inspirational stories that dominate history all follow this pattern. Blockbuster inspirational movies that hit the top of the charts follow this pattern. Why shouldn't an inspirational speech follow this pattern too?

........................Chapter Summary...............................

- Inspiring is, in large part, closing the gap between "what we need to be to do this" and "what we are."
- Inspiration and persuasion are closely associated, and many of the structures and principles carry over.

- Some inspirational structures inspire by proxy; by revealing an inspirational story of a third party.
- Other inspirational structures inspire by targeting the audience directly, and manipulating their self-estimation.
- A common mistake is only focusing on the "empowerment" aspect of inspiration; on the "you can do it" side of it.
- However, the empowerment step functions most effectively in the context of a broader structure.

KEY INSIGHT:

Inspiration Is an Act of Reconnecting People with Their Own Potential.

Inspiration In the Form of Self-Belief Is a Logical Case, To Be Conveyed with Evidence.

"You Did This. And You Did This. You Did This Too. So That? That's No Problem."

THE IRREFUTABLE PERSUASIVE SYNTAX (PART FIVE)

1	Master the Foundational Theories
1.1	Apply the Public Speaking Triad
1.2	Master the Communication Toolbox and the Three Layers
1.3	Activate, Control, and Align Your Three Languages
1.4	Satisfy the Triad Ingredients
1.5	Understand and Apply Purposeful Communication
1.6	Don't Forget the Three-Part Model of Communication
1.7	Speak to the Top of the Cone of Attention
1.8	Say the Right Things, But Also in the Right Way
1.9	Appeal to Self-Interest and "WIIFM?"
1.10	Raise Perceived Marginal Benefits, Drop Perceived Marginal Costs
1.11	Satisfy the Mental Checklist in Eight Seconds
1.12	Speak in terms of Benefits and Features
1.13	Remember the Wisdom of the Fable of the Wind and the Sun
1.14	Understand the Underlying Fact of Mental Malleability
1.15	Apply Bridge Theory to Keep Things Flowing Smoothly
1.16	Recognize the Pyramid of Human Desires
1.17	Remember Uniqueness, Personas, Ceteris Paribus and Limitations
1.18	Satisfy the Saliency, Intensity, and Stability Framework
1.19	Understand the Dilemma of One Versus Many

1.20	Master Psychological Persuasion
1.21	Speak for Action
1.22	Satisfy the 7Cs (or 14Cs) of Communication
1.23	Present Novelty and Simplicity
1.24	Achieve Emotional and Logical Certainty with the Spectrum Model
1.25	Understand the Principle of Meaning through Sequence
1.26	Recognize the Frames at Play
1.27	Communicate with Unspoken Words
1.28	Understand the Principle of Persuasive Patterns
1.29	Master the Application of All These Theories with Structure Theory
2	**Master the Basics of Structure Theory**
2.1	Build Out Structure Theory
2.2	Remember Why these Principles Matter
2.3	Understand the Crucial Truth of Speech Structure
2.4	Remember the Critical Importance of Structure
2.5	Speak as Simply as Possible
2.6	Provide Novelty of Information
2.7	Combine Novelty and Simplicity
2.8	Minimize Cognitive Load
2.9	Recognize and Apply Engineered Persuasion

2.10	Avoid Tangents and Parentheticals
2.11	Use Transitions to Maintain Audience Attention
2.12	Remember the Similarities of Structure
2.13	Engineer Your Openings
2.14	Complete Your Communication Body
2.15	Engineer Your Closing
3	**Master the Persuasive Structures**
3.1	Use Monroe's Motivated Sequence
3.2	Use the Objection-Prediction Model
3.3	Use the Path-Contrast Method
3.4	Use the Past, Present, Means Structure
3.5	Use the Problem-Solution Formula
3.6	Use the Diagnose, Problem, Solution Triad
3.7	Use Criteria Matching
3.8	Use Criteria Matching and Dematching
3.9	Use the Six-Point Punch
3.10	Use the Economic Values Structure
3.11	Use the Short-Form Rhetorical Three-Point Punch
3.12	Use the Long-Form Rhetorical Three-Point Punch
3.13	Use the Gain, Logic, Fear Trifecta

3.14	Use the Tension, Desire, Action Trifecta
3.15	Use the Persuasive Stack Sequence
3.16	Use the Last Method Strategy
3.17	Use the Past, Present, Future Method
3.18	Use the Desire, Dissonance, Decision Trifecta
4	**Master the Informative Structures**
4.1	Use the Informational Motivated Sequence
4.2	Use the Straight-Line Method
4.3	Use the Reverse-Line Method
4.4	Use the Stream of Consciousness Principle
4.5	Use the Montage Structure
4.6	Use the Attached List Structure
4.7	Use the Detached List Structure
4.8	Use the Information Stack
4.9	Use the Big Answer Strategy
4.10	Use the Back-and-Forth Method
4.11	Use the Chronological Sequence
4.12	Use the Cause-and-Effect Method
4.13	Use the Presentation, Escalation, Contrast Trifecta
4.14	Use the Narrative Structure

Email Peter D. Andrei, the author of the Speak for Success collection and the President of Speak Truth Well LLC directly.

pandreibusiness@gmail.com

Claim These Free Resources that Will Help You Unleash the Power of Your Words and Speak with Confidence. Visit www.speakforsuccesshub.com/toolkit for Access.

30 Free Video Lessons

We'll send you one free video lesson every day for 30 days, written and recorded by Peter D. Andrei. Days 1-10 cover authenticity, the prerequisite to confidence and persuasive power. Days 11-20 cover building self-belief and defeating communication anxiety. Days 21-30 cover how to speak with impact and influence, ensuring your words change minds instead of falling flat. Authenticity, self-belief, and impact – this course helps you master three components of confidence, turning even the most high-stakes presentations from obstacles into opportunities.

SPEAK FOR SUCCESS COLLECTION BOOK

X

THE PSYCHOLOGY OF PERSUASION CHAPTER

VII

THE NEXT LEVEL:

Proven Strategies for Perfecting Your Persuasion

6.1: DON'T BURY THE LEAD (OR DO...)

HAVE YOU NOTICED THAT NEWS REPORTS IMMEDIATELY start with the main events? The big ideas? The primary news? That's called starting with the lead. Why am I talking about journalism? I'll explain.

The whole point of speech structure is breaking down your speech into units and ordering them to achieve a desired impact. Each of these "sub-units" have one main idea. You can usually summarize it in one sentence. This one sentence is the "lead." It's a one-sentence summary of the entire "sub-unit," which is usually a paragraph.

And there are two strategies: First, you can *not* bury the lead. You can start each sub-unit with the lead. Here's what that does: It grabs attention, puts the rest of the paragraph in context, primes the audience for the rest of the information, and gives the main information when audience attention is highest.

So, "don't bury the lead." Or maybe *do* bury the lead. Because if you put the lead at the end of a sub-unit, here's what that does: It makes the lead seem like a natural conclusion of what came before it, gradually builds up to the lead (the lead emerges from the information), creates curiosity and suspense throughout the sub-unit, and acts as a closing summary before moving on to the next phase of your communication.

You have two choices. Pick one. They are both effective, but one likely suits you, your message, and your situation more than the other.

6.2: VERSATILITY

All of these structures can be used in multiple ways. And that's important to know. You can adapt them for different purposes. You can morph them to completely new purposes.

KEY INSIGHT:

These Structures Are Tools In Your Rhetorical Toolbox. As Such, They Are Flexible.

See the Object Behind the Label. You Can Use a Hammer for More Than Just Hammering.

6.3: LENGTHENING AND SHORTENING

This (and the next expert technique) are the two most powerful structure techniques, especially when used together. Each of these structures act as an accordion. They can be lengthened or shortened, while retaining much of their original qualities in proportion to how much they are lengthened or shortened.

For example, the problem-solution structure can be two sentences. Sentence one presents a problem, and sentence two presents the solution. It can even be a single sentence. It can be as simple as "Stagnant economy (problem)? Lower taxes (solution)."

While all of these speech structures are designed to be entire speeches, they can all be shortened until each step of the structure is one sentence, and arguably even further than that. In other words, you can use a problem-solution structure that is an entire speech. You can use 20 sentences to describe the problem, and 20 sentences to describe the solution. But you can also make a problem-solution structure in two sentences with the same impact on a smaller scale.

6.4: COMBINING

You can use all of these structures in a single speech, or make one structure an entire speech. Use them as building blocks to build a unique, customized tower. Just know this: Because all of these structures have the same effect on a smaller scale when each step is just one sentence as they do when they are full-length, you can create incredibly complex, powerful combinations of these structures.

Present a three-sentence past-present-means to build curiosity, with vague "means." Then, present a three-sentence diagnose, problem, solution structure, addressing the problem presented in the "past" stage of the previous structure, and now elaborating upon the solution. Then, present an objection prediction where each objection gets one sentence. This structure addresses the objections to the solution presented in the diagnose-problem-solution structure. Finally, present a tension-desire-action trifecta (three sentences, one sentence each step) to use emotion for a final call to action.

I gave you building blocks. The kinds of speeches you can build with them are endless. You can write a speech that is a sequence of all 18 persuasive structures if the situation calls for it. You can stack the structures in a sequence, or use one structure to complete the step of another structure. Or you can take the simple route, and organize your speech around one structure and one structure only. Let us explore some examples of different stacks that you can create out of the constituent parts we covered in the books – highly effective "meta-structures" created out of smaller structures.

An example of such a structure follows. I don't necessarily recommend this exact meta-structure. I suggest you create your own.

I present this to shed light on the strategy of structure-stacking as a whole. Think of each structure as a particular "card." You want to play the right cards in the right sequence. That's the game. And only you can know what your specific, individual situation calls for. As you take in this meta-structure, pay close attention to how the structures interact. Pay attention to how we must slightly modify some steps to ease the transition from one structure to the next. Observe the content we use in each individual structure in the stack and how it strengthens the persuasive impact of the whole (the image captions reveal this). Note the minor modifications of each core structure that ensure it flows with the whole. Look at the entire right column of the structure to understand its combined psychological impact.

KEY INSIGHT:

A Great Speech Is Really Three Speeches United Into One Whole, According to Churchill.

He's Right. In Great Speeches, Multiple Structures Combine to Form a Greater Meta–Structure, with a Deeper Persuasive Pull.

GENERATE CURIOSITY, HIDE THE "HOW"

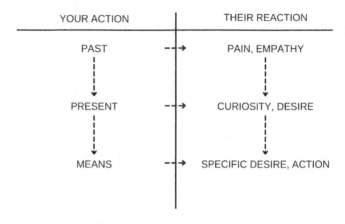

FIGURE 71: Provide one example of a success story. Only hint at the means – or the "how" – to build curiosity.

GENERATE MORE CURIOSITY, SET THE HOOK TIGHTLY

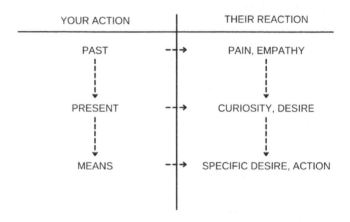

FIGURE 72: Repeat the structure with another success story. Don't tell them the "how" yet. This is only the hook.

IRREVOCABLY CAPTURE THEIR COMPLETE ATTENTION

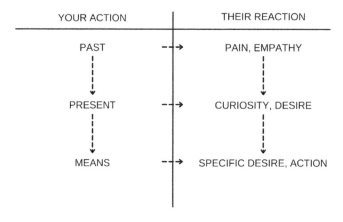

FIGURE 73: The third success story completely hooks and captivates them. Once again, be careful to only hint at the means. Provide hints that only intensify the curiosity.

SET THE GROUNDRULES, ESTABLISH CONSISTENCY

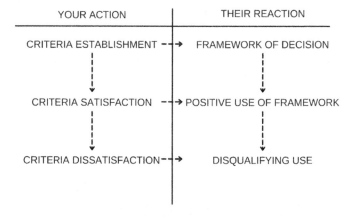

FIGURE 74: Get them to agree to the checklist they will use to judge the potential solutions to the problem. Tell them that the still undisclosed solution you are offering meets every single item on the checklist. Drop more tantalizing hints about how it meets their set of demands. Next, disqualify every other possible solution aside from yours. They still don't know what yours is at this point.

THROW STONES AT THE OLD APPROACH

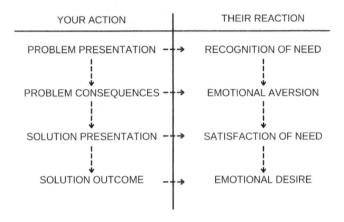

FIGURE 75: Now, present the problems they currently face, and the problems they will continue to face with any of the solutions you already disqualified. Intensify this. Promise a solution and expound on its positive outcomes. Drop more hints. Don't reveal. Keep the suspense.

COMPLETE THE EMOTIONAL SALE ONCE AND FOR ALL

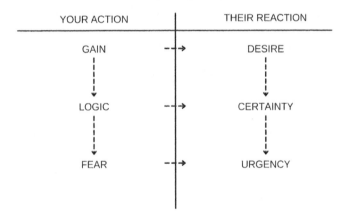

FIGURE 76: Briefly and succinctly present the gain you promise. Do so impactfully and powerfully. Support this with logical appeals that prove the gain. And show them they have a limited time to act and get this hidden, mysterious, revolutionary solution you have been teasing.

GIVE THE BIG REVEAL YOU PREFRAMED FOR VICTORY

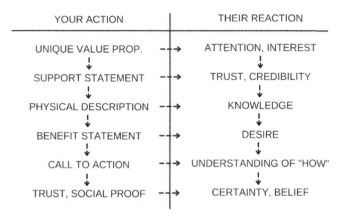

FIGURE 77: This is the big reveal. At this point, you have conveyed so much value, generated so much curiosity, and built up so much suspense that you have pre-framed the big reveal for an almost-guaranteed victory.

BUILD UP THE SOCIAL PROOF AND CERTAINTY

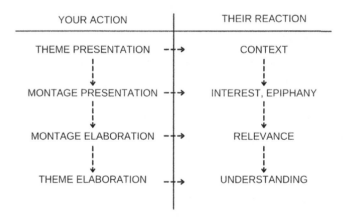

FIGURE 78: Present a montage of stories of people who adopted your solution – whatever it may be – and how it helped them. Present the theme of the montage, reveal the stories that act as testimonials, and then elaborate on both the montage and the theme itself. Tell stories that defeat their skepticism and doubt. Pile on the narrative evidence.

DELIVER THE ULTIMATE, CRYSTALIZED LIST OF BENEFITS

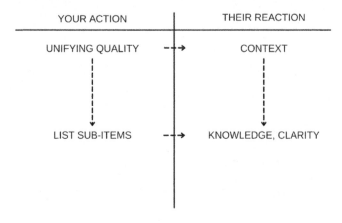

FIGURE 79: This is simple. Present an exhaustive and thorough list of the ways the solution benefits them.

DELIVER THE ULTIMATE, CRYSTALIZED LIST OF BENEFITS

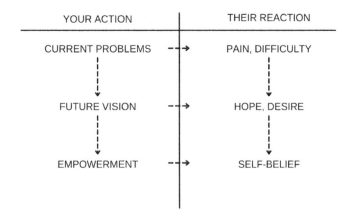

FIGURE 80: In light of everything you have revealed, return to expounding on their current problems. Do you see a meta-pattern developing of "positive, negative, positive, negative, positive, negative?" After expounding on the problems once more, cast a vision of a hopeful future your solution will give them, and then empower them to believe that they themselves have what it takes to use the solution to reach that future. Defeat their limiting beliefs.

DEFEAT OBJECTIONS AGAINST THE SOLUTION

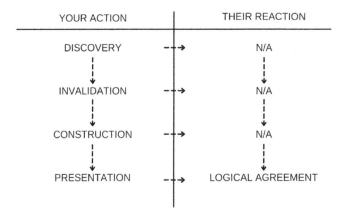

FIGURE 81: In your preparation, you should have discovered or predicted all their objections, decided how to invalidate them, and constructed a simple script to do so. Now, present this script and defeat those objections.

DEFEAT SELF-LIMITING BELIEFS THAT PREVENT ACTION

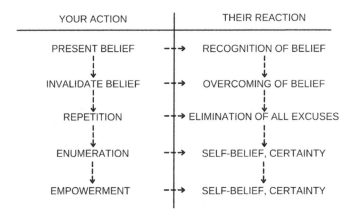

FIGURE 82: Now, after defeating logical objections against the solution itself ("it's too expensive, it's too hard to use, I don't believe it will really do this, etc.") you must use this structure to defeat their self-limiting beliefs ("I think it is a good solution, I just don't believe I have the know-how to use it or the confidence to sell it to my partners.")

DEFEAT OBJECTIONS ACROSS TIME

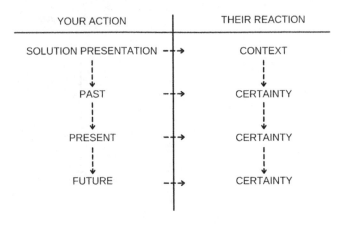

FIGURE 83: Turn your attention to time-based objections: "It may work now, but will it be rendered obsolete in the next software update?" Overcome these objections with the past, present, future structure.

DEFEAT SELF-LIMITING BELIEFS ACROSS TIME

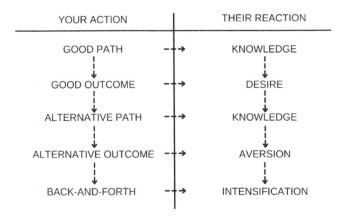

FIGURE 84: Turn your attention to time-based self-limiting beliefs: "It's a good solution, but I worry my knowledge won't keep up with updates over time." Overcome these self-limiting beliefs with the past, present, future structure.

GO IN-DEPTH AND THINK PAST THE SALE

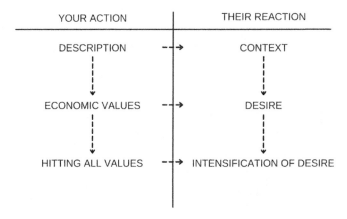

FIGURE 85: Go in-depth on the details of the solution as if they have already agreed to adopt it and you are showing them how to implement it. Show how it appeals to all economic values to complete the logical sale.

SUMMARIZE AND CALL THEM TO ACTION

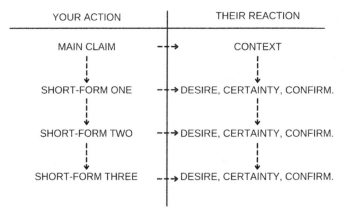

FIGURE 86: Use a simple long-form three-point punch to summarize everything you discussed and call them to action while giving them confirmation on all of the positive thoughts they are currently thinking about your solution. Close the message. Close the deal or the sale or whatever it is in your particular situation.

THE UNIFIED META-STRUCTURE WE BUILT

ACTION	REACTION
Past	Pain, Empathy
Present	Curiosity, Desire
Means	Specific Desire, Action
Past	**Pain, Empathy**
Present	**Curiosity, Desire**
Means	**Specific Desire, Action**
Past	Pain, Empathy
Present	Curiosity, Desire
Means	Specific Desire, Action
Criteria Establishment	**Framework of Decision**
Criteria Satisfaction	**Positive Use of Framework**
Criteria Dissatisfaction	**Negative Use of Framework**
Problem Presentation	Recognition of Need
Problem Consequences	Emotional Aversion
Solution Presentation	Satisfaction of Need
Solution Outcome	Emotional Desire
Gain	**Desire**
Logic	**Certainty**
Fear	**Urgency**
Unique Value Prop.	Attention, Interest
Support Statement	Trust, Credibility
Physical Description	Knowledge, Desire
Benefit Statement	Understanding of "How"
Trust, Social Proof	Certainty, Belief
Theme Presentation	**Context**
Montage Presentation	**Interest, Epiphany**
Montage Elaboration	**Relevance**
Theme Elaboration	**Understanding**
Unifying Quality	Context
Sub-Item List	Knowledge, Clarity
Current Problems	**Pain, Difficulty**
Future Vision	**Hope, Desire**
Empowerment	**Self-Belief**
Discovery	N/A
Invalidation	N/A
Construction	N/A
Presentation	Logical Agreement

Present Belief	Recognition of Belief
Invalidate Belief	Overcoming of Belief
Repetition	Elimination of Excuses
Enumeration	Self-Belief, Certainty
Empowerment	Self-Belief, Certainty
Solution Presentation	Context
Past	Certainty
Present	Certainty
Future	Certainty
Good Path	Knowledge
Good Outcome	Desire
Alternative Path	Knowledge
Alternative Outcome	Aversion
Back-and-Forth	Intensification
Description	Context
Economic Values	Desire
Hitting All Values	Intensification of Desire
Main Claim	Context
Short-Form One	Desire, Certainty, Confirm
Short-Form Two	Desire, Certainty, Confirm
Short-Form Three	Desire, Certainty, Confirm

MARKING ITS CONSTITUENT STRUCTURES

STRUCTURE	ACTION	REACTION
1	Past	Pain, Empathy
	Present	Curiosity, Desire
	Means	Specific Desire, Action
2	Past	Pain, Empathy
	Present	Curiosity, Desire
	Means	Specific Desire, Action
3	Past	Pain, Empathy
	Present	Curiosity, Desire
	Means	Specific Desire, Action
4	Criteria Establishment	Framework of Decision
	Criteria Satisfaction	Positive Application
	Criteria Dissatisfaction	Negative Application
5	Problem Presentation	Recognition of Need

	Problem Consequences	Emotional Aversion
	Solution Presentation	Satisfaction of Need
	Solution Outcome	Emotional Desire
6	**Gain**	**Desire**
	Logic	**Certainty**
	Fear	**Urgency**
7	Unique Value Prop.	Attention, Interest
	Support Statement	Trust, Credibility
	Physical Description	Knowledge, Desire
	Benefit Statement	Understanding of "How"
	Trust, Social Proof	Certainty, Belief
8	**Theme Presentation**	**Context**
	Montage Presentation	**Interest, Epiphany**
	Montage Elaboration	**Relevance**
	Theme Elaboration	**Understanding**
9	Unifying Quality	Context
	Sub-Item List	Knowledge, Clarity
10	**Current Problems**	**Pain, Difficulty**
	Future Vision	**Hope, Desire**
	Empowerment	**Self-Belief**
11	Discovery	N/A
	Invalidation	N/A
	Construction	N/A
	Presentation	Logical Agreement
12	**Present Belief**	**Recognition of Belief**
	Invalidate Belief	**Overcoming of Belief**
	Repetition	**Elimination of Excuses**
	Enumeration	**Self-Belief, Certainty**
	Empowerment	**Self-Belief, Certainty**
13	Solution Presentation	Context
	Past	Certainty
	Present	Certainty
	Future	Certainty
14	**Good Path**	**Knowledge**
	Good Outcome	**Desire**
	Alternative Path	**Knowledge**
	Alternative Outcome	**Aversion**
	Back-and-Forth	**Intensification**
15	Description	Context
	Economic Values	Desire

	Hitting All Values	Intensification of Desire
16	**Main Claim**	**Context**
	Short-Form One	**Want, Certainty, Confirm**
	Short-Form Two	**Want, Certainty, Confirm**
	Short-Form Three	**Want, Certainty, Confirm**

KEY INSIGHT:

A Technique Is a Tactical Asset. Great Strategy Comes from Combining Tactical Assets.

The Best Tactical Combinations Synergize. When They Collide, One Plus One Makes Three.

THE META-META STRUCTURE THAT EMERGES

META-ACTION	ACTION	REACTION
	Past	Pain, Empathy
Generate	Present	Curiosity, Desire
Curiosity, Build	Means	Specific Desire, Action
Suspense,	**Past**	**Pain, Empathy**
Portray Value	**Present**	**Curiosity, Desire**

	Means	**Specific Desire, Action**
	Past	Pain, Empathy
	Present	Curiosity, Desire
	Means	Specific Desire, Action
Agree to a Common Ground and Set the Stage for the Reveal	**Criteria Establishment**	**Framework of Decision**
	Criteria Satisfaction	**Positive Application**
	Criteria Dissatisfaction	**Negative Application**
	Problem Presentation	Recognition of Need
	Problem Consequences	Emotional Aversion
	Solution Presentation	Satisfaction of Need
	Solution Outcome	Emotional Desire
	Gain	**Desire**
	Logic	**Certainty**
	Fear	**Urgency**
Make the Reveal	Unique Value Prop.	Attention, Interest
	Support Statement	Trust, Credibility
	Physical Description	Knowledge, Desire
	Benefit Statement	Understanding of "How"
	Trust, Social Proof	Certainty, Belief
Prove the Solution	**Theme Presentation**	**Context**
	Montage Presentation	**Interest, Epiphany**
	Montage Elaboration	**Relevance**
	Theme Elaboration	**Understanding**
	Unifying Quality	Context
	Sub-Item List	Knowledge, Clarity
	Current Problems	**Pain, Difficulty**
	Future Vision	**Hope, Desire**
	Empowerment	**Self-Belief**
Defeat Hurdles, Objections, and Self-Limiting Beliefs	Discovery	N/A
	Invalidation	N/A
	Construction	N/A
	Presentation	Logical Agreement
	Present Belief	**Recognition of Belief**
	Invalidate Belief	**Overcoming of Belief**
	Repetition	**Elimination of Excuses**
	Enumeration	**Self-Belief, Certainty**
	Empowerment	**Self-Belief, Certainty**
	Solution Presentation	Context
	Past	Certainty
	Present	Certainty

	Future	Certainty
Emotional Resell	**Good Path**	**Knowledge**
	Good Outcome	**Desire**
	Alternative Path	**Knowledge**
	Alternative Outcome	**Aversion**
	Back-and-Forth	**Intensification**
Logical Resell	Description	Context
	Economic Values	Desire
	Hitting All Values	Intensification of Desire
Summary and Close	**Main Claim**	**Context**
	Short-Form One	**Want, Certainty, Confirm**
	Short-Form Two	**Want, Certainty, Confirm**
	Short-Form Three	**Want, Certainty, Confirm**

THE HIGHER-LEVEL EMOTIONAL FLOW AND REACTION

ACTION	REACTION	META-REACT.
Past	Pain, Empathy	*Interest, Engagement, Rapt Attention, Productive Tension*
Present	Curiosity, Desire	
Means	Specific Desire, Action	
Past	**Pain, Empathy**	
Present	**Curiosity, Desire**	
Means	**Specific Desire, Action**	
Past	Pain, Empathy	
Present	Curiosity, Desire	
Means	Specific Desire, Action	
Criteria Establishment	**Framework of Decision**	*Consistency Principle Activated; Compulsion to Act in Line with Commitment to Criteria and Desire to Do so*
Criteria Satisfaction	**Positive Application**	
Criteria Dissatisfaction	**Negative Application**	
Problem Presentation	Recognition of Need	
Problem Consequences	Emotional Aversion	
Solution Presentation	Satisfaction of Need	
Solution Outcome	Emotional Desire	
Gain	**Desire**	
Logic	**Certainty**	
Fear	**Urgency**	
Unique Value Prop.	Attention, Interest	
Support Statement	Trust, Credibility	

Physical Description	Knowledge, Desire	***Specification of Desire***
Benefit Statement	Understanding of "How"	
Trust, Social Proof	Certainty, Belief	
Theme Presentation	**Context**	***Specification of Desire***
Montage Presentation	**Interest, Epiphany**	
Montage Elaboration	**Relevance**	
Theme Elaboration	**Understanding**	
Unifying Quality	Context	
Sub-Item List	Knowledge, Clarity	
Current Problems	**Pain, Difficulty**	
Future Vision	**Hope, Desire**	
Empowerment	**Self-Belief**	
Discovery	N/A	***Elimination of Excuses and Barriers; Awareness of Valid Reasons for It, Absence of Arguments Against It***
Invalidation	N/A	
Construction	N/A	
Presentation	Logical Agreement	
Present Belief	**Recognition of Belief**	
Invalidate Belief	**Overcoming of Belief**	
Repetition	**Elimination of Excuses**	
Enumeration	**Self-Belief, Certainty**	
Empowerment	**Self-Belief, Certainty**	
Solution Presentation	Context	
Past	Certainty	
Present	Certainty	
Future	Certainty	
Good Path	**Knowledge**	***Emotional Need for Emotional Payoff***
Good Outcome	**Desire**	
Alternative Path	**Knowledge**	
Alternative Outcome	**Aversion**	
Back-and-Forth	**Intensification**	
Description	Context	***Logical Appeal***
Economic Values	Desire	
Hitting All Values	Intensification of Desire	
Main Claim	**Context**	***Memorability and Action***
Short-Form One	**Want, Certainty, Confirm**	
Short-Form Two	**Want, Certainty, Confirm**	
Short-Form Three	**Want, Certainty, Confirm**	

KEY INSIGHT:

A Powerful Speech Connects Modules of Meaning That are Sufficiently Powerful on Their Own into a Grand Orchestra of Truth. A Violin Is Beautiful on Its Own. The Parts of a Speech Should Be Too.

THE POSITIVE-NEGATIVE-NEUTRAL SENTIMENT FLOW

ACTION	REACTION	+ / - / N
Past	Pain, Empathy	-
Present	Curiosity, Desire	+
Means	Specific Desire, Action	N
Past	**Pain, Empathy**	-
Present	**Curiosity, Desire**	+
Means	**Specific Desire, Action**	N
Past	Pain, Empathy	-
Present	Curiosity, Desire	+
Means	Specific Desire, Action	N
Criteria Establishment	**Framework of Decision**	N
Criteria Satisfaction	**Positive Application**	+
Criteria Dissatisfaction	**Negative Application**	-
Problem Presentation	Recognition of Need	-

Problem Consequences	Emotional Aversion	-
Solution Presentation	Satisfaction of Need	+
Solution Outcome	Emotional Desire	+
Gain	**Desire**	+
Logic	**Certainty**	N
Fear	**Urgency**	-
Unique Value Prop.	Attention, Interest	+
Support Statement	Trust, Credibility	N
Physical Description	Knowledge, Desire	N
Benefit Statement	Understanding of "How"	+
Trust, Social Proof	Certainty, Belief	N
Theme Presentation	**Context**	N
Montage Presentation	**Interest, Epiphany**	+
Montage Elaboration	**Relevance**	+
Theme Elaboration	**Understanding**	N
Unifying Quality	Context	+
Sub-Item List	Knowledge, Clarity	+
Current Problems	**Pain, Difficulty**	-
Future Vision	**Hope, Desire**	+
Empowerment	**Self-Belief**	N
Discovery	N/A	N
Invalidation	N/A	N
Construction	N/A	N
Presentation	Logical Agreement	N
Present Belief	**Recognition of Belief**	N
Invalidate Belief	**Overcoming of Belief**	+
Repetition	**Elimination of Excuses**	N
Enumeration	**Self-Belief, Certainty**	N
Empowerment	**Self-Belief, Certainty**	N
Solution Presentation	Context	+
Past	Certainty	+
Present	Certainty	+
Future	Certainty	+
Good Path	**Knowledge**	+
Good Outcome	**Desire**	+
Alternative Path	**Knowledge**	-
Alternative Outcome	**Aversion**	-
Back-and-Forth	**Intensification**	N
Description	Context	N
Economic Values	Desire	+

Hitting All Values	Intensification of Desire	+
Main Claim	**Context**	**N**
Short-Form One	**Want, Certainty, Confirm**	**N**
Short-Form Two	**Want, Certainty, Confirm**	**N**
Short-Form Three	**Want, Certainty, Confirm**	**N**

KEY INSIGHT:

"[To Inspire] Any Emotion, He Must Be Swayed by It Himself.

Before He Can Move Their Tears His Own Must Flow. To Convince Them He Must Himself Believe." – Churchill

Breaking it down with these tables lets us see the broader strategy unfold. Using this type of analysis allows us to, for example, pick apart and reverse-engineer the rhetorical power of presidential inaugural addresses. Note that the positive-negative-neutral sentiment flow mapping refers to the explanation of states: the explanation of a negative state ("what will happen if you don't adopt this solution" or "what happened before we adopted this solution") counts as a plus, while the explanation of a positive state ("what will happen if you do adopt this solution" or "what happened when we adopted this solution") counts as a minus. Crucially, not all rhetorically useful steps accrue a plus – if that were the case, every step would earn a plus. Additionally, not every seemingly positive step (like inspiring self-belief) earns a plus. The pluses and minuses are only attributed to the explanation of positive and negative states of being, either potential or actual.

What we observe is a loose alternation throughout the entire speech, with a more dominantly positive section starting at roughly the midpoint of the speech. This evokes the ubiquitous persuasive structure – a structure which, I remind you, sits at the root of how we as humans interpret reality and meaning: the problem-solution structure, a structure that says "this is what's wrong and here's how to fix it." This pattern of tension and resolution can manifest itself in many ways. It can be quite literal, as is the case with the two-step problem-solution structure ("you have a problem and here's the solution") or it can emerge less literally, as a loose pattern of sentiments creating a "mostly bad" section describing the ramifications, from multiple perspectives, of not adopting a given solution, followed by a "mostly good" section describing the solution and its benefits and advantages.

REVISITING THE FUNDAMENTAL "PASA" STRUCTURE

STRUCTURE	"PASA" Structure			
BEHAVIORAL DUALITY	Escape		Approach	
SEMANTIC DUALITY	Problem		Solution	
EMOTIONAL DUALITY	Pain		Pleasure	
TEMPORAL DUALITY	Now		Later	
EXISTENTIAL DUALITY	Here		There	
DESIRE DUALITY	Aversion		Desire	
MODAL DUALITY	Chaos		Order	
STATE DUALITY	Actual		Potential	
KAIROS DUALITY	Conflict		Resolution	
THE SEQUENCE	**Problem**	**Agitate**	**Solution**	**Agitate**

The big-picture strategy of the positive and negative sentiments is to develop a loose pattern across the entire speech of "positive, negative, positive, negative, positive, negative" and more specifically, "what will happen if you do what I want (positive), what will happen if you don't do what I want (negative)." Humans innately respond to this pattern. It is ubiquitous in our shared narratives, mythologies, and archetypes. Developing this pattern over an entire message drives home – subtly, implicitly, and intuitively – the fundamental persuasive message at the heart of all persuasion: "I want you to do X; not X is bad, X is good." Ronald Reagan hinted at this when he said "You and I are told increasingly we have to choose between a left or right. Well I'd like to suggest there is no such thing as a left or right. There's only an up or down."

Again, this particular meta-structure achieves this particular strategy, which is suited for a particular situation. What strategy will you aim for? What does your persuasive situation call for? And what tools – what structures, what cards – will you use to achieve that strategy? What meta-structure will emerge as a result? This is the game. Enjoy it. There is literally an infinite number of possibilities. Trust your gut to narrow down the field of possible combinations. Use the knowledge of the psychology of persuasion you attained in the first section to guide you in narrowing down the endless field of possible meta-structures. And remember: You can also nest structures, using a structure to accomplish another step in a larger structure. We only applied stacking in this example. However, when we used the long-form three-point punch to close the structure, we inadvertently used the principle of layering as the long-form three-point punch is a collection of short-form three-point punches. And remember this too: These principles are universal. You can use them for a political speech, a book manuscript, a digital sales script, a face-to-face sales script, and much more.

Lastly, this was a particularly complex example of structure-stacking. Want a simpler example? Structure one: State a problem, emotionally agitate the problem, and provide the solution (problem-agitate-solution). Structure two: Present a victim or victim-group a perpetrator is harming and present your cause as the benevolent force for good that can beat back the perpetrator, heal the victim, and restore justice (victim-perpetrator-benevolence, not covered in this book). Structure-stack: Describe the problems facing a group, agitate the emotional impacts of the problems, present the best solution, and then expose how a group of perpetrators blocks the group (the victims) from getting it, and how you can beat back the perpetrators to regain access to the solution you need to solve the problems. Problem, agitate, solution, victim, perpetrator, benevolence – this is a simple, elegant, and influential two-structure stack.

KEY INSIGHT:

"The Climax of Oratory Is Reached by a Rapid Succession of Waves of Sound and Vivid Picture." – Winston Churchill

Structurally Sound Modules, Together, Make a Masterpiece.

6.5: SEPARATION OF CONCERNS

I predict that a lot of people will make the same mistake: blending the different stages of the structures. Each step is designed to have a purpose, which makes sense in the sequence of steps that come before and after, and in the sequence of purposes those steps accomplish. So, when you blend them, you blur the clarity of your message, you confuse your audience (and yourself), and you diminish the impact of the structure.

Imagine that you are using the past-present-means persuasive structure. Each step has a distinct purpose. If you blur them together, you lose that purpose. The whole point of the past and present steps is to create suspense and curiosity for the means that took you from the difficult past to the successful present. In other words, the past-present-means structure will drive your speech to success with an engine of curiosity and suspense. But if you blend the steps (even a little) and reveal the means before the proper time, you completely lose the suspense and curiosity. So, the whole thing becomes useless. Enter the solution: separation of concerns.

This means following a set of guidelines. These guidelines guarantee that your structure is executed properly, without blurring the steps. The guidelines are as follow. Each step of a speech structure should be distinct. Each step of a speech structure should be easily distinguishable from the others (which doesn't mean they shouldn't flow smoothly into and out of each other). Each step of a speech structure should fulfill its individual purpose before trying to do anything else (and once it does, probably leave it at that instead of trying to do something else). Each step of a speech structure should fulfill its own purpose, and not the purpose designed for another step. There is a place for everything in a structure, and everything should be in its place.

..............................Chapter Summary..............................

- Don't bury the lead (start with the main idea of a unit of meaning) or do (let the main idea emerge out of the unit).
- All of these structures are versatile. You can use them in multiple ways, for multiple purposes, etc.
- You can lengthen and shorten the structures and they maintain a proportional impact.
- You can combine the structures, stacking them in sequence or nesting them (using one to fill a step in another).
- Apply separation of concerns: Insofar as you can, avoid blending the steps together.
- These are the advanced principles of structure theory, allowing you to take the process to the next level.

KEY INSIGHT:

The Power of Structure Is Making the Sequence of Your Speech Speak Well.

The Absence of Structure Is Letting the Sequence of Your Speech Speak Poorly.

THREE POWERFUL OPENINGS

IF-THEN

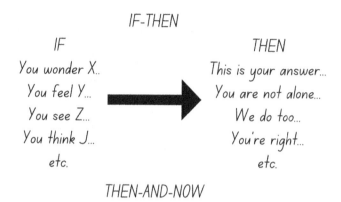

IF	THEN
You wonder X..	This is your answer...
You feel Y...	You are not alone...
You see Z...	We do too...
You think J...	You're right...
etc.	etc.

THEN-AND-NOW

X LONG AGO	NOW
Things were like this.	They are like this.

A MOMENT OF DECISION

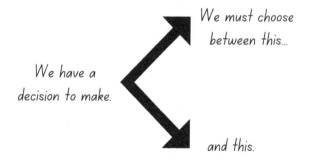

We must choose between this...

We have a decision to make.

and this.

THE IRREFUTABLE PERSUASIVE SYNTAX (PART SIX)

1	Master the Foundational Theories
1.1	Apply the Public Speaking Triad
1.2	Master the Communication Toolbox and the Three Layers
1.3	Activate, Control, and Align Your Three Languages
1.4	Satisfy the Triad Ingredients
1.5	Understand and Apply Purposeful Communication
1.6	Don't Forget the Three-Part Model of Communication
1.7	Speak to the Top of the Cone of Attention
1.8	Say the Right Things, But Also in the Right Way
1.9	Appeal to Self-Interest and "WIIFM?"
1.10	Raise Perceived Marginal Benefits, Drop Perceived Marginal Costs
1.11	Satisfy the Mental Checklist in Eight Seconds
1.12	Speak in terms of Benefits and Features
1.13	Remember the Wisdom of the Fable of the Wind and the Sun
1.14	Understand the Underlying Fact of Mental Malleability
1.15	Apply Bridge Theory to Keep Things Flowing Smoothly
1.16	Recognize the Pyramid of Human Desires
1.17	Remember Uniqueness, Personas, Ceteris Paribus and Limitations
1.18	Satisfy the Saliency, Intensity, and Stability Framework
1.19	Understand the Dilemma of One Versus Many

2.10	Avoid Tangents and Parentheticals
2.11	Use Transitions to Maintain Audience Attention
2.12	Remember the Similarities of Structure
2.13	Engineer Your Openings
2.14	Complete Your Communication Body
2.15	Engineer Your Closing
3	**Master the Persuasive Structures**
3.1	Use Monroe's Motivated Sequence
3.2	Use the Objection-Prediction Model
3.3	Use the Path-Contrast Method
3.4	Use the Past, Present, Means Structure
3.5	Use the Problem-Solution Formula
3.6	Use the Diagnose, Problem, Solution Triad
3.7	Use Criteria Matching
3.8	Use Criteria Matching and Dematching
3.9	Use the Six-Point Punch
3.10	Use the Economic Values Structure
3.11	Use the Short-Form Rhetorical Three-Point Punch
3.12	Use the Long-Form Rhetorical Three-Point Punch
3.13	Use the Gain, Logic, Fear Trifecta

3.14	Use the Tension, Desire, Action Trifecta
3.15	Use the Persuasive Stack Sequence
3.16	Use the Last Method Strategy
3.17	Use the Past, Present, Future Method
3.18	Use the Desire, Dissonance, Decision Trifecta
4	**Master the Informative Structures**
4.1	Use the Informational Motivated Sequence
4.2	Use the Straight-Line Method
4.3	Use the Reverse-Line Method
4.4	Use the Stream of Consciousness Principle
4.5	Use the Montage Structure
4.6	Use the Attached List Structure
4.7	Use the Detached List Structure
4.8	Use the Information Stack
4.9	Use the Big Answer Strategy
4.10	Use the Back-and-Forth Method
4.11	Use the Chronological Sequence
4.12	Use the Cause-and-Effect Method
4.13	Use the Presentation, Escalation, Contrast Trifecta
4.14	Use the Narrative Structure

4.15	Use the Demonstrative Sequence
4.16	Use the Short-Form Informational Three-Point Punch
5	**Master the Inspirational Structures**
5.1	Use the Quote Presentation Strategy
5.2	Use Long-Form Anaphora
5.3	Use the Want, Got, Empowerment Trifecta
5.4	Use the Present Problems, Future, Empowerment Trifecta
5.5	Use the Short-Form Inspirational Three-Point Punch
5.6	Use the Limiting Belief Prediction Strategy
5.7	Use the Visionary Structure
5.8	Use the Drama Structure
6	**Master the Advanced Principles of Structure**
6.1	Don't Bury the Lead (Or Do…)
6.2	Take Advantage of the Versatility of the Structures
6.3	Take Advantage of Lengthening and Shortening
6.4	Take Advantage of the Combining Principle (Stacking and Nesting)
6.5	Remember Separation of Concerns

SOMETHING WAS MISSING. THIS IS IT.

D ECEMBER OF 2021, I COMPLETED the new editions of the 15 books in the Speak for Success collection, after months of work, and many 16-hour-long writing marathons. The collection is over 1,000,000 words long and includes over 1,700 handcrafted diagrams. It is *the* complete communication encyclopedia. But instead of feeling relieved and excited, I felt uneasy and anxious. Why? Well, I know now. After writing over 1,000,000 words on communication across 15 books, it slowly dawned on me that I had missed the most important set of ideas about good communication. What does it *really* mean to be a good speaker? This is my answer.

THERE ARE THREE DIMENSIONS OF SUCCESS

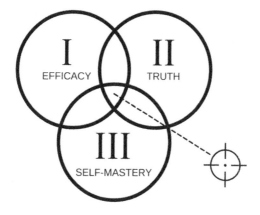

FIGURE I: A good speaker is not only rhetorically effective. They speak the truth, and they are students of self-mastery who experience peace, calm, and deep equanimity as they speak. These three domains are mutually reinforcing.

I realized I left out much about truth and self-mastery, focusing instead on the first domain. On page 33, the practical guide is devoted to domain I. On page 42, the ethical guide is devoted to domain II. We will shortly turn to domain III with an internal guide.

WHAT A GOOD SPEAKER LOOKS LIKE

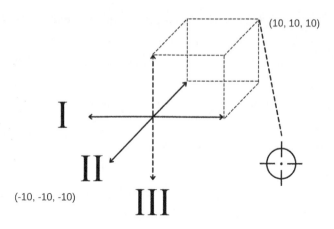

FIGURE II: We can conceptualize the three domains of success as an (X, Y, Z) coordinate plane, with each axis extending between -10 and 10. Your job is to become a (10, 10, 10). A (-10, 10, 10) speaks the truth and has attained self-mastery, but is deeply ineffective. A (10, -10, 10), speaks brilliantly and is at peace, but is somehow severely misleading others. A (10, 10, -10), speaks the truth well, but lives in an extremely negative inner state.

THE THREE AXES VIEWED DIFFERENTLY

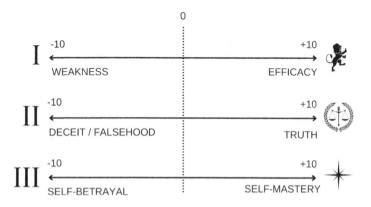

FIGURE III: We can also untangle the dimensions of improvement from representation as a coordinate plane, and instead lay them out flat, as spectrums of progress. A

(+10, -10, -10) is a true monster, eloquent but evil. A (10, 10, 10) is a Martin Luther King. A more realistic example is (4, -3, 0): This person is moderately persuasive, bends truth a little too much for comfort (but not horribly), and is mildly anxious about speaking but far from falling apart. Every speaker exists at some point along these axes.

THE EXTERNAL MASTERY PROCESS IS INTERNAL TOO

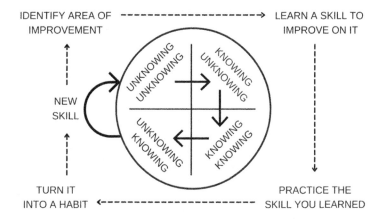

FIGURE IV: The same process presented earlier as a way to achieve rhetorical mastery will also help you achieve self-mastery. Just replace the word "skill" with "thought" or "thought-pattern," and the same cyclical method works.

THE THREE AXES, IN DIFFERENT WORDS

Domain One	Domain Two	Domain Three
Efficacy	Truth	Self-Mastery
Rhetoric	Research	Inner-Peace
Master of Words	Seeker of Truth	Captain of Your Soul
Aristotle's "Pathos"	Aristotle's "Logos"	Aristotle's "Ethos"
Impact	Insight	Integrity
Presence of Power	Proper Perspective	Power of Presence
Inter-Subjective	Objective	Subjective
Competency	Credibility	Character
External-Internal	External	Internal
Verbal Mastery	Subject Mastery	Mental Mastery
Behavioral	Cognitive	Emotional

THE POWER OF LANGUAGE

Language has generative power. This is why many creation stories include language as a primordial agent playing a crucial role in crafting reality. "In the beginning was the Word, and the Word was with God (John 1:1)."

Every problem we face has a story written about its future, whether explicit or implicit, conscious or subconscious. Generative language can rewrite a story that leads downward, turning it into one that aims us toward heaven, and then it can inspire us to realize this story. It can remove the cloud of ignorance from noble possibilities.

And this is good. You can orient your own future upward. That's certainly good for you. You can orient the future upward for yourself and for your family. That's better. And for your friends. That's better. And for your organization, your community, your city, and your country. That's better still. And for your enemies, and for people yet unborn; for all people, at all times, from now until the end of time.

And it doesn't get better than that.

Sound daunting? It is. It is the burden of human life. It is also the mechanism of moral progress. But start wherever you can, wherever you are. Start by acing your upcoming presentation.

But above all, remember this: all progress begins with truth.

Convey truth beautifully. And know thyself, so you can guard against your own proclivity for malevolence, and so you can strive toward self-mastery. Without self-mastery, it's hard, if not nearly impossible, to do the first part; to convey truth beautifully.

Truth, so you do good, not bad; impact, so people believe you; and self-mastery, as an essential precondition for truth and impact. Imagine what the world would be like if everyone were a triple-ten on our three axes. Imagine what good, what beauty, what bliss would define our existence. Imagine what good, what beauty, what bliss *could* define our existence, here and now.

It's up to you.

THE INNER GAME OF SPEAKING

REFER BACK TO THIS INTERNAL GUIDE as needed. These humble suggestions have helped me deliver high-stakes speeches with inner peace, calm, and equanimity. They are foundational, and the most important words I ever put to paper. I hope these ideas help you as much as they helped me.

MASTER BOTH GAMES. Seek to master the outer game, but also the inner game. The self-mastery game comes before the word-mastery game, and even the world-mastery game. In fact, if you treat *any* game as a way to further your self-mastery, setting this as your "game above all games," you can never lose.

ADOPT THREE FOUNDATIONS. Humility: "The other people here probably know something I don't. They could probably teach me something. I could be overlooking something. I could be wrong. They have something to contribute" Passion: "Conveying truth accurately and convincingly is one of the most important things I'll ever do." Objectivity: "If I'm wrong, I change course. I am open to reason. I want to *be* right; I don't just want to seem right or convince others I am."

STRIVE FOR THESE SUPERLATIVES. Be the kindest, most compassionate, most honest, most attentive, most well-researched, and most confident in the room. Be the one who cares most, who most seeks to uplift others, who is most prepared, and who is most thoughtful about the reason and logic and evidence behind the claims.

START BY CULTIVATING THE HIGHEST VIRTUES IN YOURSELF: love for your audience, love for truth, humility, a deep and abiding desire to make the world a better place, the desire to both be heard and to hear, and the desire to both teach and learn. You will find peace, purpose, clarity, confidence, and persuasive power.

START BY AVOIDING THESE TEMPTING MOTIVES. Avoid the desire to "outsmart" people, to overwhelm and dominate with your rhetorical strength, to embarrass your detractors, to win on the basis of cleverness alone, and to use words to attain power for its own sake. Don't set personal victory as your goal. Strive to achieve a victory for truth. And if you discover you are wrong, change course.

LISTEN TO YOURSELF TALK. (Peterson, 2018). See if what you are saying makes you feel stronger, physically, or weaker. If it makes you feel weaker, stop saying it. Reformulate your speech until you feel the ground under you solidifying.

SPEAK FROM A PLACE OF LOVE. It beats speaking from a desire to dominate. Our motivation and purpose in persuasion must be love. It's ethical *and* effective.

LOVE YOUR ENEMIES (OR HAVE NONE). If people stand against you, do not inflame the situation with resentment or anger. It does no good, least of all for you.

AVOID THESE CORRUPTING EMOTIONS: resistance, resentment, and anger. Against them, set acceptance, forgiveness, and love for all, even your enemies.

PLACE YOUR ATTENTION HERE, NOW. Be where you are. Attend to the moment. Forget the past. Forget the future. Nothing is more important than this.

FOCUS ON YOURSELF, BUT NOW. Speaking gurus will tell you to focus solely on your audience. Yes, that works. But so does focusing on yourself, as long as you focus on yourself *now*. Let this focus root you in the present. Don't pursue a mental commentary on what you see. Instead, just watch. Here. Now. No judgment.

ACCEPT YOUR FEAR. Everyone fears something. If you fear speaking, don't fear your fear of speaking too. Don't reprimand yourself for it. Accept it. Embrace it, even. Courage isn't action without fear. Courage is action despite fear.

STARE DOWN YOUR FEAR. To diminish your fear, stare at the object of your fear (and the fear itself), the way a boxer faces off with his opponent before the fight. Hold it in your mind, signaling to your own psyche that you can face your fear.

CHIP AWAY AT YOUR FEAR. The path out of fear is to take small, voluntary steps toward what you fear. Gradual exposure dissolves fear as rain carves stone.

LET THE OUTER SHAPE THE INNER. Your thoughts impact your actions. But your actions also impact your thoughts. To control fear, seek to manage its outward manifestations, and your calm exterior will shape your interior accordingly.

KNOW THAT EGO IS THE ENEMY. Ego is a black storm cloud blocking the warm sunlight of your true self. Ego is the creation of a false self that masquerades as your true self and demands gratification (which often manifests as the destruction of something good). The allure of arrogance is the siren-song of every good speaker. With it comes pride and the pursuit of power; a placing of the outer game before the inner. Don't fall for the empty promises of ego-gratification. Humility is power.

DON'T IDENTIFY WITH YOUR POSITIONS. Don't turn your positions into your psychological possessions. Don't imbue them with a sense of self.

NOTICE TOXIC AVATARS. When person A speaks to person B, they often craft a false idea, a false avatar, of both themselves and their interlocuter: A1 and B1. So does person B: B2 and A2. The resulting communication is a dance of false avatars; A1, B1, B2, and A2 communicate, but not person A and B. A false idea of one's self speaks to a false idea of someone else, who then does the same. This may be why George Bernard Shaw said "the greatest problem in communication is the illusion that it has been accomplished." How do you avoid this dance of false avatars? This conversation between concepts but not people? Be present. Don't prematurely judge. Let go of your *sense* of self, for just a moment, so your real self can shine forth.

MINE THE RICHES OF YOUR MIND. Look for what you need within yourself; your strengths and virtues. But also acknowledge and make peace with your own capacity for malevolence. Don't zealously assume the purity of your own motives.

RISE ABOVE YOUR MIND. The ability to think critically, reason, self-analyze, and self-criticize is far more important than being able to communicate, write, and speak. Introspect before you extrospect. Do not identify as your mind, but as the awareness eternally watching your mind. Do not be in your mind, but above it.

CLEAR THE FOG FROM YOUR PSYCHE. Know what you believe. Know your failures. Know your successes. Know your weaknesses. Know your strengths. Know what you fear. Know what you seek. Know your mind. Know yourself. Know your capacity for malevolence and evil. Know your capacity for goodness and greatness. Don't hide any part of yourself from yourself. Don't even try.

KNOW YOUR LOGOS. In 500 B.C. Heraclitus defined Logos as "that universal principle which animates and rules the world." What is your Logos? Meditate on it. Sit with it. Hold it up to the light, as a jeweler does with a gem, examining all angles.

KNOW YOUR LIMITS. The more you delineate and define the actions you consider unethical, the more likely you are to resist when they seem expedient.

REMEMBER THAT EVERYTHING MATTERS. There is no insignificant job, duty, role, mission, or speech. Everything matters. Everything seeks to beat back chaos in some way and create order. A laundromat doesn't deal in clean clothes, nor a trash disposal contractor in clean streets. They deal in order. In civilization. In human dignity. Don't ignore the reservoir of meaning and mattering upon which you stand. And remember that it is there, no matter where you stand.

GIVE THE GIFT OF MEANING. The greatest gift you can give to an audience is the gift of meaning; the knowledge that they matter, that they are irreplaceable.

HONOR YOUR INHERITANCE. You are the heir to thousands of years of human moralizing. Our world is shaped by the words of long-dead philosophers, and the gifts they gave us: gems of wisdom, which strengthen us against the dread and chaos of the world. We stand atop the pillars of 4,000 years of myth and meaning. Our arguments and moral compasses are not like planks of driftwood in a raging sea, but branches nourished by an inestimably old tree. Don't forget it.

BE THE PERSON YOU WANT TO BE SEEN AS. How do you want to be seen by your audience? How can you actually be that way, rather than just seeming to be?

HAVE TRUE ETHOS. Ethos is the audience's perception that the speaker has their best interests at heart. It's your job to make sure this perception is accurate.

CHANGE PLACES WITH YOUR AUDIENCE. Put yourself in their shoes, and then be the speaker you would want to listen to, the speaker worthy of your trust.

ACT AS THOUGH THE WHOLE WORLD IS WATCHING. Or as though a newspaper will publish a record of your actions. Or as though you're writing your autobiography with every action, every word, and even every thought. (You are.)

ACT WITH AUDACIOUS HONOR. As did John McCain when he called Obama, his political opponent, "a decent family man, [and] citizen, that I just happen to have disagreements with." As did Socrates and Galileo when they refused to betray truth.

ADOPT A MECHANIC'S MENTALITY. Face your challenges the way a mechanic faces a broken engine; not drowning in emotion, but with objectivity and clarity. Identify the problem. Analyze the problem. Determine the solution. Execute the solution. If it works, celebrate. If not, repeat the cycle. This is true for both your inner and outer worlds: your fear of speaking, for example, is a specific problem with a specific fix, as are your destructive external rhetorical habits.

APPLY THE MASTERY PROCESS INTERNALLY. The four-step mastery process is not only for mastering your rhetoric, but also for striving toward internal mastery.

MARSHAL YOURSELF ALONG THE THREE AXES. To marshal means to place in proper rank or position – as in marshaling the troops – and to bring together and order in the most effective way. It is a sort of preparation. It begins with taking complete stock of what is available. Then, you order it. So, marshal yourself along three axes: the rhetorical axis (your points, arguments, rhetorical techniques, key phrases, etc.), the internal axis (your peace of mind, your internal principles, your mental climate, etc.), and the truth axis (your research, your facts, your logic, etc.).

PRACTICE ONE PUNCH 10,000 TIMES. As the martial arts adage says, "I fear not the man who practiced 10,000 punches once, but the man who practiced one punch 10,000 times." So it is with speaking skills and rhetorical techniques.

MULTIPLY YOUR PREPARATION BY TEN. Do you need to read a manuscript ten times to memorize it? Aim to read it 100 times. Do you need to research for one hour to grasp the subject of your speech? Aim to research for ten.

REMEMBER THE HIGHEST PRINCIPLE OF COMMUNICATION: the connection between speaker and audience – here, now – in this moment, in this place.

KNOW THERE'S NO SUCH THING AS A "SPEECH." All good communication is just conversation, with varying degrees of formality heaped on top. It's all just connection between consciousnesses. Every "difference" is merely superficial.

SEE YOURSELF IN OTHERS. What are you, truly? Rene Descartes came close to an answer in 1637, when he said "cogito, ego sum," I think therefore I am. The answer this seems to suggest is that your thoughts are most truly you. But your thoughts (and your character) change all the time. Something that never changes, arguably even during deep sleep, is awareness. Awareness is also the precondition for thought. A computer performs operations on information, but we don't say the computer "thinks." Why? Because it lacks awareness. So, I believe what makes you "you," most fundamentally, is your awareness, your consciousness. And if you accept this claim – which is by no means a mystical or religious one – then you must also see yourself in others. Because while the contents of everyone's consciousness is different, the consciousness itself is identical. How could it be otherwise?

FORGIVE. Yourself. Your mistakes. Your detractors. The past. The future. All.

FREE YOUR MIND. Many of the most challenging obstacles we face are thoughts living in our own minds. Identify these thoughts, and treat them like weeds in a garden. Restore the pristine poise of your mind, and return to equanimity.

LET. Let what has been be and what will be be. Most importantly, let what is be what is. Work to do what good you can do, and accept the outcome.

FLOW. Wikipedia defines a flow state as such: "a flow state, also known colloquially as being in the zone, is the mental state in which a person performing some activity is fully immersed in a feeling of energized focus, full involvement, and enjoyment in the process of the activity. In essence, flow is characterized by the complete absorption in what one does, and a resulting transformation in one's sense of time." Speaking in a flow state transports you and your audience outside of space and time. When I entered deep flow states during my speeches and debates, audience members would tell me that "it felt like time stopped." It felt that way for me too. Speaking in a flow state is a form of meditation. And it both leads to and results from these guidelines. Adhering to them leads to flow, and flow helps you adhere to them.

MEDITATE. Meditation brings your attention to the "here and now." It creates flow. Practice silence meditation, sitting in still silence and focusing on the motions of your mind, but knowing yourself as the entity watching the mind, not the mind itself. Practice aiming meditation, centering your noble aim in your mind, and focusing on the resulting feelings. (Also, speaking in flow is its own meditation).

EMBARK ON THE GRAND ADVENTURE. Take a place wherever you are. Develop influence and impact. Improve your status. Take on responsibility. Develop capacity and ability. Do scary things. Dare to leap into a high-stakes speech with no preparation if you must. Dare to trust your instincts. Dare to strive. Dare to lead. Dare to speak the truth freely, no matter how brutal it is. Be bold. Risk failure. Throw out your notes. The greatest human actions – those that capture our hearts and minds – occur on the border between chaos and order, where someone is daring to act and taking a chance when they know they could fall off the tightrope with no net below. Training wheels kill the sense of adventure. Use them if you need to, but only to lose them as soon as you can. Speak from the heart and trust yourself. Put yourself out there. Let people see the gears turning in your mind, let them see you grappling with your message in real time, taking an exploration in the moment. This is not an automaton doing a routine. It's not robotic or mechanical. That's too much order. It's also not unstructured nonsense. That's too much chaos. There is a risk of failure, mitigated not by training wheels, but by preparation. It is not a perfectly practiced routine, but someone pushing themselves just beyond their comfort zone, right at the cutting-edge of what they are capable of. It's not prescriptive. It's not safe either. The possibility that you could falter and fall in real-time calls out the best from you, and is gripping for the audience. It is also a thrilling adventure. Have faith in yourself, faith that you will say the right words when you need to. Don't think ahead, or backward. Simply experience the moment.

BREAK THE SEVEN LAWS OF WEAKNESS. If your goal is weakness, follow these rules. Seek to control what you can't control. Seek praise and admiration from others. Bend the truth to achieve your goals. Treat people as instruments in your game. Only commit to outer goals, not inner goals. Seek power for its own sake. Let anger and dissatisfaction fuel you in your pursuits, and pursue them frantically.

FAIL. Losses lead to lessons. Lessons lead to wins. If there's no chance of failure in your present task, you aren't challenging yourself. And if you aren't challenging yourself, you aren't growing. And that's the deepest and most enduring failure.

DON'T BETRAY YOURSELF. To know the truth and not say the truth is to betray the truth and to betray yourself. To know the truth, seek the truth, love the truth, and to speak the truth and speak it well, with poise and precision and power… this is to honor the truth, and to honor yourself. The choice is yours.

FOLLOW YOUR INNER LIGHT. As the Roman emperor and stoic philosopher Marcus Aurelius wrote in his private journal, "If thou findest in human life anything better than justice, truth, temperance, fortitude, and, in a word, anything better than thy own mind's self-satisfaction in the things which it enables thee to do according to right reason, and in the condition that is assigned to thee without thy own choice; if, I say, thou seest anything better than this, turn to it with all thy soul, and enjoy that which thou hast found to be the best. But if nothing appears to be better than [this], give place to nothing else." And as Kant said, treat humans as ends, not means.

JUDGE THEIR JUDGMENT. People *are* thinking of you. They *are* judging you. But what is their judgment to you? Nothing. (Compared to your self-judgment).

BREAK LESSER RULES IN THE NAME OF HIGHER RULES. Our values and moral priorities nest in a hierarchy, where they exist in relation to one another. Some are more important than others. If life compels a tradeoff between two moral principles, as it often does, this means there is a right choice. Let go the lesser of the two.

DON'T AVOID CONFLICT. Necessary conflict avoided is an impending conflict exacerbated. Slay the hydra when it has two heads, not twenty.

SEE THE WHOLE BOARD. Become wise in the ways of the world, and learned in the games of power and privilege people have been playing for tens of thousands of years. See the status-struggles and dominance-shuffling around you. See the chess board. But then opt to play a different game; a more noble game. The game of self-mastery. The game that transcends all other games. The worthiest game.

SERVE SOMETHING. Everyone has a master. Everyone serves something. Freedom is not the absence of service. Freedom is the ability to choose your service. What, to you, is worth serving? With your work and with your words?

TAKE RESPONSIBILITY FOR YOUR RIPPLE EFFECT. If you interact with 1,000 people, and they each interact with 1,000 more who also do the same, you are three degrees away from one billion people. Remember that compassion is contagious.

ONLY SPEAK WHEN YOUR WORDS ARE BETTER THAN SILENCE. And only write when your words are better than a blank page.

KNOW THERE IS THAT WHICH YOU DON'T KNOW YOU DON'T KNOW. Of course, there's that you know you don't know too. Recognize the existence of both of these domains of knowledge, which are inaccessible to you in your present state.

REMEMBER THAT AS WITHIN, SO (IT APPEARS) WITHOUT. If you orient your aim toward goals fueled by emotions like insecurity, jealousy, or vengeance, the world manifests itself as a difficult warzone. If you orient your aim toward goals fueled by emotions like universal compassion and positive ambition, the beneficence of the world manifests itself to you. Your aim and your values alter your perception.

ORIENT YOUR AIM PROPERLY. Actions flow from thought. Actions flow from *motives*. If you orient your aim properly – if you aim at the greatest good for the greatest number, at acting forthrightly and honorably – then this motive will fuel right actions, subconsciously, automatically, and without any forethought.

STOP TRYING TO USE SPEECH TO GET WHAT YOU WANT. Try to articulate what you believe to be true as carefully as possible, and then accept the outcome.

LEARN THE MEANING OF WHAT YOU SAY. Don't assume you already know.

USE THE MOST POWERFUL "RHETORICAL" TACTIC. There is no rhetorical tool more powerful than the overwhelming moral force of the unvarnished truth.

INJECT YOUR EXPERIENCE INTO YOUR SPEECH. Speak of what you know and testify of what you have seen. Attach your philosophizing and persuading and arguing to something real, some story you lived through, something you've seen.

DETACH FROM OUTCOME. As Stoic philosopher Epictetus said: "There is only one way to happiness and that is to cease worrying about things which are beyond the power of our will. Make the best use of what is in your power, and take the rest as it happens. The essence of philosophy is that a man should so live that his happiness shall depend as little as possible on external things. Remember to conduct yourself in life as if at a banquet. As something being passed around comes to you, reach out your hand and take a moderate helping. Does it pass you? Don't stop it. It hasn't yet come? Don't burn in desire for it, but wait until it arrives in front of you."

FOCUS ON WHAT YOU CONTROL. As Epictetus said, "It's not what happens to you, but how you react to it that matters. You may be always victorious if you will never enter into any contest where the issue does not wholly depend upon yourself. Some things are in our control and others not. Things in our control are opinion, pursuit, desire, aversion, and, in a word, whatever are our own actions. Things not in our control are body, property, reputation, command, and, in one word, whatever are not our own actions. Men are disturbed not by things, but by the view which they take of them. God has entrusted me with myself. Do not with that all things will go well with you, but that you will go well with all things." Before a high-stakes speech or event, I always tell myself this: "All I want from this, all I aim at, is to conduct what I control, my thoughts and actions, to the best of my ability. Any external benefit I earn is merely a bonus."

VIEW YOURSELF AS A VESSEL. Conduct yourself as something through which truth, brilliantly articulated, flows into the world; not as a self-serving entity, but a conduit for something higher. Speak not for your glory, but for the glory of good.

Want to Talk? Email Me:

PANDREIBUSINESS@GMAIL.COM

This is My Personal Email.
I Read Every Message and
Respond in Under 12 Hours.